FIGHTING TECHNIQUES
OF NAVAL WARFARE

PRAISE FOR THE FIGHTING TECHNIQUES SERIES:

"Solid historical essays on topics like naval warfare in the ancient world, or the role of infantry in early modern times, with ingenious color illustrations of key battles…. Although written for adults, these books would have thrilled me starting at about the age of 9."

—William Grimes, *The New York Times*

FIGHTING TECHNIQUES
OF NAVAL WARFARE

1190 BC ~ PRESENT

STRATEGY, WEAPONS, COMMANDERS, AND SHIPS

IAIN DICKIE MARTIN J. DOUGHERTY PHYLLIS J. JESTICE CHRISTER JÖRGENSEN ROB S. RICE

THOMAS DUNNE BOOKS
ST. MARTIN'S PRESS ☆ NEW YORK

Thomas Dunne Books.
An imprint of St. Martin's Press

FIGHTING TECHNIQUES OF NAVAL WARFARE.
Copyright © Amber Books Ltd 2009. All rights reserved.
For information, address
St. Martin's Press, 175 Fifth Avenue,
New York, N.Y. 10010.

www.thomasdunnebooks.com
www.stmartins.com

Library of Congress Cataloging-in-Publication Data
on file at the Library of Congress

ISBN-13: 978-0-312-55453-8
ISBN-10: 0-312-55453-2

Editorial and design by
Amber Books Ltd
Bradley's Close
74-77 White Lion Street
London N1 9PF
United Kingdom
www.amberbooks.co.uk

Project Editors: Michael Spilling
Design: Jerry Williams
Picture Research: Terry Forshaw

Printed in Thailand

First U.S. Edition June 2009

10 9 8 7 6 5 4 3 2 1

CONTENTS

CHAPTER 1

THE AGE OF THE GALLEY

A universal truth in the military arena is that battles tend to happen along lines of communication. Until steam power became widely available, waterways – salt and fresh – were the preferred means of transportation for armies, supplies and building materials. Thus, after the fall of the Romans, a vacuum in naval power allowed the Vikings to land armies where wanted. Not only did they make the sea their motorway, they also sailed far inland along rivers, even besieging Paris in 885 AD.

D uring the late twelfth century BC, Egypt was beset by foreign invaders. The cities and fertile territories subject to the pharaoh Ramses III were eyed enviously by all around him. He only had to turn his attention to one corner of his empire for his enemies to make inroads into another.

THE SEA BATTLE OF SALAMIS *by German artist Wilhelm von Kaubach (1804-74). The Greek goddess Athene watches from above as her city burns and her people plead for salvation while the Greek fleet takes on and beats the superpower of the day, Persia. Despite the fanciful setting, the clothing depicted is reasonably accurate.*

7

To the south were the Nubian Kushites, probably the enemy most familiar to the Egyptians since there was some level of trade between the peoples. The waters of the Nile, which brought shipping and fertilized Egypt's fields, formed a highway from these southern lands into the heart of the Egyptian kingdom. South of the second cataract (one of the shallow stretches of rocky, turbulent rapids), the Nile also fertilized the lands of the Nubians, allowing their wealth to grow and become a serious rival to Egyptian power. Ramses had 15 sophisticated fortresses, each garrisoned by up to 300 regular troops, in the region of the second cataract, plus a naval base at the first cataract to defend against the Nubians from Ethiopia. For the moment, these defences were sufficient; a few centuries later, however, the Kushites would break through to conquer Egypt.

To the west of Egypt, the Libyans, with their seemingly alien customs, lurked menacingly. Periodically they migrated in huge armies made of several different tribes, searching for fertile land to settle. They had little in the way of horses or metal, however, and at the battle of Hatsho in the fifth

year of his reign, Ramses was easily able to defeat the Libyans. Lines of archers backed by spearmen advanced directly towards the tribesmen while chariots and javelin men harassed their flanks. When the Libyans broke, they were pursued for over 80km (50 miles), a victory attributed to superior Egyptian technology and organization.

In the north of his kingdom, to the west of the Nile Delta, Ramses built a fortified zone to protect against invasion by the Libyans and the mysterious Sea Peoples. It was here that his predecessor, Merneptah, had defeated a Libyan and Sea Peoples alliance just 50 years earlier. This zone would give early warning of an incursion from the Mediterranean by the Sea Peoples or along the coastal route from the west by the Libyans. To the east of Egypt, there were civilized peoples, the Hittites, with whom messages and ambassadors could be exchanged. However, the Hittites were weak and unable to hold back their own enemies, including the Sea Peoples.

Ramses III and the Sea Peoples: Battle on the Nile

The identity of these invaders, referred to in Egyptian inscriptions as the 'foreign peoples of the sea', is still something of a mystery. It seems likely that the Sea Peoples originated from Greece and islands in the Mediterranean. They are depicted by the Egyptians as two distinct groups. One group, known to

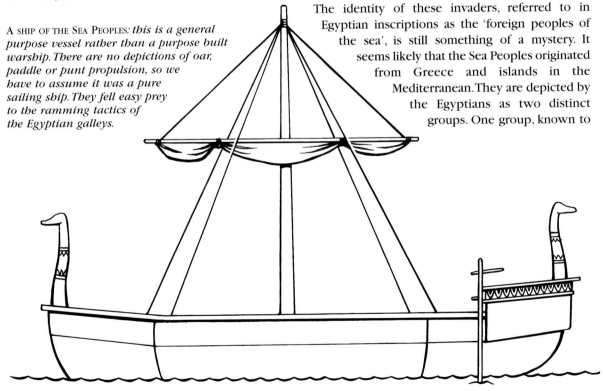

A SHIP OF THE SEA PEOPLES: *this is a general purpose vessel rather than a purpose built warship. There are no depictions of oar, paddle or punt propulsion, so we have to assume it was a pure sailing ship. They fell easy prey to the ramming tactics of the Egyptian galleys.*

Egyptian Marine
(1200 BC)

Armed with a javelin that had a range of about 30m (98ft), and a mace or club, the marine also carried a shield. He may have discarded this when the sea was rough, preferring to hold onto the boat.. The tunic was made from small pieces of metal or leather, known as scales. These were sewn onto a linen backing and overlapped each other, covering the stitches and affording some degree of protection against light missiles. The kilt was a design copied from earlier contact with the Sea Peoples. Note the bare feet, which gave better grip on the wooden deck than leather sandles.

Philistines, who gave their name to Palestine. During the twelfth century BC, the Peleset swept aside the once-great Hittite Empire in a huge migration of men, women, children and flocks.

It is possible that the Sherden and Peleset joined together in the southern part of the collapsing Hittite Empire. While the main body approached Egypt across the Sinai desert, the ships of the Sea Peoples moved ahead and entered the Nile Delta. Such a movement could be neither rapid nor secret, so Ramses III had plenty of time to assess his enemy's strength and to prepare a response.

At his disposal, Ramses had two armies in the eastern delta, facing the Libyans. Another army was held in reserve in the centre of the kingdom, possibly at Thebes, and one was in the south facing the Nubians. The soldiers were conscripted, one man in 10 being liable for service. The Egyptian population was organized into generations of roughly 100,000. By this means, it has been calculated that 10,000 fresh recruits were available each year. We do not know the length of service, but we do have details of a force of 8362, including non-combatants, sent on an expedition to the south in the reign of Ramses IV. If this was a portion of the army of the south and we assume a prudent two-thirds of that army were left behind, that would make an army of about 25,000 men and a term of service of 10 years. The infantry were organized

the Egyptians as the Sherden, wear horned helmets very similar to those worn by the Acheans who fought at Troy. Indeed, although dates are difficult to establish, one theory places the end of the siege of Troy close to the beginning of the reign of Ramses III. The second group are shown sporting headdresses made of vertical stalks, possibly feathers. These are the Peleset, better known as the

into units of 250, the charioteers into units of 50. Military police accompanied the force.

Although Ramses maintained a fleet of ships, these were considered to be a part of the army. In addition, tribesmen from the fringes of the empire were recruited as auxiliary troops. We can assume he also used some of these tribesmen as scouts and spies, since they could more easily blend with the advancing horde and discover the final destination of the enemy's fleet. How else could Ramses have known to position his ships in the delta when there were so many possible landing sites on the Egyptian coast? For the coming

campaign, Ramses summoned his land forces to Pi-Ramses, about 8km (5 miles) north of Suez, and commandeered all sorts of craft from the Nile and coastal areas.

His warships were equipped with 10 oars per side, a single mast with crow's nest, castles fore and aft, and a single steering oar. At the prow was a ram shaped like a lion's head and sheathed in metal, probably bronze. A slinger was posted in the crow's nest, a man with a grappling hook on the forecastle, and a boarding pike was wielded from the bow. For the rest of the fighting crew, a part of the army was selected and trained as marines, and

THE EGYPTIAN RAM *strikes its victim on the bulwark, knocking the crew over and many of them into the water. Then it backs off to seek another enemy ship. The capsized ships can later be recovered relatively intact and form part of the 'prizes of war'.*

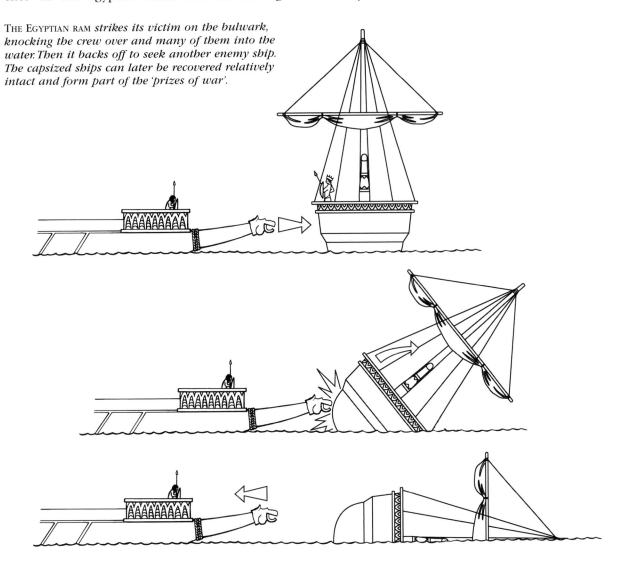

armed with bows or javelins. The marines wore knee-length, linen kilts, possibly reinforced with leather strips. Above the waist they wore armour in the form of overlapping bronze scales sewn onto a cloth backing. An armoured helmet was made in the same way. The oarsmen were also expected to fight. The total crew numbered just 50 men.

A SHERDEN (SEA PIRATE), *wearing a leather, or metal, cuirass and a leather helmet with cow horns or boar tusks. He carried a sword 1m (3ft) long and a large leather shield with bronze bosses.*

The hulls of the Egyptian ships had a distinct belly in the centre and were relatively narrow, perhaps 16m (50ft) long and just 2m (7ft) wide. This made them a fairly good shape for rowing. They had sides high enough to protect all but the heads of the oarsmen. On the Medinet Habu monument and Queen Nefertiti's barge, the bows and sterns of the boats are shown extending fore and aft in a graceful arc above the waterline. Their leaf-shaped oars appear through the hull sides and the rowers face the stern. The planks of the hulls were lashed together with fibrous rope. We can also assume that the hulls were built from dry wood; when this became wet, it would expand and seal the gaps between the planks, keeping the lashings taut.

The ships of the Sea Peoples are depicted on Egyptian monuments with a similar hull shape to the Egyptian vessels: with castles and crow's nests but without rams or oars. They may have had paddles, although these are not shown. The stem and sternposts seem to be decorated with duck's head shapes. Their crews appear to have used the javelin but not the bow. They also wore knee-length kilts, of a type also worn by the Egyptians. Above the waist, their armour is shown as made of either leather, muscled corselets or strips of overlapping leather, similar to that worn by the Egyptians.

Clash in the Nile Delta

While the Sea Peoples approached the Nile Delta in their ships, their families and goods travelled on slow-moving ox-drawn carts, presumably with a military escort. These convoys were attacked by the Egyptian chariots, auxiliaries and skirmishers and destroyed, those who were not killed becoming slaves. The attacking force, a small proportion of the whole Egyptian army, is another indication that Ramses had good intelligence of his enemy's plans and movements.

Meanwhile, the naval assault sailed into the mouth of the Nile, presumably on a northerly wind. Once inside the reed-bound, meandering channels of the Nile Delta, they were trapped. It was difficult to find the right channel without a local pilot and the papyrus sedge formed great clumps 4–5m (13–16ft) high, making it hard to see the masts of lurking ships.

As the wind slackened – which it always does moving from the sea inshore – they would have found it hard to manoeuvre. As the southerly flow of the Nile competed with the northerly wind, the Egyptian ships appeared behind and in front of the Sea Peoples' fleet.

The Egyptians fired a shower of arrows from a range of 150m (500ft) and javelins from 15m (50ft) as their ships closed to ram. When the rams crashed into the gunwales of the enemy ships, these tended to roll as the Egyptian ships, their rams high out of the water, pushed over the top. The crew of the enemy ship, already distracted by the incoming missiles, would tumble to the far side, causing a sharp list. If the Egyptians were lucky, the opposite gunwale would go under water and the ship would roll onto its side, throwing the crew into the water. The high prow and stem shapes on the vessels of both sides would have provided an element of counter-buoyancy, helping to prevent a complete roll over. The usual effect, however, was to overturn the ships of the Sea Peoples, as depicted on Ramses' monument to the battle at the mortuary temple at Medinet Habu.

Even a few casualties would cause a lot of disruption to the smooth running of such small ships. With no medical facilities on board, the injured were left to suffer. Both sides fought with their masts and yards standing, the sail still furled. This would have contributed to the ships' instability and the Sea Peoples' vulnerability to the Egyptian ram. Crews of both sides were spilled into the water during the fighting, but it was the Sea Peoples whose fleet was finally destroyed.

Some of the Sea Peoples were pulled out of the water or dragged to shore and tied up as prisoners for sale as slaves later. Ramses III's inscription at Medinet Habu records the fate of the invading fleet: 'They were dragged, overturned and laid low on the beach; slain and made heaps from stern to bow of their galleys.'

The Development of the Bireme

It would be wrong to think that the ships used by the Egyptians in this battle laid down the model for subsequent warship development. The materials available – wood, rope and cloth – lent themselves most readily to the sorts of ships used by either side. The next development that we are able to trace was deep in the bowels of the vessel: the maximum speed of a ship is proportional to the square of its length, so the longer the ship, the faster it can go. By changing the way the planks were fixed together, ship builders were able to construct longer and therefore faster ships.

'...the unruly Sherden whom no one had ever known how to combat, they came boldly sailing in their warships from the midst of the sea, none being able to withstand them.'
— INSCRIPTION OF RAMSES II
ON A STELA FROM TANIS

To achieve this, a slot was cut into the edge of one plank to match a slot cut into the edge of its neighbour. A tongue of wood was then hammered (it had to be a tight fit) into the first slot and the neighbouring plank, carefully aligned, was hammered onto the protruding tongue. Each end of the tongue was secured by a dowel going through the plank and tongue and out the other side. When seawater soaked the wood, it would swell and tighten the joint. Planed smooth, this gave the ships an efficient shape with minimal water resistance. As well as joining the planks edge to edge, this allowed them to be securely joined end to end, meaning that the length of the ship was no longer limited to the tallest tree available. An internal frame was added after the planking was complete.

The Greeks evolved such ships up to around 30m (100ft) in length. They were powered by

Battle of the Sea Peoples

1190 BC

The end of the great conspiracy of the Sea Peoples was achieved by the greater organization of the Egyptian empire. The Sea Peoples' deeply flawed plan left their women and children with insufficient protection in open country – easy prey for the maurading Egyptian chariotry backed by their tribal allies. The invaders' strike force used outdated technology and failed to achieve surprise or numerical superiority. Indeed, they were themselves surprised by Egyptian ships lurking unseen amongst the tall papyrus reeds of the Nile delta. The Egyptians also employed superior tactics, with their ships ramming and then withdrawing to ram again – and again. The survivors from the Sea People's army were captured and used as slaves. Very few escaped, bringing an end to the culture of the Sea Peoples and the threat they posed in the Eastern Mediterranean.

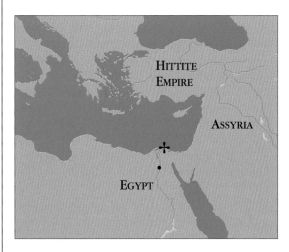

The Nile is the heart of Egypt and her principal line of communication. Trying to enter from the north, the Sea Peoples were trapped in the labyrinthine channels and reed beds of the delta.

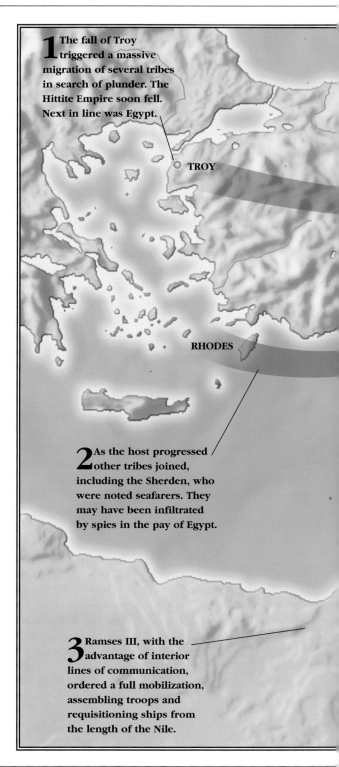

1 The fall of Troy triggered a massive migration of several tribes in search of plunder. The Hittite Empire soon fell. Next in line was Egypt.

2 As the host progressed other tribes joined, including the Sherden, who were noted seafarers. They may have been infiltrated by spies in the pay of Egypt.

3 Ramses III, with the advantage of interior lines of communication, ordered a full mobilization, assembling troops and requisitioning ships from the length of the Nile.

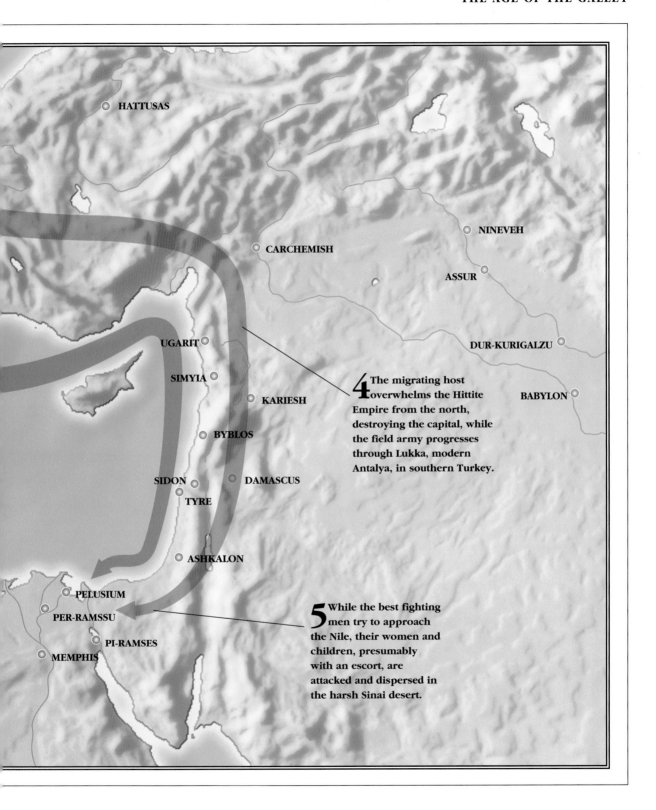

HATTUSAS

NINEVEH

CARCHEMISH

ASSUR

DUR-KURIGALZU

UGARIT

SIMYIA

BABYLON

KARIESH

4 The migrating host overwhelms the Hittite Empire from the north, destroying the capital, while the field army progresses through Lukka, modern Antalya, in southern Turkey.

BYBLOS

SIDON
TYRE

DAMASCUS

ASHKALON

PELUSIUM

5 While the best fighting men try to approach the Nile, their women and children, presumably with an escort, are attacked and dispersed in the harsh Sinai desert.

PER-RAMSSU

PI-RAMSES

MEMPHIS

Persian Marine
(480 BC)

Persia was a vast empire and drew its fighting men from all quarters, including the Greek cities on the Asia mainland and Egypt. This, however, is a true Persian marine, dressed in the Median style with tunic, trousers and a cap that covers his ears.

His principal weapon was the bow. In fact, almost every man in the Persian army was equipped with one. For close fighting, he used a hand axe, favoured for centuries for boarding actions. Although he carried a large shield, this did not compensate for his lack of armour.

At the battle of Salamis, Xerxes relied heavily on marines, placing at least 30 on each vessel. At the heart of this decision was probably Persian distrust of sea power and failure to recognize the effectiveness of the ship itself as the primary weapon. Impressive as they appeared, the marines probably did Xerxes' cause more harm than good. They were so tightly packed on the ships that they could not fight effectively and their lack of body armour and light weapons were no match for the Greeks.

30 oarsmen (the *triakonter*) or 50 oarsmen (the *pentekonter*) and by a square sail on a single mast. A small forecastle held between two and five marines, but the main weapon was a waterline ram designed to smash through the planks of the opposing ships and sink them. These ships would also leave their masts and sails on shore before a battle. This lightened the ship, making it faster, and cleared the deck of clutter.

The difficulty with further increasing the motive power of the vessel was that each oarsman rowed a single oar and had to sit adjacent to the outside edge of the ship. The Phoenicians solved this problem by using the space between oarsmen to slide another oar through, with the extra man sitting inboard and slightly higher than the outer row. The holes through which the oars protruded also had to be staggered vertically. Each rowing station now sported two oarsmen and the type became known as the *bireme*.

A variant on this design was the *hemiola*, with one-and-a-half banks of oars. While merchantmen of the period operated under sail and warships fought under oar power, this ship was designed for the chase. She could supplement wind power with her oars and was capable of sustained faster speeds to catch her prey or evade capture – an ideal pirate craft.

More Oarsmen

The next development was to add a third row of oarsmen, creating the *trireme*. This third row was not accommodated within the hull of the ship but on an outrigger projecting from the side of the hull, which allowed the *trireme* to retain its sleek, fast, narrow hull shape. This ship could carry 14 marines in a small forecastle and was powered by 170 oarsmen. Her ram delivered more power and momentum to break through the hulls of the enemy vessel. To stop the enemy ship riding too far up the ram and damaging the forecastle, the stem post now appeared forward of the forecastle. In battle, leather side screens were rigged to protect the crew from enemy missiles. An additional mast was added near the bow, angled forwards like a bowsprit. The main mast and sail were still left ashore when battle was imminent, but the bow mast would be retained on board to facilitate

escape, if necessary. It was the *trireme* that was the backbone of the Ancient Greek fleet at the Battle of Salamis in 480 BC.

Salamis, 480 BC: Battle in the Straits

The rich and powerful rulers of Ancient Persia commanded a huge empire that stretched from the Caspian Sea and the borders of the Russian steppe in the north to the great river Indus beyond the mountains in the south. To the east, their writ ran as far as the edge of the Gobi desert and in the west beyond the land of the Pharaohs along the shores of the Mediterranean Sea to the province of Skudra, today part of Turkey. It was only here in the west that anyone continued to defy their will for here, on the Asiatic coast of the Persian Empire, there were many quarrelsome and disobedient Greek colonies. These colonies argued not only with the Persians but also amongst themselves and with the Greek city-states across the Aegean Sea.

In 500 BC, the Greek cities of the Asiatic mainland rose in revolt against the Great King. In a long campaign characterized by repeated Greek betrayal of their fellow Greeks, the overwhelming Persian forces crushed the revolt. In the final battle at Lade in 494 BC, some 600 Persian *triremes* defeated a fleet of 353 *triremes* from the Greek Ionian colonies. During the Ionian revolt, the rebels had often been supported by city-states in Greece, principally the Athenians. The Persian emperor Darius I resolved to punish the Greeks for their defiance of his authority.

Darius' first plan in 492 BC involved a fleet supporting the Persian land army's advance. Unfortunately his fleet was wrecked in a storm off Mount Athos and, after a reverse ashore, the army was forced to retire. Two years later, a new expedition set off from the Asiatic coast in 600 *triremes* plus transports with the intention of attacking Athens and Eretria for their part in the rebellion. After capturing several islands, the Persian fleet duly landed an army and took the city of Eretria.

The Persian fleet then transported the army to the bay of Marathon. This wide beach was on the edge of a broad plain just two days hard marching from Athens. It was ideal for a naval landing and a good cavalry ground – an arm of the military in which the Persian army far exceeded the power of the Athenians. The wily Greeks, however, declined to come down from the safer ground of the adjacent mountainside to fight their more mobile foe. A stand-off ensued. With 150,000 soldiers and crewmen to feed and water, the Persian supply train could not keep up and the Persians were forced to re-embark their forces. As they were so doing, the Athenians attacked and inflicted a minor victory on an enemy already trying to leave. News of the victory was carried from Marathon to Athens by runner, an event now commemorated in the race of the same name. The Persian fleet with the remainder of the army on board sailed round to Athens (having lost fewer than 7000 casualties), but the Greek army, marching overland, arrived first. Seeing that the opportunity for a landing had been lost, the Persian fleet returned to Asia.

OPPOSITE: A WOODCUT OF XERXES watching the battle of Salamis from the hill called Xerxes' Throne. Depicted here as a spectator, in reality Xerxes needed a full view of the straight to command effectively.

Darius' son Xerxes was next to try in 480 BC. Xerxes' plan was similar to his father's first scheme but much bigger. He had a fleet of 1207 warships and 3000 supply ships built or requisitioned, stripping bare the coastal areas of his empire. The fleet included ships from Egypt and Cyprus and from the formerly rebellious Greek cities in his empire. More than half the fleet was crewed by Greeks. This fleet was the largest in history and its size would not be exceeded until the D-Day landings in June 1944. The historian Herodotus claimed that over a million soldiers marched against Greece in the Persian army. Modern estimates of 150,000 are more credible, but still a

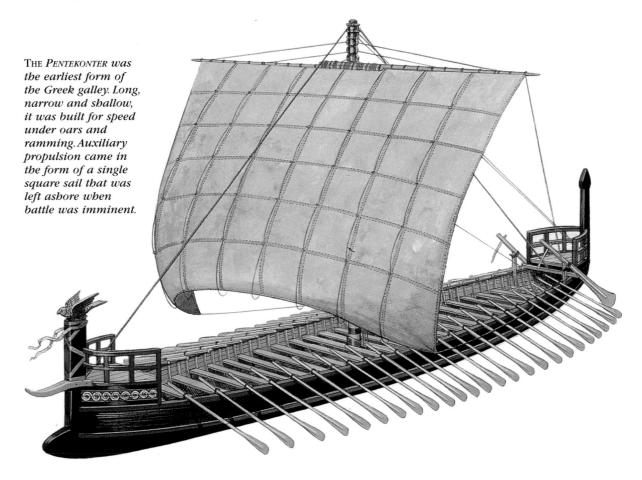

THE PENTEKONTER was the earliest form of the Greek galley. Long, narrow and shallow, it was built for speed under oars and ramming. Auxiliary propulsion came in the form of a single square sail that was left ashore when battle was imminent.

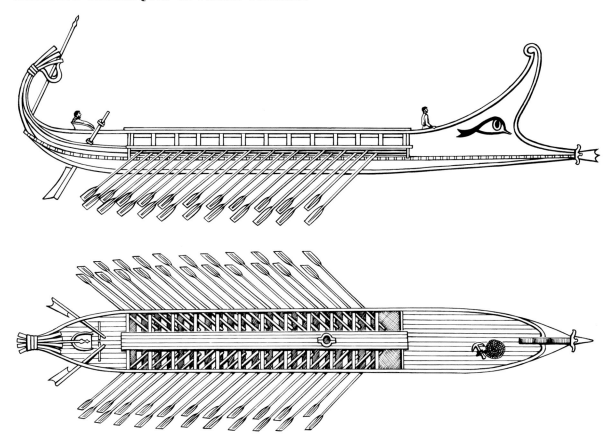

THE GREEK *BIREME: by adding an extra oarsman, the bireme packed double the power into the same hull length. The hull was heavier to accommodate the extra men, but was able to maintain higher speeds for longer than the* pentekonter.

remarkable figure. By comparison, Athens, which was one of the largest Greek city states, could boast barely 30,000 men of fighting age.

The Armies Advance

The Persian army assembled at Sardis in modern Asiatic Turkey, a city the Athenians had burned to the ground during the Ionian revolt but which had since been rebuilt. The Greeks sent three spies, who were captured. Instead of executing them, Xerxes ordered them to be taken on a guided tour of the preparations and then released to carry back news of the vast host assembling to attack Greece. While the army was gathering, advanced supply depots were established along the invasion

route. It took four years before all the preparations were complete.

Finally the army – which Herodotus claims numbered 1.7 million men, including camp followers, servants and soldiers – set off towards the Hellespont, the modern Bosporus Strait between the European and Asian landmasses. A bridge of boats 2km (1.2 miles) wide was constructed across the Hellespont, but the strength of the current broke the cables and the boats drifted away. A Greek engineer supervised the construction of two replacement bridges using nearly 674 *triremes, pentekonters* and other ships from the invasion fleet. In addition to stronger cables, the ships employed extra large anchors to prevent the bridge being swept away. It reputedly took seven days and seven nights for the huge Persian army with all its baggage animals to cross over the bridge. Worried by the fate of his father's fleet, wrecked off Mount Athos in 492, Xerxes had also ordered a canal dug through the

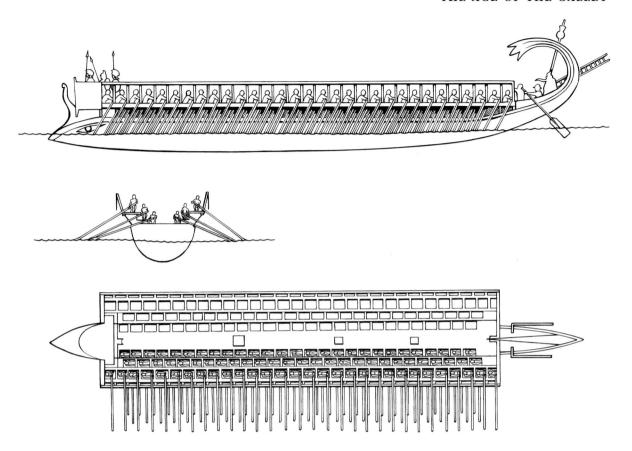

THE *TRIREME: extending the rowing benches beyond the confines of the bull on an outrigger, a third tier of oarsmen generates even more power. But it is still a ramming machine with just 14 marines.*

Mount Athos peninsular to allow his fleet to avoid the dangerous headland. Dug using local forced labour, the canal was 1.6km (1 mile) long, 60m (200ft) wide and at least 2.5m (8ft) deep.

As the army advanced, the northern Greek cities, no doubt greatly intimidated by the vast force, capitulated without a fight. A further 24 cities were forced to contribute more men and 120 ships to the already mighty host. As the army marched, it was organized into three columns. One moved along the shore within sight of the fleet, another inshore via tracks and roads, and the third, with Xerxes himself, in the middle. Such a huge enterprise was well known in Greece. It was obvious that the emperor coveted the whole of Greece, not just those cities that had supported

the rebellious Greek colonies on the Asiatic shore. Conferences were called and oracles consulted, but even then the Greek cities were unable to present a unified front. Different cities demanded sole command of the combined army and argued bitterly amongst themselves.

In the end, terrified Athens ploughed all the revenues from her silver mines into building *triremes*, the wooden wall prophesied by the Oracle at Delphi. Working flat out, her shipwrights had completed 127 vessels, mainly *triremes*, by the time the fleet had to set sail. Each ship required a crew of 170 oarsmen, 20 sailors and 14 marines. Thus the 127 ships required about 26,000 men. This could be achieved only by heavily depleting the army and relying on her allies to make up the combined land force. Both sides knew from experience that in equipment, motivation and training the Greeks soldiers were better prepared than the Persians. But the difference was much less marked in the fleets than on shore. The ships

were virtually the same and at least half the Persian ships were crewed by Greek sailors. Moreover, the Egyptian marines were possibly even better than the Greeks. So the Greek strategy was to seek confined or restricted battle sites to confront the overwhelming Persian host.

First Clashes

Geography pointed to the narrow pass at Thermopylae as the best site to meet the Persian land army and the narrow channel between the island of Euboea and the Greek mainland near Artemisium, some 64km (40 miles) to the west, as the best point to position the Greek fleet. A mere 300 Spartans and 4900 allies from other cities gathered at Thermopylae and set about repairing the wall built during an earlier conflict between the Phocians and Thessalians. Meanwhile, the Greek ships took their station by Artemisium. The Athenian fleet was supplemented by 40 Corinthian ships, 20 Megaran ships, 20 ships from Chalcis and 64 from various other states. A Spartan named Eurybiades was appointed as commander because the other contingents refused to serve under an Athenian. The whole fleet, some 271 ships strong, required more than 55,000 sailors and marines. Ashore, lookouts were posted and a contingent left to guard a mountain track that bypassed the wall. Afloat, a piquet of three *triremes* was posted at the island of Skiathos, 30km (20 miles) to the northeast. Alarm

"Forward, sons of the Greeks,
Liberate the fatherland,
Liberate your children, your
women, the altars of the gods of
your fathers
And the graves of your
forebears:
Now is the fight for
everything.'
— *A PAEAN THOUGHT TO HAVE BEEN*
SUNG BY GREEK SAILORS AT SALAMIS

OPPOSITE: THIS PICTURE *gives a good impression of a seaborne mêlée, but note that the oarsmen did not have shields to hang on the sides for protection and that the wind appears to be blowing from three different directions at the same time! Sails were normally left ashore during battle. Note too the flanking galleys coming into ram from the top left.*

beacons were arranged on the hills and headlands and the fastest *pentekonter* was allocated the duty of liaising between fleet and army.

While the Persian army approached the position at Thermopylae, 10 of their fastest ships chased down and captured the three Greek piquets. They also marked a dangerous submerged rock in the channel off Artemisium using a large stone pillar. When their main fleet arrived, some 200 ships were dispatched to sail south around Euboea and take the Greek fleet from the rear. To counter this, the Greeks sent 53 ships to hold the other end of the inshore channel. Meanwhile, the main Persian fleet anchored at Aphetae on the northern side of the Euboea channel. Then the wind took a hand. A great storm from the east blew up and damaged or scattered about 400 of the Persian ships, including the squadron detached to encircle the Greeks. This reduced the Persian strength to around 727 ships, still outnumbering the Greeks by more than three to one. When the storm abated, the Persians sailed to attack. The Greeks, however, formed a defensive circle and the Persian attack lost 30 ships without inflicting any significant losses on the Greek side.

Delayed Offensive

The next day, neither side made a move – both fleets were presumably busy repairing damage. As the day wore on, the 53 Greek ships previously despatched to hold the end of the channel returned and the Persians must have realized that their flank force had been lost. On the third day, however, the Persians returned to the offensive. By the end of the action, about 100 Greek ships and more than 100 Persian ships had suffered some form of damage. This was a tit-for-tat battle, which the numerically weaker Greek fleet could ill afford. Now the news arrived that the Greek force at Thermopylae had been defeated. The desperate last stand of the Spartan-led army had bought valuable time, but the road to Athens now lay open. So, despite the post-battle weariness and trauma, the Greek sailors had to leave their dead and sail by moonlight down the inshore channel and back to defend the now vulnerable city of Athens.

While the gallant few had fought and died at Thermopylae, other Greeks had been busy preparing their defences. The next natural line of defence on the mainland was the Isthmus of Corinth and here another wall was being built. But the great cities of Athens and Thebes were on the wrong side of the new wall. And unless the Persian fleet could be neutralized, the Persian army would be able to land wherever it wished, regardless of the wall. Clearly drastic action was required to counter the remaining 600-odd Persian ships.

The city of Thebes submitted to the Persian king, a dreadful blow to the morale of the free Greeks. Those cities that refused to submit were burned and the countryside around them ravaged. Most of the remaining population of Athens – men, women and children - was ferried to the offshore islands of Salamis and Aegina and to Troezen on the far side of the Saronic Gulf. When the land army under Xerxes arrived at the almost deserted city, they found that the guardians of the Acropolis and a few others had barricaded themselves inside. A frontal attack with fire missiles failed but a secret way in was found and the defenders slaughtered.

Meanwhile the reinforced Greek fleet, now up to 378 ships, stationed itself between Salamis and the head of the Saronic Gulf. The Persian fleet settled in at the beaches around Phaleron and other beaches nearby. Divisions still racked the Greek ranks. The contingents from the lands south

'Remember also, thou goest home having gained the purpose of thy expedition; for thou hast burnt Athens!'

— QUEEN ARTEMESIA TO XERXES AFTER SALAMIS, FROM HERODOTUS

of the new wall wanted to return to their homes to join in the defence there.

At this crucial moment a little artifice went a long way. The Athenian commander Themistocles gave the impression that the Greeks were planning to escape. The Persians deployed their fleet that night to block both exits from the Salamis basin, preventing the Greek contingents from escaping. All night, the Persians stayed at sea. Their crews, unable to rest other than on their rowing benches, must have been exhausted by morning.

Battle Begins

The western channel was blocked by the still powerful Egyptian flotilla of perhaps 150 ships. To face this deployment, the Greeks placed around 80 ships of the Corinthian contingent. At the mouth of the eastern channel, to the west of the island of Psyttaleia, the Persian commander placed around 300 ships from the Greek cities in Asia. To the east of the island were positioned around 100 ships from the Ionian contingent. Psyttaleia itself was occupied by Persians so that any beached ships could be captured. Meanwhile, the great king Xerxes set up his throne on the hillside overlooking the Gulf, guarded by his elite force, the Immortals, to watch the battle.

Surviving accounts of the battle, like all such accounts, are confusing. It seems that the Egyptians and the Corinthians vessels fought all day. The main Greek fleet deployed as if to break out but then started to back water into the narrowest part of the strait, which was just 1.8km (1 mile) wide. This position suited the Greeks since their ships were on the outside of the curve and could enjoy local numeric superiority and the advantages of a flank attack. The Persians took the bait and pursued the Greeks into the narrow waters.

Although the rams used on both sides could cripple opposing ships, the victims tended not to sink. Having little in the way of ballast and being made largely of wood, stricken vessels would continue to float and become obstacles to manoeuvre. So, after the initial clash, naval battles of the period would usually break down into shipboard mêlées, with each side trying to reinforce their own beleaguered comrades. This is exactly what happened at Salamis. As they crowded into the strait, the Persian ships became so bunched up that they could not row without interfering with the neighbouring vessels, never mind manoeuvre to ram or counter ram. Consequently the Greeks, being better able to manoeuvre, had a field day for a while, at least until the water was so choked with waterlogged ships that they had to resort to boarding where they could and fighting hand to hand on blood-soaked decks.

During the vicious hand-to-hand fighting, the superiority of the Greek hoplite's equipment, training and motivation quickly began to tell and the Persian king's men fell in droves. Morale is an important factor in any battle and it appears that the Persian morale gave way first. As Xerxes watched from his throne on the hillside overlooking the strait, the unengaged ships from the head of the Persian column turned to try and escape back out to sea, some unintentionally ramming others from their own side. Many of the Persian sailors who were thrown into the water drowned because they were unable to swim. Among the thousands of Persian casualties during the battle was Xerxes' own brother.

This defeat did not spell the end for Xerxes. Fearing that the victorious Greeks would sail off to the Hellespont and destroy his bridge of boats, cutting off his retreat, the emperor ordered some of his troops to build a mole out to the island of Salamis to mask his other preparations for retreat. As the remaining Persian fleet fell back to Asia, Xerxes left an army behind in his newly won northern Greek provinces. This army was beaten at the Battle of Platea the following year and the Persian fleet was caught in its winter base and destroyed. Greco-Persian animosity festered for

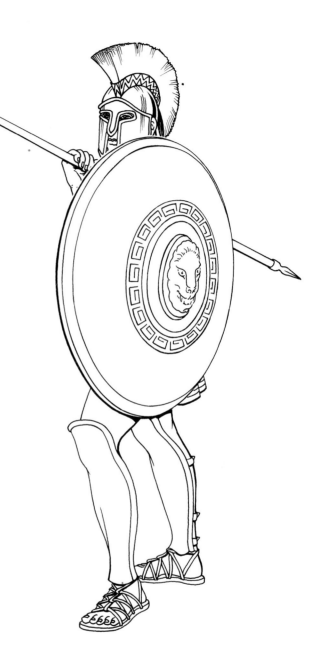

A GREEK HOPLITE, WHO *fought shoulder to shoulder and face to face. The principal weapon was a heavy 3.5m (11ft) spear made from hard cornel wood with a metal head and counterweight. He also carried a short sword for really close work. He wore bronze greaves, breast and back plate, and a helmet. The shield was bronze-faced wood with a painted design.*

Battle of Salamis

480 BC

Both the previous land and naval battles between the Greeks and Persians had been fought on lines of communication, but this was not. If Xerxes could establish command of the seas he could bypass the next line of Greek defence, a wall being built near Corinth across the isthmus connecting the Peloponnese to the Greek mainland. So, he had to further reduce the already depleted Greek fleet or it would hamper his further conquest of Greece or harry his return home. The Greeks in turn knew that they had to establish naval superiority despite their inferior numbers or become vassals of the Great King. The Greek plan was to achieve locally superior numbers by forcing the Persian fleet to fight in narrow channels where their much larger fleet could not fully deploy. Once they had gained comparable or superior numbers the better-armed Greek marines would make mincemeat of the unarmoured Persian crews.

Just off shore from the city of Athens, the island of Salamis provides a waterway with just two narrow entrances and enough deep water to shelter the entire Greek fleet.

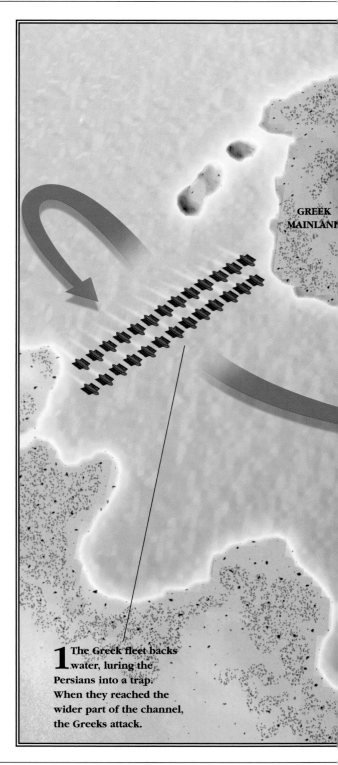

1 The Greek fleet backs water, luring the Persians into a trap. When they reached the wider part of the channel, the Greeks attack.

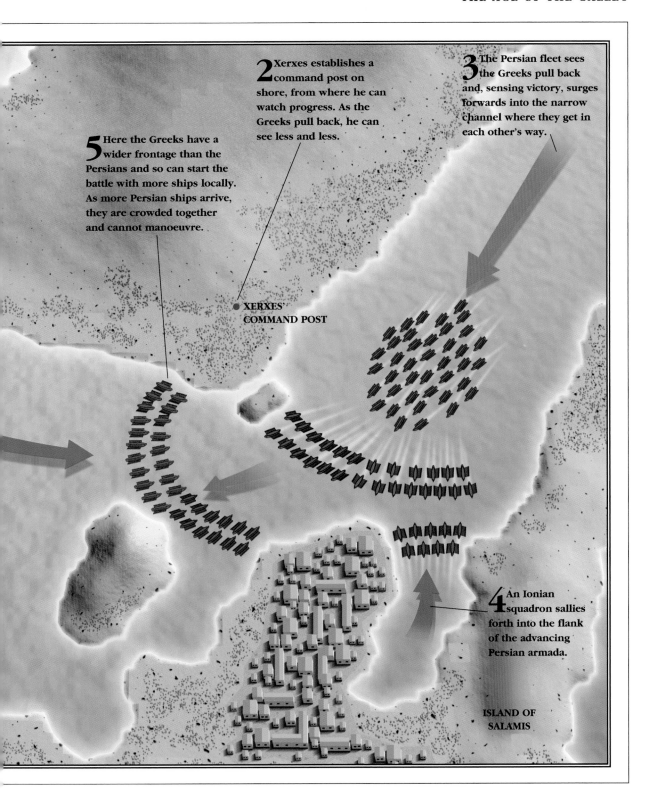

2 Xerxes establishes a command post on shore, from where he can watch progress. As the Greeks pull back, he can see less and less.

3 The Persian fleet sees the Greeks pull back and, sensing victory, surges forwards into the narrow channel where they get in each other's way.

5 Here the Greeks have a wider frontage than the Persians and so can start the battle with more ships locally. As more Persian ships arrive, they are crowded together and cannot manoeuvre.

● XERXES' COMMAND POST

4 An Ionian squadron sallies forth into the flank of the advancing Persian armada.

ISLAND OF SALAMIS

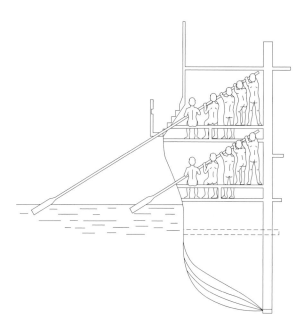

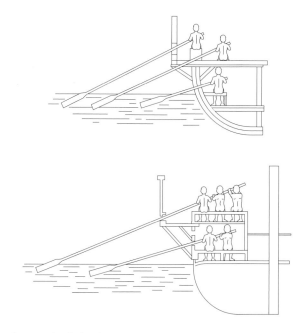

ABOVE: THE ROWING ARRANGEMENT OF THE DECERES –
*10 men pulling on two oars at each rowing station.
Top right: the rowing arrangement of the* trireme *–
three men pulling three oars. Lower right: the rowing
arrangment of the* quinquireme *– five men pulling
on two oars at each rowing station.*

years until Alexander the Great crossed the
Hellespont in 334 BC and conquered Persia, finally
ending the Achaemenid Persian Empire.

Costs, Crews and Storage

Although slavery was commonplace in the ancient
world, slaves were not usually used on board ship
in this period. The role of oarsman was considered
an honourable trade and was at least partially
skilled. The practice of beaching ships at night
to allow the crews to come ashore to cook, eat
and sleep would have made it difficult to prevent
slaves from escaping. Moreover, in a battle, free and
willing rowers meant that a substantial military
reserve existed below decks to supplement the
marines. The oarsmen were therefore paid as semi-
skilled labourers.

During the great Peloponnesian War between
Athens and Sparta in the early fifth century BC, the
oarsmen earned half a drachma per day. The
captain of the ship earned 5000 drachma per year,

from which he had to cover maintenance as well
as his own salary. So, a *trireme* with a crew
of 300 rowers, sailors and marines would cost,
allowing for one day off in ten, around
55,000 drachmas per year to run. The cost to build
was just 6000 drachmas. By the time of the Roman
Empire, inflation had pushed the pay for crewmen
up to 1 drachma per day.

Considering the number of trees required to
build each ship - perhaps 50 - and the size of the
fleets launched throughout the ancient period, it is
small wonder that the forested shores of the
Mediterranean were soon denuded of trees. It was
clearly important for the owners to preserve the
wooden ships for as long as possible. To shield
them from the fierce summer sun and cold winter
rain, they were stored while ashore in huge sheds,
perhaps 50m (165ft) long.

The ship sheds in one harbour at Athens were
capable of storing 350 ships. At Carthage in North
Africa, a circular basin around the harbour was
entirely lined with ship sheds, while more sheds
were sited on an island in the centre of
the harbour.

Ramming Tactics

There were two key tactics used by ramming ships
in the ancient world: the *periplus* and the

diekplus. The *periplus* involved manoeuvring to one side of the enemy ship and ramming the vessel full in the beam. The *diekplus* required more skill and nerve. The attacking ship would head for a gap between two enemy vessels and then swerve to one side, intending not to ram the ship but to break off all the oars down one side. This would have had a devastating effect on the oarsmen, crushing rib cages and breaking backs. Having lost propulsion along one side, the victim would inevitably turn across the stern of the attacker, leaving it vulnerable to a beam ram from a following ship.

Alternatively, the crippled ship could simply be ignored and dealt with later. The attacker could then gather speed from behind the enemy line and was thus ideally placed to use a *periplus* attack on another ship in the line. The best counter to this tactic was to have a second line of ships so that there was a vessel to ram the *diekplus* attacker in the beam as it emerged from the first line.

The Corinthian admiral Machaon, heavily outnumbered at the Battle of Patras in 429 BC, deployed his ships in a circle facing outwards with a small reserve in the centre. The attacking Athenian fleet sailed round like Native Americans circling a wagon train. Finally a wind came up and disrupted the circle, and the Athenian ships pounced. The Corinthians eventually discovered that if they greatly reinforced the bow timbers of their ships they could take on the lighter Athenian

A *DECERES,* THE BACKBONE *of the Roman fleets. The deck was fully covered and able to support several light artillery pieces and 400 marines. There were 600 oarsmen, all of whom had to row in unison.*

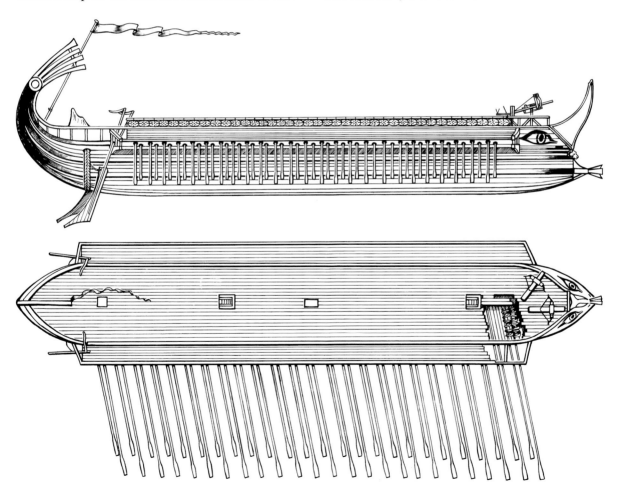

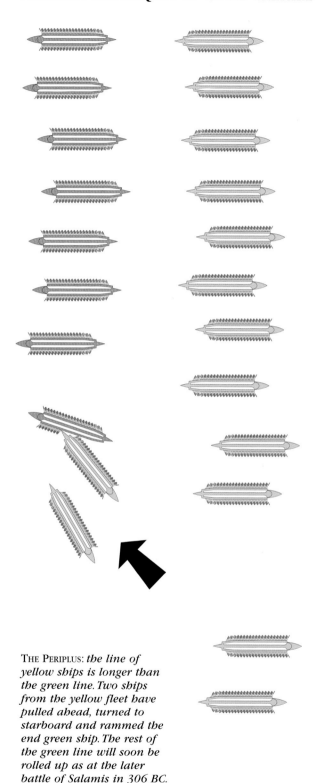

THE PERIPLUS: *the line of yellow ships is longer than the green line. Two ships from the yellow fleet have pulled ahead, turned to starboard and rammed the end green ship. The rest of the green line will soon be rolled up as at the later battle of Salamis in 306 BC.*

ships bow to bow and come off best. This tactic led to the victory over the Athenian fleet in the harbour of Syracuse in 415 BC and the disastrous end of the Athenian expedition to conquer Sicily.

Although it ended badly for the Athenians, the Sicilian Expedition was a classic example of the projection of authority by a dominant naval power. When that authority is absent or focused elsewhere, piracy prevails. The war that followed the fall of Athens from her predominant position involved four different groupings, all trying to command the trade routes between Athens and the grain harvests of the Crimea. At the battle of Cyzicus in 410 BC, a fleet from the Peloponnesian faction beached their ships stern first to avoid being rammed by a larger Athenian fleet. An Athenian squadron did, however, ram the ships on one flank, landing a force of marines and capturing the improvised camp. The losing admiral sent a message back to Sparta: 'Ships lost. General dead. Men starving. Don't know what to do.' Sadly, the reply is not recorded.

By 406 BC, the quality and number of experienced Athenian seamen had dwindled disastrously and the navy had to resort to hastily trained labourers and freed slaves. This fleet of 150 ships set off to raise the siege of Methymna on the island of Lesbos. The Athenians were faced by 120 ships of the Peloponnesian faction manned with experienced crews. To counter the *diekplus* manoeuvre, the Athenians lined up in two ranks, which made their line much shorter than the enemy's. To prevent their ships being outflanked, they deployed with an island in the middle of their line, allowing them to match the length of the enemy line. The tactic worked. The battle became a giant slogging match, devoid of manoeuvre, in which Athenian numbers counted for more. Athens lost 25 ships compared with 69 of the enemy.

The next development in naval technology came from the Greek colony of Syracuse in Sicily. This was to make the ships wider and add additional oarsmen to each oar. Thus the *quadreme* carried four oarsmen per rowing station and the *quinquereme* five oarsmen. Having made this breakthrough in design, there was no limit and the Greeks soon built *heptares*

THE DIEKPLUS: *the leading yellow ship aims to knock the oars off the opposing brown ship and pass through the gap. With no propulsion on that side, it turns to the left, exposing its righthand side to the following ship. The first yellow ship through can now turn onto the rear of the next brown one in line. If the brown ships had been in two lines, the tactic would be a disaster for the yellow ships.*

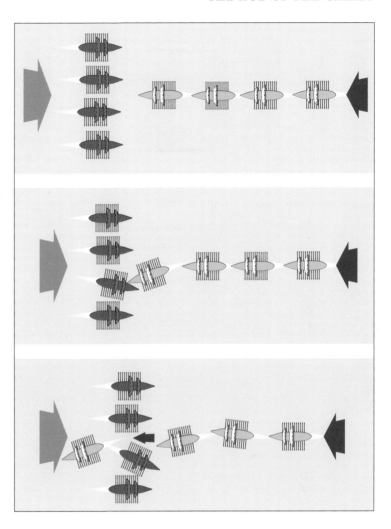

and *hexares* with seven and eight oarsmen per rowing station respectively. The deck was extended from the narrow walkway in the centre of the ship across the full width of the ship, giving much greater protection to the oarsmen and creating a much enlarged platform for marines or even artillery. Even so, these ships were lightly constructed – the Roman ships of the Punic Wars period particularly so. It was found that the oars had to be in the water to steady a ship sufficiently for grapples to be thrown. On one occasion, a Roman ship was able to slide over a boom across the mouth of a harbour by moving all the non-rowing crew to the stern to lift the front of the ship while the rowers worked intensely, and then moving them forward to the bow to alter the way she sat in the water, thereby bringing the ship over the boom.

The Battle of Salamis in Cyprus, 306 BC

Following the death of Alexander the Great in 323 BC, his successor generals carved out their own individual empires, initiating a series of wars that lasted for more than 20 years. Antigonos, known as 'One Eye', held much of Alexander's Asian empire and was at war with Ptolemy I, who held Egypt. Antigonos' son Demetrius invaded Egyptian territory in 312 BC, when he was beaten by Ptolemy at the battle of Gaza. Early in 306 BC, Demetrius went on to invade the Egyptian-held island of Cyprus, laying siege to the governor in the capital of Salamis on the eastern coast. Ptolemy raised a relief force in Egypt and set sail directly from the mouth of the Nile to Paphos, at the western end of Cyprus.

The trip of 400km (250 miles) was an extremely risky undertaking, involving a night passage in an age before the compass. A fleet that left at first light would need to maintain an average speed of over 7 knots to arrive at Cyprus before the second nightfall. Even with the *pharos* (lighthouse) at Alexandria, some 122m (400ft) high, the fleet would have lost sight of land after just five-and-a-half hours at sea and would not have seen it again for 28 hours. To steer a straight course for all that time must have taken nerve and skill in equal measures. Indeed, it must have been an enormous relief to see a thin dark line on the horizon mature and grow into the recognizable silhouette of Cyprus.

Ptolemy's force comprised 140 *quadremes* and *quinqueremes*, plus 10,000 soldiers carried on 200 sail-only transports. Bottled up in the harbour at Salamis were a further 60 Egyptian ships, again *quadremes* and *quinqueremes*. Demetrius had only 108 ships, including seven *heptares* and 10 *hexares* plus 30 Athenian *quadremes*. But he did have the advantage of internal lines of communication. As Ptolemy sailed south and east around the island, Demetrius laid out his plans. He would leave 10 *quinqueremes* to hold the narrow entrance to Salamis harbour, thereby neutralizing the 60 ships inside. To supplement his remaining fleet, he would use his own 53 transports, which were built with a deeper draft like merchantmen but also equipped with three banks of oars. These were well manned with soldiers to act as marines. Stone and dart throwing artillery was stationed on the decks of his ships along with the usual archers and marines. Demetrius also deployed units of cavalry on shore to mop up any enemy crews who made it to land.

Ptolemy expected to outflank his enemy and thought that Demetrius would therefore keep one flank of his line close to shore. Both sides therefore deployed their ships in the traditional two lines with one end as close to the shore as was prudent. Ptolemy placed his own ship about 12 ships out from the coast and, presumably, put his heaviest ships in his front line.

Demetrius' deployment was more interesting. His shore-side wing comprised his *quadremes* and *quinqueremes*, his centre the transports, and on his seaward side the *heptares* and *hexares* were backed by more *quinqueremes* including his own ship. To lengthen his line and ensure he could outflank the Egyptian line, he deployed some of this squadron only one rank deep.

It must have been a staggering sight, with the ships all colourfully painted using the traditional eyes on the bow and stretched out into a line over 1km (0.6 miles) in length. The 141 Greek ships closed with 140 Egyptian ships at a combined speed of about 16 knots. The artillery had a range of around 370m (1215ft) and would have opened

fire at the earliest opportunity; they had only six or seven minutes before the fleets clashed and the rams started their work. The effect of the artillery – torsion catapults firing heavy bolts or stones – was mainly psychological. Aiming when both ships were rolling in the swell and closing at 16 knots would have been difficult to say the least.

As the fleets met in a crash of ships and rams, the two ranks of ships on both sides provided a counter to *diekplus* ramming tactics. The exposed flank of the Egyptian line, however, proved more vulnerable to the longer Greek line. Demetrius's ships overwhelmed the seaward end of Ptolemy's line and rolled it up. The Governor of Salamis eventually broke through the Greek blockade of the harbour and Ptolemy managed to break through the Greek line near the shore, but the

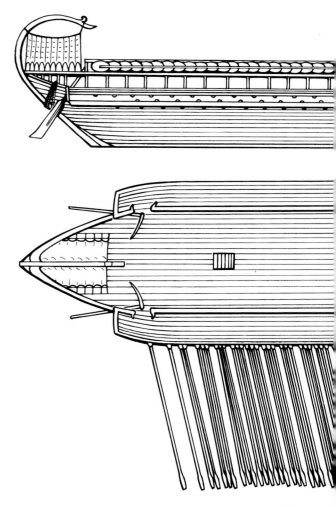

battle was already lost. Around 8000 of Ptolemy's soldiers were captured together with 120 ships before the remainder, including Ptolemy, escaped. The island surrendered to Demetrius, who controlled the eastern Mediterranean for the next 20 years. Antigonos was killed in battle five years later, fighting his former fellow generals in central Turkey. Ptolemy survived until 283 BC, founding the dynasty that ended with Queen Cleopatra.

Campaign Against the Pirates, 66–67 BC

The early period of Roman expansion was marked by a succession of wars with neighbours near and far. First there were the other states in Italy and then Carthage. When Carthage was beaten, the Rome turned its gaze to the east. Macedonia, Greece and then Pontus (modern Asiatic Turkey)

fell to Rome over a number of years. But it was while Rome was focused on these wars that piracy raised its head in the eastern Mediterranean.

For many years, the island of Rhodes had used its navy to suppress piracy in order to protect her position as a transit port in the lucrative east-west trade. However, Rhodes fell foul of the Macedonian kingdom and appealed to Rome, who sent a force of *quinqueremes* to defend her ally. The combined force compelled the Macedonians to sue for peace. Under the treaty, the Romans gained the small island of Delos, which they returned to Macedonia on the condition that it was run as a free port with no taxes or dues on goods entering or leaving. Unfortunately for Rhodes, the presence of this offshore tax haven undermined the revenues from her trade and the island and her

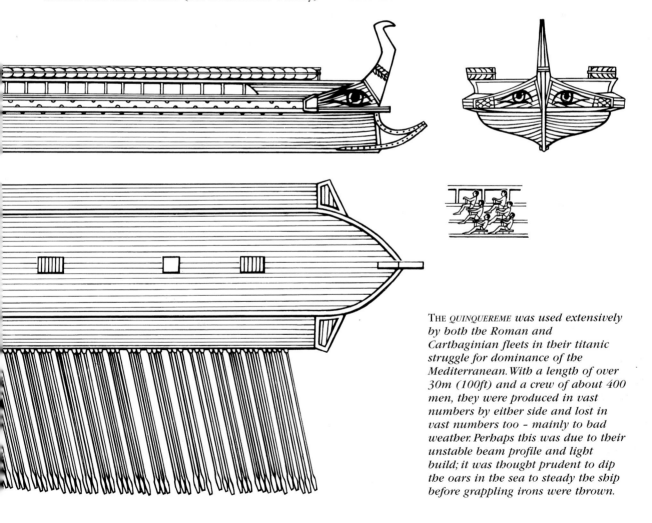

THE *QUINQUEREME was used extensively by both the Roman and Carthaginian fleets in their titanic struggle for dominance of the Mediterranean. With a length of over 30m (100ft) and a crew of about 400 men, they were produced in vast numbers by either side and lost in vast numbers too - mainly to bad weather. Perhaps this was due to their unstable beam profile and light build; it was thought prudent to dip the oars in the sea to steady the ship before grappling irons were thrown.*

AN EARLY ROMAN *QUINQUEREME* POWERS *through the sea, propelled by oarsmen seated on three levels. It is equipped with a* corvus *at its prow, ready to entrap any enemy ship attempting to withdraw from a ramming contact.*

navy went into long-term decline. With Rhodes no longer able to police the waters of the Mediterranean, the pirates spread their depredations beyond the eastern Mediterranean. Ports and coastal towns were sacked, shrines desecrated and cargoes, crews and ships taken at sea. The goods, ships and their crew were then sold off at various markets. Wealthy captives were held to ransom.

The ordinary merchants of the ancient world sailed in ships far simpler in design than the warships of the period. Such ships could not afford the expensive oarsmen of the warship and had to rely instead on the single main mast and single square sail with the optional refinement of bowsprit and second, smaller square sail. Later ships added a triangular sail above the main for extra propulsion. The merchant ships could be as much as 60m (200ft) in length, possibly with more than one mast, but were more usually just 30m (100ft) long and 8m (26ft) in beam, drawing just 3m (10ft) of water and carrying loads of around 100–150 gross tons. Built for capacity rather than speed, they were not fast – perhaps 5-6 knots if the wind permitted. Crews were kept to a minimum since they ate into the profits: 10-15 men were usual on a medium-sized ship; less on a smaller ship and more on a larger one.

While the sail-powered merchantman was dependent on the wind for speed, the oar-powered warship or pirate ship was unhampered by head winds or rough seas. Since the square sail meant the merchantman would sail fastest heading down wind, the pirate tactics were simple: cruise into the wind so that any prey coming the other way would find it next to impossible to escape. Alternatively, the pirates would lurk behind headlands for a quick spurt to catch any passing trader. Fear and intimidation were the best weapons to induce a quick surrender. Faced by a pirate ship apparently bristling with armed men and with no way to escape, most merchant ships would be forced to capitulate. The pirates could

then use their oars to spin the ship around and bring their bows up to the victim's stern, where it was safe to board. The crew would be bundled below and well trussed up and the pirates would install their own crew to sail the prize for home.

So widespread and powerful did the pirates grow that when the rebel leader Spartacus and his army of ex-slaves became trapped in the toe of Italy in 72 BC they negotiated with the pirates to evacuate the whole army – some 90,000 men, women and children – by ship. The pirates were then paid even more by the Roman politician Crassus not to fulfil the contract. The problem with piracy reached such a pass that two Roman Praetors, together with their staff, were captured by the pirates. Another squadron attacked Rome's port at Ostia and sacked other towns in the region.

Pompey's Appointment
In many ways, the Roman elite benefited from the pirate's activities. For those who could afford to buy, piracy kept the price of slaves low and supply plentiful. On the other hand, it did interrupt trade.

THE ROMANS EXPERIMENTED with ship-borne ballistae as an effective missile arm to soften up enemy ships before engaging in ramming or ship-boarding operations. The type shown here would have operated by winching back and shooting a cord, pulling against the tension created by the wound rope spools.

So the wealthiest classes in Rome, who needed to buy slaves to work their estates, benefited while the lower, merchant classes and their workers suffered. In 69 BC, however, the pirates excelled themselves and plundered the island of Delos. It comes as no surprise, then, that the consul Metellus was voted an army to reduce the pirate base in Crete. He headed off and set about his task, rounding up some pirates and settling down to besiege others in the main pirate base on the island.

In 67 BC, the Roman tribune Aulus Gabinus presented a bill to the Peoples' Assembly to appoint the most famous general of the age, Pompeius Magnus – better known as Pompey – to sweep the pirates from the seas once and for all.

The ramifications were enormous. Clearing the Mediterranean of the pirates would greatly ease the lot of the ordinary man. Indeed, prices in the markets of Rome fell significantly simply at the presentation of this bill. The Roman citizens, the *plebs*, were right behind the idea. However, the wealthy ruling classes, the senators and, to a lesser extent, the knights were almost universally against the bill. The one notable exception was Julius Caesar. Ever the populist, he supported the motion. It was passed.

Pompey had already enjoyed a very distinguished military career. He had first been appointed commander of an army at the age of 24, supporting Sulla's side in an earlier civil war. Although he was occasionally accused of cruelty, he proved so successful during campaigns in Sicily and in Africa that he was acclaimed 'Great' by Sulla. He even asked for and was granted a triumphal procession that should not have been permitted given his youth and junior rank. No sooner had Sulla died than another civil war loomed and Pompey found himself in Spain, leading an army against Sertorius. Although he was supported by a second army under Metellus, it was Pompey who gained a second triumph. It was a truly remarkable achievement.

The resources initially proposed for Pompey in this next task were huge. They comprised some 200 ships plus oarsmen, sailing crew and marines totalling over 40,000 men. He was to be given 15 legates (military commanders), an unlimited treasury, and unlimited powers over the whole of the Mediterranean and up to 7km (4.5 miles) inland.

However, the vote was postponed for a day and when the final amended version was passed the Assembly voted through an even bigger force. This consisted of no less than 500 ships, 120,000 infantry and 5000 cavalrymen, 24 senior military commanders and a pair of quaestors (magistrates responsible for military finances). Against this,

GNAEUS POMPEIUS MAGNUS *(106–47 BC), Roman soldier and statesman, circa 48 BC. He had a meteoric rise to fame and power through early military success. But he backed the wrong aristocratic side against the populist Julius Caesar.*

Pompey versus the Sea Pirates

67 BC

The pirates needed to avoid contact with more powerful military elements so that they could continue to extract plunder from less well defended ports and communities in the Mediterranean, while the Roman squadrons sought to round up the pirates and bring them to a very rudimentary justice. Pompey chose to divide the Mediterranean into discrete areas and conquer each in turn, starting in the far west off the coast of Spain. This drove the pirates steadily towards the southern shore of Turkey and the final bloody confrontation happened near Soli, in modern-day southern Turkey. There, Pompey's assault routed the pirates, destroying their sttongholds in the area. Although hailed as a great victory Empire, it was not successful in the long term. Just a few years later in Sicily, Anthony and Octavian had to combine to combat Pompey's son, who had turned to piracy.

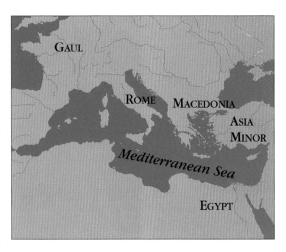

The long Mediterranean shore includes many small inlets relatively inaccessible from the shore and ideal as places for pirates to hide undetected, before launching further raids.

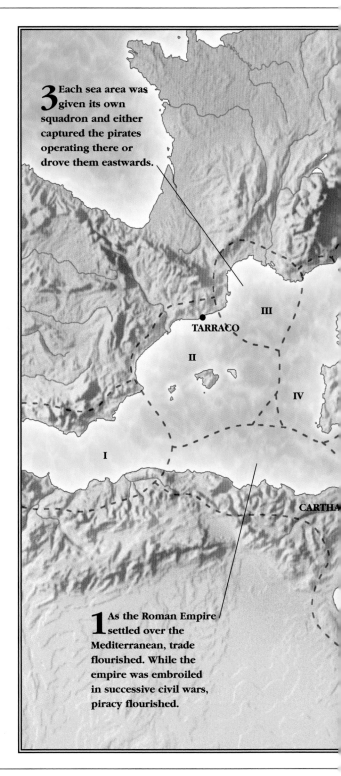

3 Each sea area was given its own squadron and either captured the pirates operating there or drove them eastwards.

TARRACO

III

II

IV

I

CARTHA

1 As the Roman Empire settled over the Mediterranean, trade flourished. While the empire was embroiled in successive civil wars, piracy flourished.

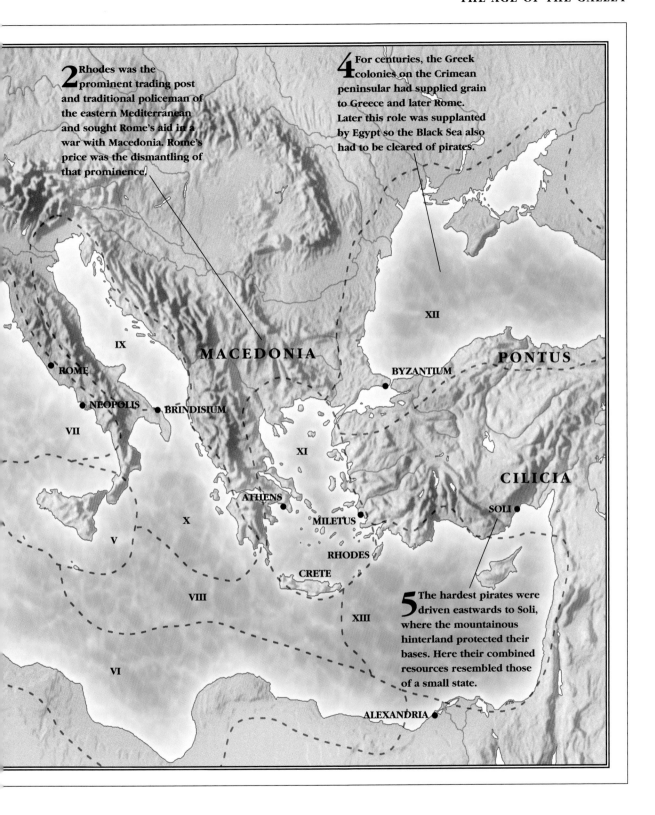

2 Rhodes was the prominent trading post and traditional policeman of the eastern Mediterranean and sought Rome's aid in a war with Macedonia. Rome's price was the dismantling of that prominence.

4 For centuries, the Greek colonies on the Crimean peninsular had supplied grain to Greece and later Rome. Later this role was supplanted by Egypt so the Black Sea also had to be cleared of pirates.

MACEDONIA

PONTUS

XII

IX

ROME

BYZANTIUM

NEOPOLIS

BRINDISIUM

VII

XI

CILICIA

ATHENS

SOLI

X

MILETUS

V

RHODES

VIII

CRETE

XIII

5 The hardest pirates were driven eastwards to Soli, where the mountainous hinterland protected their bases. Here their combined resources resembled those of a small state.

VI

ALEXANDRIA

THE GREEK-STYLE *TRIREME, the ship that laid
the foundations for galley design for the next
2000 years. It had just one purpose: to ram, and
ram again.*

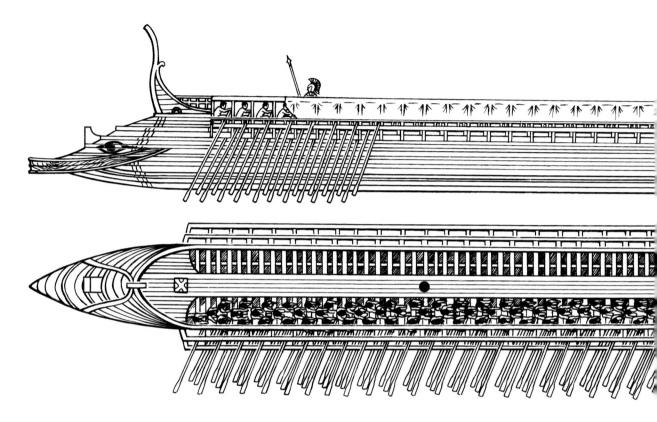

however, the pirates were reputed to have 1000 ships at their disposal and bases both large and small all around the Mediterranean.

Planning and preparation are key to the success of any enterprise and Pompey's orders were decisive. The Mediterranean was divided into 13 areas and each one was allocated a commander and a force appropriate to the threat in that area. Pompey retained direct control over a reserve of 60 of his best ships – almost certainly *quinqueremes* with well-trained crews. Starting with the waters west of Italy, the local commanders restricted the seaborne movements of the pirates and forced them ashore, where they were destroyed. It took only 40 days to sweep these seas clean of the menace. Those pirates that escaped, made their way back to bases along the inhospitable Cilician coast in what is now Turkey.

The greatest threat to Pompey's success came from inside Rome. The general's wide powers were both envied and feared, especially by those who benefited most from the activity of the pirates. The consul Piso, safe within the walls of Rome, went so far as to countermand Pompey's orders, paying off some of the ships' crews. While Pompey's fleet sailed south around the foot of Italy to tackle the pirates in the Adriatic, Pompey himself hurried back to Rome. There, his friend and supporter Gabinius had already started the process of dismissing Piso from his position as consul. This would have been a dreadful and permanent stain on his family honour and reputation. Having got his crews back, however, Pompey had the bill withdrawn, and thus Piso lwas let off. Meanwhile, Rome had been transformed – the markets were full of foodstuffs from all over

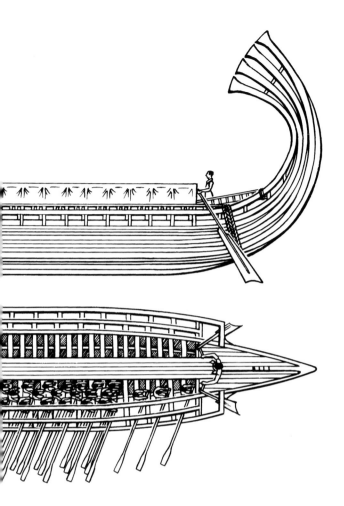

the Mediterranean and prices were almost back to normal. From Rome, Pompey made his way to Brundisium on the east coast of Italy and took ship for Greece and the final part of the war.

Some of the more cut-off pirate squadrons surrendered to Pompey, who confiscated their ships and arrested the men. He stopped short of having the pirates crucified – the normal form of execution for such a crime (all the survivors of Spartacus' rebellion had been crucified). Thus encouraged, a large number of pirates also sent a message of surrender from Crete, where they were sitting out a siege by Metellus. Pompey accepted their surrender and despatched one of his own commanders, Lucius Octavian, with instructions that no one should pay heed to Metellus but only to Octavian. Mettelus was understandably livid and continued the siege. Octavian, following Pompey's orders, now

masterminded the defence of the city on behalf of the pirates. Eventually the city - and Octavian – were forced to surrender. Metellus humiliated his rival in front of the assembled army before sending him back to Rome with a flea in his ear.

Pompey's rehabilitation worked. Around 20,000 former pirates were eventually settled in underpopulated inland areas like Dyme in Achea, on the northern coast of the Peloponnese, and Soli, in what is now Turkey. However, a substantial body of the miscreants occupied the mountain fastnesses of Cilicia with their families. The inevitable battle with Pompey's men took place at Coracesium in Cilicia in 67 BC. That there was a battle and that the pirates lost it is about all that is known. Pompey's victory was not surprising, however. The trained and experienced men of Pompey's army and navy, with their proper equipment, were more than a match for the undisciplined pirates. It is worth recording that among the spoils of war after that last battle were 90 ships equipped with bronze-headed rams.

The *Cataphract* and Roman Artillery

The *trireme* as a warship had a number of weaknesses. First, the rowers were exposed to high-trajectory missile fire and, being unarmoured, were extremely prone to head and shoulder injuries. Injured oarsmen flailing about in agony tended to disrupt the stroke of the others and thereby slow the progress of the ship just when speed and power were needed most. Second, the narrow walkway between banks of oarsmen and the small decks fore and aft severely limited the number of marines or archers a ship could carry.

The solution to the first two problems was the same: to raise the deck of the ship to above the height of the oarsmen's heads and to board over the whole thing. These vessels were known as *cataphract* ships, from the Iranian term that literally meant 'baking oven' and which was used to describe a fully armoured man on an armoured horse. This enlarged deck space protected the rowers and provided more room for marines and even for small pieces of torsion-powered artillery.

The *ballista* was a Roman artillery-piece made by holding two loops of animal gut and hair in a wooden, or later iron, frame. Through each of these was passed a horizontal arm. Both the top and bottom halves of the loop were then twisted away from the frame and clamped, thus spring-loading the arms in opposition. The individual strands of the loops were tensioned to the same musical note to ensure consistent results. A cord strung between the extremities of the arms could, when pulled back, provide the power to launch a heavy dart to a distance of about 400m (1300ft) with sufficient power to impale more than one victim.

Alternatively, the *ballista* could be used to shoot a spherical stone projectile. Although the balls were not heavy enough to sink the opposing galleys, they would cause considerable damage as they smashed into the ships or crews. The balls could also be made of flammable material to set fire to the target – dangerous to use but very effective against a wooden ship. Another novelty was to hurl earthenware pots filled with poisonous snakes. The pot would shatter on impact, releasing the snakes and causing pandemonium on board the enemy ship. Although much larger artillery was available and capable of hurling missiles of around 40kg (88lb), such machines were too large to be accommodated on board ship and were confined to the defence of cities and harbours.

The third problem, and the most significant for the Romans, was that each ship needed skilled oarsmen and helmsmen. Learning to row is in itself

ROWING ARRANGEMENTS *on a Carthaginian* quinquireme. *Rowing was a respected and skilled profession. With poor ventilation on the later ships, it must have been hard and unpleasant work.*

not so much of a problem; during the Punic Wars, the Romans famously set up rowing benches on shore and taught thousands to row before their ships were even completed. However, helming a 35m (115ft) ship well enough to ram an enemy who is simultaneously attempting to avoid your ram and to ram you in turn is a lot less easy to teach. The Romans concluded that the best answer was to board the enemy rather than attempting to ram and to treat the fight as if it were a shore battle. The Roman solution to an enemy who did not want to be boarded was the *corvus,* or raven. A narrow bridge 1.2m (4ft) wide was constructed and one end slotted over an extra mast, some 7m (23ft) high, erected near the bow. The free end of the bridge was raised to a near vertical position by a hoist at the mast head. Underneath the outboard end of the bridge was a large spike. When the hoist was released, the bridge fell with great force, impaling the spike into the deck of the enemy ship. The direction of fall was controlled by sailors or marines on the deck. Once the *corvus* had been dropped, the Roman marines could storm across two abreast to attack. It is arguable that this one device did more to secure Rome's ultimate victory over Carthage than any other factor.

Actium 31 BC: Anthony and Cleopatra's Last Stand

In 48 BC, Julius Caesar travelled to Egypt to try to restore the grain shipments that were so vital to the Roman masses and which had been disrupted by civil war between Cleopatra and her brother Ptolemy. He also intended to hunt down Pompey,

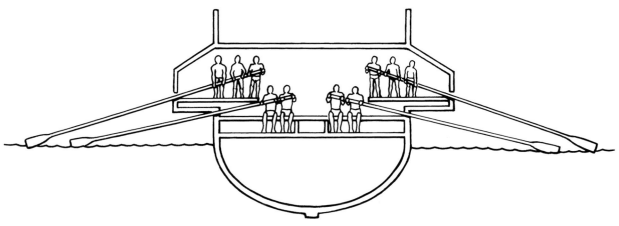

his deadly rival. Cleopatra used every device at her disposal to secure Caesar's affection and protection for herself as the Queen of Egypt. Nine months later, in 47 BC, Cleopatra gave birth to Julius Caesar's son, Ptolemy Caesar, nicknamed Caesarion. Caesar never named Caesarion as his heir, instead nominating his grand-nephew Gaius Octavian. Nonetheless, Caesar restored Cleopatra to her throne and they remained lovers until his death in 44 BC.

One of Caesar's most trusted subordinates was Mark Antony, the grandson of a man who had backed the wrong side in the civil war with Sulla. Despite a frugal upbringing, Antony had still managed to misspend his youth on wine and women, landing up in considerable debt. Summoned to join the army, however, he quickly came to prominence as a gifted leader of his men. Caesar needed good leaders and Antony rose to be his trusted commander of cavalry. Indeed, he was left in charge of Rome for some of the time when Caesar was away campaigning in Spain.

'...suddenly Cleopatra's sixty ships were seen hoisting their sails for flight and breaking away through the mass of fighting ships...'

— *PLUTARCH*

In 44 BC, Caesar was assassinated by a faction headed by the Roman senators Brutus and Cassius. Following Caesar's murder, Mark Antony formed an alliance with Caesar's nominated heir Gaius Octavian to proscribe and eliminate their rivals, the conspirators in Caesar's murder. In time, however, Octavian fell out with the much older Antony and they separated to raise their own armies to hunt down Julius Caesar's killers and the supporters they had recruited.

Brutus and Cassius had meanwhile fled to Macedonia with an army of 17,000. At the battle of Philippi in 42 BC, Octavian was so badly defeated by Brutus that he only narrowly missed being captured himself. He fled to Rome, pleading ill health. Antony, however, defeated Cassius and had him executed. A few days later, he defeated Brutus' contingent too, forcing him to commit suicide. Other collaborators, real or perceived, were also terminated. Antony and Octavian now had a problem. They had promised their soldiers 5000 drachmas each to ensure their loyalty, but with Octavian apparently near to death in Rome it was left to Antony to collect the funds.

He planned a grand tour of the Eastern provinces of the empire to extract the annual tribute/protection money. Unfortunately, it was in Antony's nature to be lavish with gifts and entertainment, so he had to resort to demanding double tribute to pay for the expenses of travel and the soldiers' bounty. Antony received information suggesting that Cleopatra had supported Cassius, one of the prime movers in Julius Caesar's assassination, with funds. He summoned the Egyptian queen to meet with him in Cilicia, now southern Turkey, to give an account of herself. Cleopatra arrived for the meeting on the royal barge surrounded by slave boys dressed as Eros and 'crewed' by slave girls. Antony was captivated. He spent the winter with Cleopatra in Alexandria and soon the queen had borne him two children.

In 40 BC, there was trouble on the eastern frontiers of the empire. An invasion by the Parthians had been blocked by the local commander, Antony's subordinate. Now Antony had to counterattack. But he was more focused on Cleopatra's delights. He rushed the job, leaving behind his siege train, which was captured and destroyed. In 36 BC, the army was very nearly trapped and annihilated while trying to besiege the city of Phraata without the necessary equipment. Antony managed to extricate some of the men, but not before having to resort to decimation - the systematic execution of one in every ten men - to enforce discipline. By the time the roll was called, they had lost 32,000 casualties, fully one third of his force. Eventually, Antony reached the coast of modern Syria and Cleopatra arrived by ship, bringing supplies and money to pay the troops.

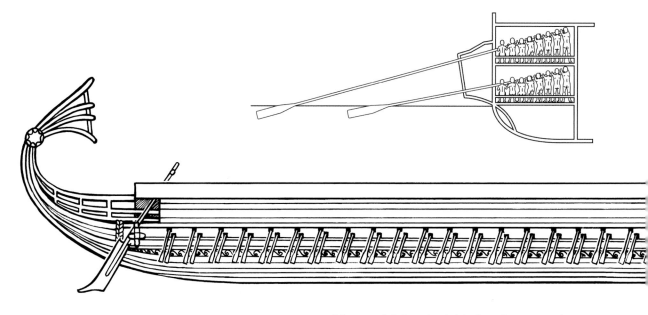

A 'SIXTEEN' FROM THE FIRST CENTURY AD: *introducing a second team on the same oar but facing the first team and pushing when the first team pulls increases the force on the oar.*

While he was recovering on the coast, news arrived that his wife Octavia, a sister of Octavian, was on her way from Rome with reinforcements and supplies. He instructed her to wait at Athens and began planning to duck the confrontation by tackling the easier task, a return expedition to Parthia. A war of words erupted with Octavian in Rome. While Antony continued his affair with Cleopatra from her capital Alexandria, where they indulged in a continuous round of parties, his wife Octavia had no choice but to return to Rome, having been rejected in a most public way.

Declaration of War

Meanwhile, Antony at last set off to Armenia, the first move in the campaign against Parthia. There he received news of Octavian's denunciation, which galvanized him into action. He ordered 16 legions to move to the coast and the combined fleet of all the Egyptian and eastern Roman client territories to assemble at Ephesus on the west coast of modern Turkey. While the fleet was getting together, he and Cleopatra lavishly entertained the client kings on the nearby island of Samos. Seizing the initiative, they moved across to Athens. In Rome, Octavian was working hard to alert the Senate to Antony's betrayal. The key issue was Antony's will. Contrary to Roman custom, Octavian had the scroll removed from the custody of the Vestal Virgins and read before the Senate. It revealed that Antony had bequeathed his portion of the split empire to Cleopatra. Incensed, the Senate agreed to Octavian's declaration of war in 33 BC. Since he had commenced his preparations for war before getting the required decree ratified by the Senate, he was was ready to move instantly.

Since Antony and Cleopatra controlled much of the eastern Mediterranean, the size of their combined fleet was considerable: 520 warships, including a number of huge *octaremes* and *decaremes*, ships with eight and ten rowers per station respectively. The huge *decaremes* alone had a crew of around 1000 men. The vessels were organized into eight flotillas, each consisting of 60 heavy warships and five light ships as scouts. The force also included 300 transports, carrying 100,000 soldiers and 12,000 cavalry – the equivalent of 19 legions.

Much of the navy was Egyptian and the ships were rather short of crew following an outbreak of disease. Many of those pressed into service were therefore largely untrained. In addition, many recruits to the army were from subject kingdoms

and forcing the vast amount of supplies required by Antony's fleet to come over the narrow mountain passes.

At full strength, Antony's host can be calculated as amounting to nearly 400,000 men. Feeding even half that number given the transport resources of the era would have been extremely difficult. And by the time that Antony was able to react to the news of one raid, another was occurring in a completely different part of his territory. Under cover of all this activity, Octavian moved his army across from Italy to Epirus on the Greek coast, just north of Antony's base in Actium. Not only had they firmly gained the initiative, but Agrippa and Octavian had also started to hurt Antony where he was most vulnerable. The restricted rations of his men and the unanswered raids had begun to damage the morale of his soldiers and sailors; more importantly, Antony's supporters had started to wonder whether they had backed the wrong horse.

Agrippa kept up the pressure. He had Octavian's fleet sail out in battle formation across the mouth of the Gulf. Antony matched this challenge by parading every cook and bottle washer on the decks as fighting crew but keeping the ships as close as possible, blocking the entrance to the Gulf. Agrippa recognized this as an impossible situation and retired to let the shortages take more effect. He moved the army south from its landing site to the Ionian shore just 16km (10 miles) from Antony's base, and set up his own camp there at the end of March 31 BC. Through the late spring and all summer, Antony tried everything he could to gain the upper hand. He had the wells of the neighbouring villages salted to make the water undrinkable. He mounted a cavalry raid, sending the troopers all around the shore of the Gulf to attack the camp from an unexpected direction. Then he shipped troops across the narrow entrance to attack the eastern wall of the camp. It was all to no avail.

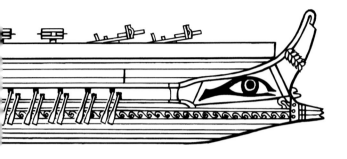

and were not trained or equipped to the same standard as the Roman legionaries. Trudging along on foot, they struggled to keep up with the fleet.

This huge armada moved from Athens to the Gulf of Ambracia on the western seaboard of Greece. This Gulf forms an almost complete circle with Actium, and Antony's first camp, on the southern tip of its narrow mouth. Octavian meanwhile collected some 250 warships, 150 transports, 80,000 infantry and 12,000 cavalry at the southeast Italian ports of Tarentum and Brundisium, just 320km (200 miles) from Antony's headquarters. Although he had a few big ships, most of his galleys were lighter and more manoeuvrable than Antony's.

Octavian may have been a master of political manoeuvring, but for the leadership of his fleet he relied on the older and more experienced general Marcus Vipsanius Agrippa. Agrippa's first move was to cut Antony's fleet off from the supplies that were being shipped from Egypt, by capturing the southern port of Methone. Then, as Antony focused on this problem and was forced to re-route supplies through Corinth, Agrippa raided the watch stations located immediately north and south of Actium. Finally he launched a raid up the length of the Gulf of Corinth, 160km (100 miles) into the heart of Antony's territory, capturing Corinth as well as Patras on the southern shore

Battle Commences

By August, Antony was in desperate straits. Having to match his available manpower to his ships, he took the drastic measure of burning 140 ships that he could not fully crew. Clearly he had no expectation of recovering them after the impending battle – he was already planning to break out rather than to defeat his arch rival. The remaining vessels were supplemented with 20,000 legionaries and 2000 archers. For four days the weather was too poor to venture out, but on the fifth day, 2 September 31 BC, the skies cleared and the fleet sallied forth.

Agrippa was ready. He deployed his fleet in three divisions, each in two ranks to counter the *diekplus* tactic. Octavian took the southern command, Arruntius controlled the centre while Agrippa commanded the northern division. His plan was straightforward but risky: to lure the enemy away from the shore in an ever lengthening crescent. He needed several of his smaller ships to be able to attack the sides of each of Antony's monsters at the same time. When the gaps between the enemy's ships were wide enough, his fleet would attack. Antony was not looking for a decisive battle; he was looking for an escape to regroup, rebuild the strength of his hungry men and try again. He needed to force Octavian's fleet away from the land to gain space to hoist his masts and sails and flee south. It was usual in this period for ships to leave their masts and sails ashore to keep the decks clear of clutter and to retain just the bowsprit and small fore sail on board, for escape or pursuit.

Main Masts in Place

Antony, however, retained his main mast and sails, betraying his intention to flee – although it is unlikely that Octavian or Agrippa would have known this until after they joined battle. He organized his fleet, still larger than that of his rivals, into four commands. Facing Octavian in the south was Caelius, in the centre another Octavian, while Antony led the northern command. Each of these divisions was larger than the one facing it. In reserve waited Cleopatra with her Egyptian contingent and the pay chest.

MARK ANTHONY *was a soldier's soldier. He led his men well and was a good tactician but was a poor planner. Despite the ignominy of his death, his descendants included three emperors.*

In war, morale and confidence are everything. At the Battle of Philippi just nine years earlier, when Antony had saved Octavian from disaster, he was at his peak as a leader. Now, after the disasters in Parthia and having being continually wrong-footed by Agrippa, he no longer had the dash and drive that had won Caesar's confidence. He was defeated before he fought.

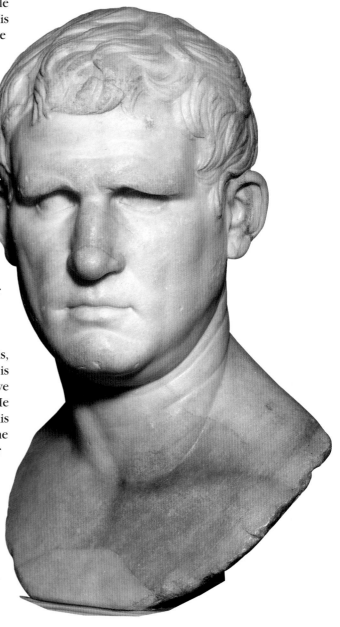

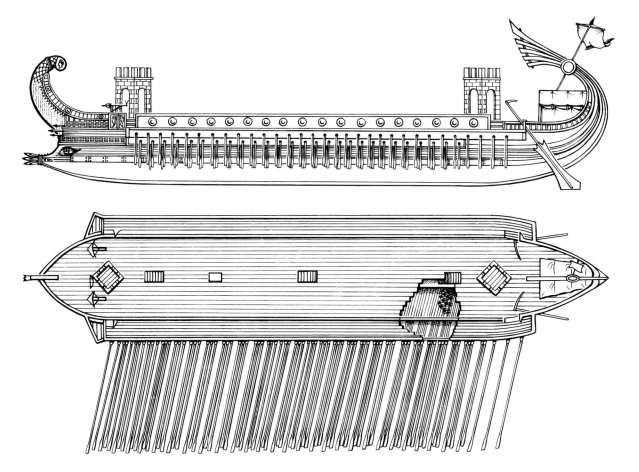

Agrippa's plan gave him the initiative. At first, Antony's line held fast and for a while the two fleets faced one another 1.5km (1 mile) apart. Then Agrippa appeared to move northwards to overlap the end of Antony's line. This was a potentially disastrous position for Antony. He had to attack. As Antony's ships moved forwards, Agrippa's backed water and slowed down, the crescent formation opening the gap between the individual ships. Antony pushed the ships under his command forward while Agrippa edged further back and to the north. The other divisions of Antony's fleet were obliged to do the same or let their leader be outflanked. When he was satisfied that the enemy line had opened and that his own ships outflanked the enemy, Agrippa signalled the attack.

The vessels on both sides were fully decked *cataphract* ships crammed with marines and

A SECOND CENTURY AD ROMAN DECERES, fitted with towers for missile troops. This was the biggest practical size for a battleship powered by oars. Fully manned with a good crew, it could do tremendous damage. Unfortunately, a poor or underfed crew negated that advantage.

augmented with artillery. The bigger ships in Antony's fleet had these mounted on small deck towers to fire over the heads of their own marines. Both sides flung burning missiles at the opposition. There are few things more frightening on a wooden ship than fire, and under the hot summer sun the decks were as dry as matchwood. Where fires started, the sailors flapped at them with leather cloaks, hurled buckets of water, and even piled the bodies of the dead to try to smother the flames.

Amid this chaos Agrippa's ships darted in to shatter the oars on one side or the other or to ram

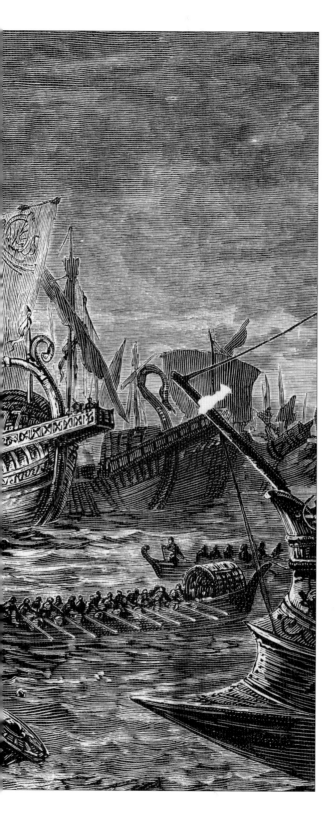

THIS ANONYMOUS *English print showing the battle of Actium presents the Augustan propogandists' view of events, suggesting that Cleopatra deserted Antony's fully engaged ships at the height of the battle.*

the reinforced sides of the bigger enemy. Sometimes they grappled in an attempt to board; sometimes they withdrew to gather speed and try again. Each of the bigger ships was assailed by three or four smaller *quadremes* or *quinqueremes*. Meanwhile, the lumbering giants with their weakened and hungry crews struggled to get up to ramming speed and catch the manoeuvrable smaller ships. The ships in the centre of Antony's fleet engaged their counterparts, but a gap opened between them and the northern flotilla. The southern flotilla did not try so hard; there was more posturing than fighting against Octavian's division, which continued to back water.

In this part of the world, a wind often springs up from the west in the late afternoon and then veers round to blow strongly from a northerly direction. Suddenly Cleopatra's reserve flotilla of 60 ships sprang into action, shouldering their way through the gap that had appeared between the northern and central divisions. Throwing these fresh ships into action could have decisively turned the course of the battle. Had they attempted, they could surely have rolled up Octavian's central or northern commands. Instead, they continued past the fray, raised their masts, hoisted their sails and set off south.

Antony's final act of betrayal was to abandon his own ship, transfer to a lighter *quinquereme* and set off after his queen. Some 40 ships of his fleet also managed to escape the fight. Only three *Liburnian* scout ships from Octavian's fleet made any attempt at pursuit, capturing one of the fleeing ships. The rest of Antony's fleet fought on for nine hours before exhaustion overtook them and the survivors surrendered.

The naval battle cost 5000 lives, less than two per cent of the total numbers of men involved and a measure of how localized the fiercest fighting was. Nearly 300 ships were captured by Octavian and his commander Agrippa. For three days, Antony sulked in the bows of his ship. Only when

Battle of Actium

31 BC

Anhony's best hope for success over Octavian was at sea as he had a greater number of well-equipped ships than his opponent. Moreover, he could not risk invading Italy with his Egyptian soldiers, since his attack would be regarded as a foreign invasion of the homeland rather than an act of civil war. He therefore planted his fleet and army at Actium, as a challenge to Octavian to come out and fight. However, this surrendered the initiative to Octavian, whose general, Agrippa, took full advantage, interrupting food supplies and waging a war of attrition that left Antony's men seriously under strength. They also suffered from the diseases associated with large numbers living in the same place without proper sanitation. Mark Antony's warships were mostly gigantic *quinqueremes*, huge galleys with massive rams that could weigh up to three gross tons. Agrippa had smaller, more mobile ships and better-trained crews who were fresh and healthy.

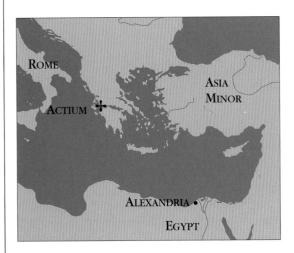

The Gulf of Actium provides a large, sheltered, area for Anthony's fleet with seaborne lines of communication and supply back to Egypt.

3 Agrippa's command edges northwards to outflank Anthony's command. Anthony matches the move and the melee is joined.

4 Octavian backs water to try and pull the enemy away from the shore. Little fighting takes place on this flank. He is not keen to lose another battle and Anthony's commander is reluctant to close.

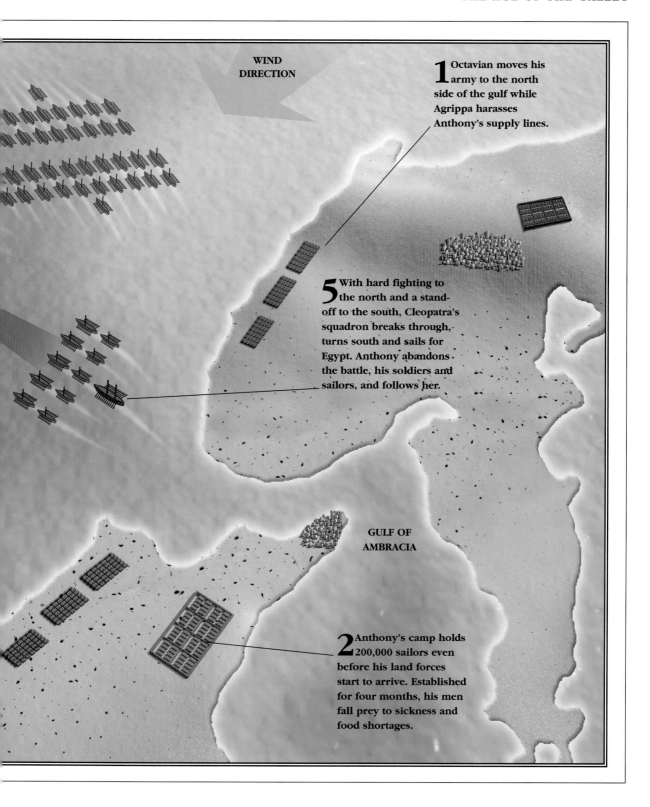

WIND
DIRECTION

1 Octavian moves his army to the north side of the gulf while Agrippa harasses Anthony's supply lines.

5 With hard fighting to the north and a stand-off to the south, Cleopatra's squadron breaks through, turns south and sails for Egypt. Anthony abandons the battle, his soldiers and sailors, and follows her.

GULF OF
AMBRACIA

2 Anthony's camp holds 200,000 sailors even before his land forces start to arrive. Established for four months, his men fall prey to sickness and food shortages.

they rendezvoused off Taenarum Point, at the southern tip of the Peloponnese, could he be persuaded to talk to Cleopatra. At first, Antony's desertion was not widely believed. After all, he still had a very substantial army at his disposal. Antony and Cleopatra were pursued to Egypt, where their men deserted them in droves as Octavian and Agrippa approached. The lovers famously, and separately, committed suicide, leaving the Roman Empire in the hands of just one man, Octavian. He adopted the title Caesar Augustus and ruled the empire like a benevolent father figure for 45 years until he died in AD 14. He remained firm friends with Agrippa until his death in 12 BC.

Final Evolution of the Ancient Galley

Although Actium was the final great battle of the classical world, it did not feature the most spectacular ships seen in the age of the galley. In 350 BC, the Macedonians had joined two *quinqueremes* together to form a catamaran and mounted a huge siege tower four storeys high on top. Designed to assault city walls, the inner sets of oars were removed as unnecessary. But the greatest of the ancient galleys was the *tessarakonteres* ('forty'). Built by Cleopatra's ancestor Ptolemy IV of Egypt in 215 BC, this monster was nearly 130m (425ft) long with a catamaran hull form and nearly 18m (60ft) beam. There were three banks of oars: the lowest oar was manned by four standing oarsmen, the middle by two seated and five standing, and the uppermost oar by five standing and three seated oarsmen. The total crew came to 4000 rowers, 2900 marines and 100 sailors.

In accordance with the custom of the time, the crew boarded in the

A HIGHLY ROMANTICIZED *rendering of Cleopatra aboard her flagship, named* Anthonia, *at Actium. Like her husband Mark Antony, she succeeded in escaping the battle and returning to Egypt.*

morning and disembarked each evening, there being no space for sleeping and certainly no chance of cooking for 7000 hungry men. Unfortunately this took so long, there was little time for this showpiece galley to actually go anywhere.

The Battle of Actium and the annexation of Egypt, Rome's last serious rival with a Mediterranean seaboard, effectively pushed the boundaries of the empire beyond the middle sea. Fleets of smaller ships were still required on the frontiers: the Rhine and Danube, the English Channel and the Irish Sea all supported fleets, mainly *biremes*, nothing bigger being required. The threats they faced were from open boats with a single small square sail and low freeboard, like the Saxon and Viking longships that rafted together to fight or the Irish *curragh*, a leather boat of about 6m (20ft), designed only for raiding.

No major challenge to the Roman Navy came until after the separation of the empire into eastern and western portions. It was the efforts of the Eastern, or Byzantine, Empire to reimpose its

THE ARMIES OF BOTH SIDES *deployed on their respective hillsides to watch the battle. The Romans illustrated here are wearing armour from a later period.*

authority that restarted the trend for building large warships. They were now generally shorter, 36m (120ft), with just 25 sets of oars per side. The lower oar was pulled by just one man and the upper oar by one to three men. All were armed and the upper oarsmen also wore armour. The ships now sported two masts with lateen fore and aft sails giving better performance to windward. The ram was raised above the waterline, like the ships of Ramses III, designed to damage enemy ships rather than to sink them, and they carried up to three towers.

The principle weapon now was fire. A naptha-like inflammable substance – 'Greek fire' – was projected using a bellows device from a nozzle in the bow, with short range but truly horrific results. Long into the medieval era, these ships were able to wade into a mêlée and cause death and destruction all around them.

CHAPTER 2

THE AGE OF CANNON

A shower of flame announced a new era in maritime warfare. A secret super weapon saved the Byzantine Empire from the very jaws of jihad, and the rest of the world realized that, despite improving ships and increasingly skilled sailors, the only way to secure victory was with new technology. The necessities of national survival financed research and lethal innovation. Over the course of centuries, one final weapon came to be the ultimate arbiter of victory at sea.

In 678, Constantinople and the West appeared doomed. An Arab fleet lay unchallenged before the Golden Horn, and the Muslim tide of conquest seemed ready to engulf the last fragment of the Roman Empire in the Eastern Mediterranean. The Arabs had their new religion, one of the central tenets of which was the necessity of jihad in the name of their faith.

MUZZLE-LOADING CANNON *on wheeled carriages announced their presence and potency in gouts of smoke and flame. The vast size and equipment of the Spanish Armada made England's doom seem certain – but standardized calibers on wheeled gun carriages kept the Spanish out to sea and Elizabeth on the throne.*

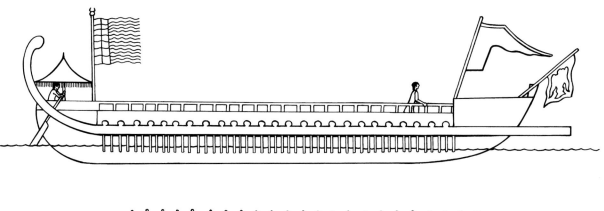

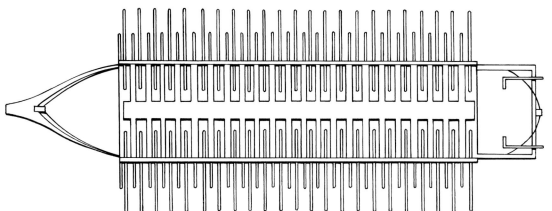

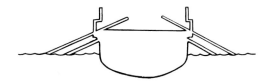

THE BYZANTINE *DROMON*, or 'runner', of the sixth and seventh centuries was a fast descendant of the galleys that had guarded Rome's final years. Covered decks protected hulls and oarsmen, while twin steering oars made for an agile, swift ship that could sail up rivers and beach itself to land troops.

Alexandria, with its docks and shipyards, had fallen to the Arabs in 641, bringing an empire's resources and a vast fleet of well-designed ships. An Arab army surrounded the city on the landward side while the blockading fleet kept food from reaching the city via the harbour.

Unbeknown to the besieging Arab army, however, a Syrian Christian refugee named Kallinikos had mounted a secret weapon known as a *siphon* (pump) on the warships of the Byzantine Emperor's aging navy, turning the *dromon* galleys into an entirely new sort of warship called a *siphonophore*. As the Byzantine Navy sailed out to meet the Arab fleet near Syllaeum, bronze tubes fitted into armoured casemates on the ships' bows shot streams of liquid fire into the Arab armada. Ships and men caught in the fountains of flame burned fiercely as the Arab besiegers fled in the face of this terrifying new weapon. The new incendiary weapon, which became known as Byzantine or 'Greek' fire, provided a striking demonstration of the role that military technology can play at sea.

The realization of the possibilities of naval technology began with the *siphon*, an ingenious combination of pump and incendiary chemical mixture, the details of which were so carefully guarded by the Byzantines that even today the details of both remain obscure. But with the technological salvation of Constantinople never

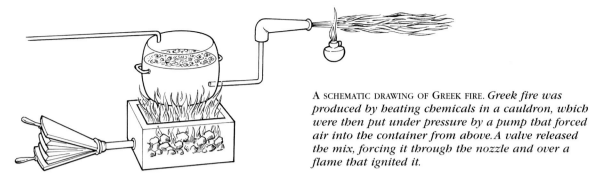

A SCHEMATIC DRAWING OF GREEK FIRE. *Greek fire was produced by heating chemicals in a cauldron, which were then put under pressure by a pump that forced air into the container from above. A valve released the mix, forcing it through the nozzle and over a flame that ignited it.*

far from mind, an interest and justified faith in technology became a permanent fixture of naval warfare worldwide.

New inventions on old ships, or ships built to exploit new tactical possibilities, could alter naval fighting techniques almost overnight. For a millennium, kings and commanders would pursue this or that invention in the hope of finding the next Greek fire. A great many failures were left behind and forgotten as one particular weapon came to dominate the technological arms race at sea. It was the cannon that would eventually come to determine the direction of naval combat throughout the world, becoming the central focus of warfare at sea.

The Evolution of the Warship
The distinction between the 'round ships' of peace and the 'long ships' of war had lasted throughout

classical antiquity. The period from 500 to 1600 would see this distinction between sailing merchant ships and military galleys gradually disappear. Rowed war galleys would continue to be used up until the end of this period and beyond, but by the time of the Battle of Sluys, in 1340, navies were already experimenting in the use of exclusively sailing vessels for war.

With no major rival naval power, the Roman Navy in its final years had dwindled down to lighter and lighter galley designs, most notably the slim, fast, but seaworthy *liburniae* – at its largest a light cruiser with 250 crew, able to patrol and suppress any serious outbreak of piracy. Along the coasts of the Empire and up the largest rivers, these liburnians shared the duties of patrol and reconnaissance with slimmer, lighter vessels known as *naves lusoria* (pleasure yachts), which carried as few as 24 crew and were used for

LARGER AND MORE LETHAL, *the later* dromons *of the ninth to twelfth centuries provided platforms for missiles and protection from boarding in a fast, seaworthy platform. A single row of heavy oars replaced the old layered system, while the basic design became a larger, heavier, main-line unit meant to stand in the line of battle.*

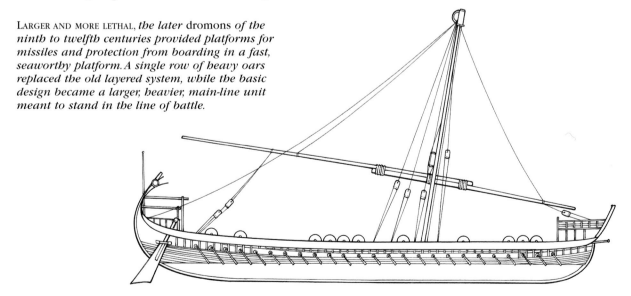

patrols and landing light raiding parties on the far sides of rivers.

With the disintegration of the Roman Empire at the hands of the roving barbarian peoples, however, there came a need for larger vessels capable of extended cruising and the heaviest of fighting. In 533, the Byzantine Roman emperor Justinian destroyed the Vandal kingdom in North Africa with an expeditionary army carried in 500 transports. These vessels were protected by 92 warships of a new design, the *dromons*.

Dromons were initially small ships not very different from their predecessors. They were fast and capable of operating on inland waterways like the patrol craft that had preceeded them. The ships of Justinian's African fleet were probably around 15m (50ft) long, with crews of 30-35 men manning some 22 oars. The oarsmen acted as marines when required, engaging in boarding combat. Like their Homeric ancestors, these galleys featured sailing gear for use while cruising rather than in combat. Unlike the earlier ships, these smaller vessels featured a covered deck and high sides, which offered additional protection to their oarsmen from the arrows of the enemy archers. The *dromon*, increasing in size with the years, remained the backbone of the Byzantine fleet for centuries and was the archetype for the heavier version of the war galley.

The Northern Vessels

In the waters around northern Europe, a simpler, more robust design of war galley gave its possessors a reach and a

BEARERS OF FLAME *and destruction to the Emperor's enemies, vessels such as this* siphonophore, *or pump carrier, annihilated the Arabic fleet in the Golden Horn in 678, and later Viking and Muslim forays against Constantinople. The bronze head around the siphon's nozzle added a dramatic touch and protection to crew directing liquid flame onto enemy ships and sailors.*

reputation far out of proportion to what might otherwise have been the case. As early as 700, fleets of Viking long ships were sailing up the Seine to ravage Paris. The tenth-century voyages of Bjarni Herjulfsson, Erik the Red and Leif Ericsson across the stormy North Atlantic are deservedly legendary.

Mediterranean galleys, with their flimsy hulls, found the rough Atlantic waters a difficult and dangerous proposition. These galleys were typically built of lapped planks, carvel fashion, to preserve timber rare after centuries of exploitation in the more civilized areas. The Viking long ship had the same low freeboard required for rowing, but a hull made of overlapping wooden strakes, in the 'clinker' style of construction. Such building consumed more wood but produced an intensely strong and flexible hull that could survive large waves. Viking long ships sailed down rivers from Scandinavia as far south and east as Moscow and the frontiers of the Byzantine Empire.

There, however, Greek fire proved as effective against the Viking long ships as it had been against the Arab galleys.

The crews of these northern European long ships rowed and fought at sea or ashore as in the millennia previously, every galley having a considerable reserve of manpower. When wood and expertise permitted, the clinker-built long ship could grow to a considerable size. William of Normandy's knights and their mounts crossed the Channel in 1066 on vessels estimated from their depiction on the Bayeux tapestry to be as long as 18m (60ft), and with a freeboard low enough for the horses to disembark on the beach at Pevensey. The tapestry shows the long ships with training gear, which in combination with the inherent 'V' shape of a clinker-built hull allowed ships to make way with the wind abeam, vastly increasing their sailing ability. The use of a keeled hull in sailing vessels would be the most enduring legacy of the Viking design in subsequent shipbuilding.

The shape of the big grain freighters of the Roman era lived on in the early medieval round ship. Like the southern galleys, these were carvel-built – the one difference from their Roman forerunners being a bowsprit raised up until

THIS ILLUMINATED MEDIEVAL GREEK manuscript depicts a smaller Byzantine cheland destroying an Islamic attacker with what the Greeks also called 'automatic fire.' The details of all but the mixture's stunning lethality are lost, leaving other powers to cast about for a super weapon of their own.

it became a second vertical mast. In the Mediterranean's shifting winds, the versatile, easily handled, triangular lateen sail prevailed for all types of shipping; in the Atlantic, the hard-pulling square sail endured.

A 'round ship' with the double-ended design of the Viking craft and its clinker hull would become the most famous of medieval ship types, the celebrated cog. The cog combined the same robust construction and superior sailing ability of the Viking ships with labour efficiency and longevity. A concession to simplified construction was a heavy stern rudder and a tiller, somewhat more robust, if no more functional, than the Greco-Roman steering oar.

Converging Developments
Asian shipbuilders had a different tradition of ship construction but reached a similar level of success

independently of Western innovations. The river *sampan* and the deep-sea junk evolved over the centuries into two supremely capable designs that could and did carry cargoes, weapons and warriors to the western world. Asian versions of the tiller could also be lifted out of the water to facilitate operations in the shallows.

The keelless 'three plank' design of the *sampan* made for the most efficient use of human labour in shallow water, and its wedge-shaped high-sterned design expanded easily and naturally into the seagoing junk. The large and small ships of Asia remained easy to beach and unload quickly – for trade or war, as the situation required. Reinforced, compartmented hulls lent Asian ships a seaworthiness and cargo capacity that would not be matched by the West for centuries and which would call for the development of iron hulls.

Early Inventors

Kallinikos's *siphon* was only the most celebrated manifestation of incendiary weaponry in this period. The Byzantines used their lungs and a reed pipe to discharge a blast of flame, or a simple plunger-piston affair to expel a gout of fire in the course of boarding combat. The Arabs and other powers employed more primitive incendiary devices, such as clay pots filled with naptha and thrown by hand or catapult onto the enemy deck. Fire arrows were the Vikings' counter to the Byzantine devices.

Classical Greek warships, most notably those from Rhodes, had employed catapults. The great naval battle at Actium featured large engines throwing stone shot at hulls and iron bolts at men. By the Middle Ages, however, the catapult was no longer a major weapon of naval combat. The ratchets and relatively precision metallurgy required for the torsion-driven weapons of the Roman era had not survived in the technology of the West. In the East, the Greek fire of the *siphon* gave the Byzantine Empire something dramatically more lethal and less temperamental.

For land sieges, the huge and immensely powerful trebuchet proved a viable replacement for the torsion catapult, but the trebuchet had little success as a ship-to-ship weapon. In 1217, the flagship of the French mercenary and pirate

Eustace the Monk carried a trebuchet intended for use against London itself, but it could not be employed in the resulting naval battle at Dover, a French defeat. In 1274, the ships of the Mongol fleet in the invasion of Japan carried and employed their own trebuchets – but these fired iron bombs against the samurai on the beaches. Other weapons would fill the gap between the catapult and the cannon.

Byzantine marines threw pots filled with powdered quicklime at the crews of enemy vessels. Upon impact, quicklime choked and blinded those exposed to it. Both Byzantine and Arab marines threw pots filled with poisonous snakes and scorpions, which shattered on the enemy decks to release their distracting contents. Particularly unpleasant were spiked wooden balls wrapped in cloth and soaked with inflammables before being ignited and thrown on the enemy's deck. Sailors unfortunate enough to try stamping out the flames would find themselves disabled during the height of battle, even as their ship burned. Byzantine warships featured cranes and derricks to drop burning material on a grappled enemy, while merchant vessels might employ their yardarms and anchors for similar gravity-powered attacks. Other pyrotechnic devices survived even the introduction of gunpowder. The Spanish *bomba* was a military 'Roman candle' – a chemical mixture on a long pole ignited to throw a shower of sparks over an enemy's deck, crew and hull. *Bombas* and ceramic fire grenades were found in the wrecks of ships from the Spanish Armada of 1588.

Gunpowder: The 'Fire Drug'

The Byzantines closely controlled knowledge of the composition of Greek fire, but its efficacy remained well-known and it continued to be used in battle down to the final fall of Constantinople in 1453. The search for some comparable weapon drove scientists and inventors such as the thirteenth-century English scholar Roger Bacon and the fourteenth-century Korean scientist Choe Mu-Seon to extremes of experimentation.

The Chinese had first appreciated the explosive effects of the 'fire drug' (*huo yao*) – a mixture of sulphur, saltpetre and other ingredients

- as far back as the ninth century. At first, they used the gunpowder mixture in the construction of their own version of 'fire arrows,' simple rockets, and in what would be called today 'shock grenades', to stun and confuse an enemy. In between its Chinese inventors and European developers were the Arab traders who brought the gunpowder mixture to the West. It is not certain who first thought of enclosing the explosive to drive a projectile, but the Arab accounts refer to a weapon called a *midfa* - a section of reinforced bamboo (and later iron pipe) driving an arrow

COMPARTMENTS, RUDDER *and multiple masts made this Ming Dynasty 'treasure ship' supremely sea-worthy. Innovations such as the 'fire drug' (*buo yao*) *and the arquebus traveled in such vessels along the coasts of Asia, arming the Koreans and the Japanese even as Arab traders brought the new military technology to the West.*

with a gunpowder charge. The Muslim Mamelukes successfully employed this weapon against the Mongol armies at the Battle of Ayn Jalud in 1260. The first firearms had been invented and the world had changed once again.

At this point in history, the English scholar and Franciscan monk Roger Bacon did something new. Having determined by experimentation a functional composition of gunpowder, he recorded and published the result in 1242, albeit in an encoded form. The formula and its military applications apparently found a ready reception in England since the inventories of the Tower of London include artillery and components dating back to at least 1344 and almost certainly earlier. When the fleet of Edward III bore down upon the French fleet in the estuary at Sluys in 1340, the mouths of cannon already pointed forth in the direction of the enemy.

The precise story of how the cannon evolved into the rest of the world's substitute for Greek fire is largely unknown, but the story of what happened in Korea, at least, is preserved. The raiders besetting the kingdom of Korea were Japanese pirates called *wako*, but the need was the same. With the Chinese keeping a similar control over the knowledge of gunpowder that the Byzantines did with Greek fire, the Korean scientist Choe Mu-Seon had to combine curiosity, persistence and great resourcefulness. Hearing that a travelling Chinese merchant knew the proper proportions of saltpetre and sulfur to charcoal, Mu-

Seon was able to bribe the exact recipe out of him and produce his own versions, which he refined, like Roger Bacon, through experimentation.

Like other inventors throughout the world, Choe Mu-Seon found government support in an era long before the concept of capitalized invention had dawned in any but a military context. Demonstrations before the Korean royal court led to the first weapons laboratory since the original Museum at Alexandria, and resulted in improved leaching methods for nitrates from soil, a rocket-firing cart and a Korean version of the cannon. Preference or practicality drove the Korean line of

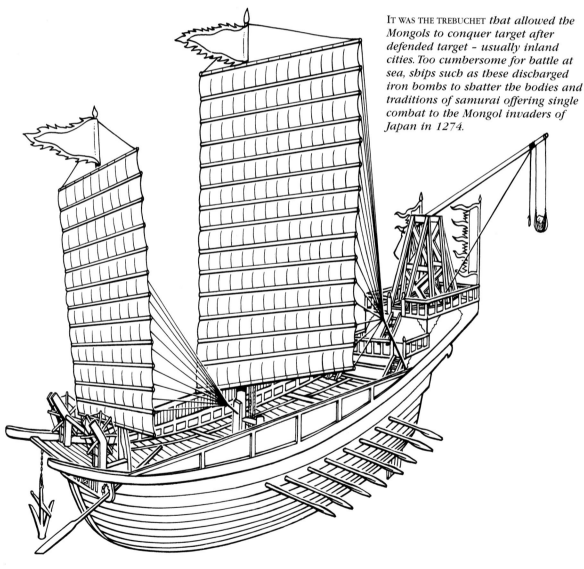

IT WAS THE TREBUCHET *that allowed the Mongols to conquer target after defended target – usually inland cities. Too cumbersome for battle at sea, ships such as these discharged iron bombs to shatter the bodies and traditions of samurai offering single combat to the Mongol invaders of Japan in 1274.*

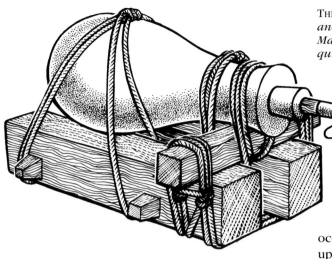

THE *POT DE FER,* KNOWN TO THE ARABS *as* midfa, *was the ancestor of all subsequent forms of cannon. Materials evolved from bamboo to wood to iron quickly enough for the Egyptian Mamelukes to employ the weapon against the Mongols at the battle of Ain Jalut in 1260, which ended the Mongol advance into the Mediterranean world. A wooden cup on the end of the arrow trapped gas behind the projectile.*

development into artillery and away from infantry weapons. This choice would find considerable vindication before two centuries had passed.

Sluys 1340: The Land Battle Fought at Sea

The key elements of any naval engagement are the weapons available and the vessels used to carry these weapons into battle against an enemy. The rowed galley was still the warship *par excellence* in the period, even in the waters around England. The galley's combination of a shallow draught and a large crew continued to recommend it as a raider in most battles of the time. Vessels that the Vikings would have found familiar persisted in most navies until the sixteenth century. The Battle of Sluys is notable not so much for the presence of a few cannon – the main weapons were still swords and arrows – but for the use of sailing vessels instead of war galleys to carry the archers and men-at-arms into battle. The French ships, moreover, were lashed together to form a stable platform, allowing the two armies to fight a battle that owed more to land battles of the period than the naval engagements of the Classical era.

In 1338, French and Genoese mercenary galleys had raided the English fishing fleet, burned Portsmouth and attacked Jersey. The French proceeded to add insult to injury by capturing Edward III's own ship *Christopher* and the *Cog Edward* while the ships were at rest in a German port, presumably engaged in the vital wool trade, a trade that Philip VI of France was doing his best to

destroy. The French and Genoese then gleefully turned *Christopher* and the three cannon that she carried upon her original owners.

The French went on to burn and temporarily occupy Southampton, burn Hastings and then sail up the Solent to seize the ships in Plymouth harbour. What had begun as a quarrel over Norman estates between two Angevin monarchs seemed to be shaping into a second French invasion of England. While Philip VI's commanders collected men and supplies in Flanders in readiness of this invasion, Edward III made preparations for a massive pre-emptive assault on the French fleet at their roadstead.

The Battle of Sluys is often considered – mostly because of its convenient date – as a classic sea battle of medieval times. It was nothing of the sort. Edward did not have a great many galleys, the typical warship of the period; conventional preparations for a set-piece battle of the time would have required him to build or hire many more galleys and then intercept the invaders off his coast or theirs to fight it out with ram, arrow and sword. Instead, Edward chose to make his attack with ships larger and heavier than human muscle was capable of moving.

Edward's decision to employ a fleet of cogs in 1340 gave him a number of advantages. The high and thick bulwarks of a fourteenth-century cog formed an effective wall against boarding and a rampart for the defenders. Wooden castles could be built on the bows and sterns of the ships to provide a platform to increase the range and lethality of any of a variety of missile weapons. Any galley attempting to employ the ancient weapon of the ram also risked destruction from the crushing weights that the cog's mobile yardarm could drop through their hulls from above.

Another factor was the nature of their objective. The invasion fleet that Philip VI was gathering along the Flemish coast was meant to carry men, horses, armour and siege engines. To carry this weight of men and equipment, the French fleet would need to use cogs. Edward needed ships capable of carrying corresponding amounts of men and armament and of a height and strength to match the French vessels. Moreover, the large crews of war galleys had to be fed and housed ashore if their ships were to play any role, creating difficulties in supply and

PRMITIVE GUNS AND advanced bows bear the brunt of the fighting as an anchored cog's defenders fight for their ship and their lives as an attacker bears down. Merchant ships could become men o' war by the simple addition of infantry, leaving the skill of sailors and marksmen to vie with weapons technology as decisive factors.

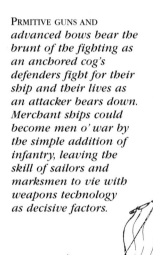

THE FRENCH FLEET at Sluys (1340) thought to take full advantage of their numbers and armour by chaining their fleet together. While any ship in each line could reinforce the others, the tactic sacrificed the single greatest asset of any warship - manoeuvrability. The English took cruel advantage.

coordination. Sailing vessels could use fewer men and rely on the wind for propulsion.

Edward collected outlying squadrons from London and the Channel to form a grand fleet of 120-160 warships and perhaps 40 support vessels. On 23 June 1340, this force bore down on the Sluys Estuary, where Philip was marshalling his forces. Edward came prepared for a long war - his fleet included his queen and her ladies of waiting, one of whom would perish in the coming day's fighting. The French invasion fleet found itself unexpectedly transformed from an instrument of aggression into a vulnerable target.

Floating Fortress

Caught in the midst of their preparations, the two French admirals, Nicolas Béhuchet and Hugues Quiéret, had already surrendered the initiative to Edward when the news came that the English fleet had arrived and was certain to attack the following day. The Genoese mercenary admiral, Pietro Barbavera, counseled them to put out to sea, where they could manoeuvre or escape. Instead, the French began to chain their ships together, beam to beam, in three lines across the windward opening of the estuary. Given the subsequent French defeat, the decision to bind their fleet together in this way has been severely criticized. It should be noted, however, that the French had been preparing for an invasion, not a naval battle. Their main naval escort was intended to be Barbavera's galley squadron. On Barbavera's orders, however, the galleys stood so far out to sea that they played little part in the day's fighting before disappearing over the horizon.

The French cogs carried armoured infantry with as many as 600 heavy crossbowmen. With the ships chained together, they could transfer men along the lines in support of any beleaguered individual vessel. The French ships were also equipped with grapnels to hold to an attacking ship while it was boarded, and with the ships linked together they could have poured more than one ship's worth of combatants onto the enemy's decks. Two decades later, the Chinese Han fleet on Lake Poyang would employ similar tactics in one of the largest naval battles in history and protract a startlingly similar combat into five months of bitter struggle. The initial choice of tactics had much to justify it.

Quiéret and Béhuchet used the time between Edward's arrival and his attack to make still further preparations, which included hoisting their ships' boats aloft to provide impromptu fighting tops for their archers and crossbowmen – this also removed the temptation to use the boats to escape to a not-very-friendly shoreline.

HEAVY INFANTRY: *this fourteenth-century man-at-arms is well equipped for everything but swimming, a fatal liability for the French at Sluys. The brimmed helmet provided protection against missiles from above, while the chain mail corselet offered better defence against edged weapons than the English longbow. His long sword is less useful at sea than his axe, which could kill boarders or clear away debris at need.*

The captured warship *Christopher* carried the only guns present at the battle, although the question remains whether the French had the skill to fire them before the ship and her cannon were recaptured.

The English Longbow

Edward finally gave the signal to engage at around 3 p.m., when he decided that the afternoon breeze and the position of the summer sun were acceptable to his needs. These needs became apparent for the first time, but not the last, when a shower of English arrows preceded the crushing onslaught of the largest English ships as they bore down upon the waiting French. Edward III, who had reason only to exaggerate, later wrote that the French met his own forces with 180 sailing ships and heavy rowed barges.

Given the legend of the English archers at Crécy and Agincourt, it is worth pointing out that the first time the English longbow (actually a Welsh invention) was used to slaughter armoured French soldiers was at sea. The longbow and the Genoese crossbow were both deadly weapons with much to recommend them in battle, but the longbow had a dramatically faster rate of fire. Its arrows were 1m (37in) long and have been reliably recorded as penetrating field plate and oak planks as much as 10cm (4in) thick. At Sluys, as at Crécy and Agincourt, neither French courage nor armour was proof against the showers of arrows.

The French responded in kind. When English knights and men-at-arms finally recaptured *Christopher*, they found 400 French and Genoese crossbowmen on her. The French commanders had shrewdly

Battle of Sluys

1340

Caught between the two halves of the French and Scottish alliance, Edward III of England made the decision to forestall further French raids along his southern coast with a pre-emptive attack. Striking with more force and supplies than human muscle and galleys could transport, Edward assembled a large fleet of 120–160 armed cogs and as many as 40 support vessels, and set sail for the Flemish Coast, with both queen and courtiers in tow. Suddenly cast onto the defensive, the French commanders on the scene decided to chain their fleet together in three lines in the shelter of the Sluys estuary, and await battle. Edward pressed his advantage and the attack, his longbowmen and war fleet hammering the French until the local Flemish completed the rout by hitting the French from the rear.

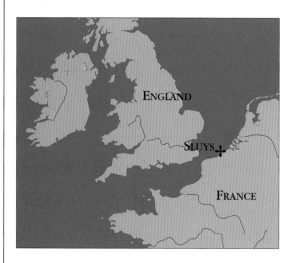

Neither rare nor unthinkable, the threat of a French invasion drove Edward III into drastic action. In between the years 1660 and 1688, nine separate invasions of England turned a foreign war into a domestic one. In his own century, Edward thrust the French permanently upon the defensive with a sudden attack.

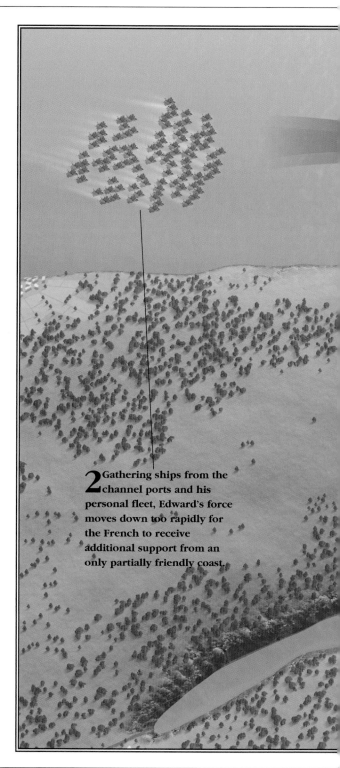

2 Gathering ships from the channel ports and his personal fleet, Edward's force moves down too rapidly for the French to receive additional support from an only partially friendly coast.

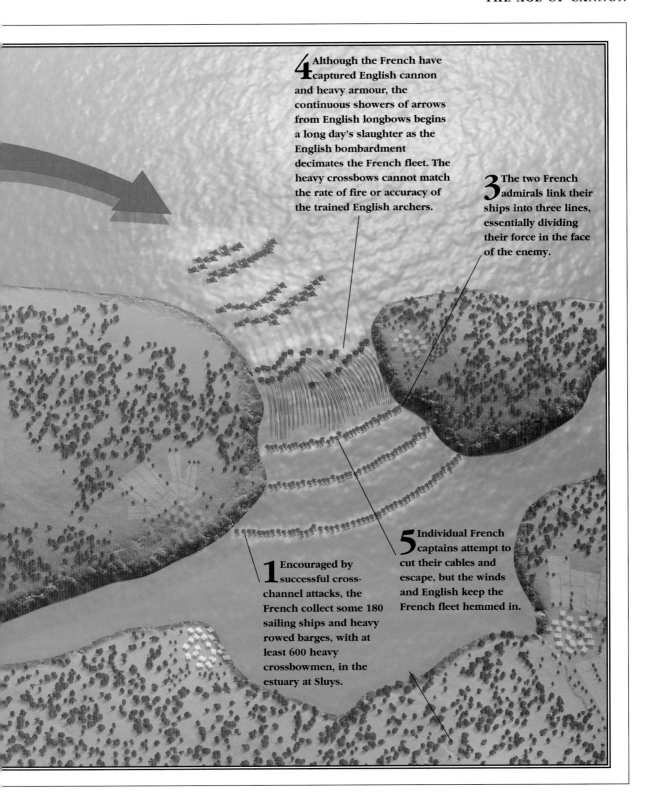

4 Although the French have captured English cannon and heavy armour, the continuous showers of arrows from English longbows begins a long day's slaughter as the English bombardment decimates the French fleet. The heavy crossbows cannot match the rate of fire or accuracy of the trained English archers.

3 The two French admirals link their ships into three lines, essentially dividing their force in the face of the enemy.

5 Individual French captains attempt to cut their cables and escape, but the winds and English keep the French fleet hemmed in.

1 Encouraged by successful cross-channel attacks, the French collect some 180 sailing ships and heavy rowed barges, with at least 600 heavy crossbowmen, in the estuary at Sluys.

English Longbowman (1340)

The English Longbowman was the decisive combatant at Sluys, Agincourt and Crécy. The archer shown here wears a gambeson, a padded garment usually worn under heavier armor to cushion the blows of combat, more practical than mail at sea. He carries a short dagger – short enough to draw at the last moment when the enemy was too close for the continued use of his main weapon. Originating in Wales, the 'English' longbow could discharge six arrows a minute as far as 350m (383 yards), its accuracy being a function of range and the time taken by the archer to mark his target. Archers were expected to shoot 'at the mark' on a barrel target (butt), and to drove a certain number of miles each month – droving being the discharge of an arrow at a distant mark and the retrieval of the arrow, the process being repeated at a different mark further on. Accounts of the penetrating power of the longbow are legendary, the 178cm (70in) of English or Russian yew able to drive an arrow through an oak door, a ship's hull, and, at close range, through chain or plate armor – with murderous results.

concentrated their most effective missile weaponry on the ship that they knew Edward would be the most eager to recapture.

Disintegration

Before attacking, Edward sent word of his plans to the Flemish, who for their part had long been enraged by French interference in the wool trade. Surviving accounts mention that, as the battle heated up, the Flemings attacked the French rear by way of the waterways emptying into the estuary, using what were probably small rowed craft. It was most likely at this point that French cohesion finally – and fatally – disintegrated.

Having refused to follow the Genoese galleys out to sea while manoeuvre and escape had still been possible, the French now began to unchain their ships from their anchored lines, abandoning the idea of mutual support in the vain hope of flight.

One by one, the largest French vessels fell to the English. English missile fire cleared decks and gunwales, allowing armoured men-at-arms to board and conquer. The French soldiers had no way to retreat and little hope, given the raids of previous years, that they would be given quarter. Philip VI's jester acquainted his master with the sad news by joking, 'Our soldiers are braver than those of the English, for they have jumped into the sea in their armour'.

Edward himself took a wound in the battle, but chivalry yielded to revenge when Béhuchet was brought before him. Finding out that Béhuchet had commanded the ships responsible for the destruction of Portsmouth, Edward ordered his execution using a noose over the yardarm. The English victory was staggeringly complete. The

most reliable reckonings of the French casualties include 190 ships and as many as 18,000 men. The battle set the pattern for the Hundred Years War: from then on it would be the English who crossed the Channel to make war on the French; never again would the French make the attempt.

Monsters of the Sea

As the Hundred Years War wore on, the lessons of Sluys remained strong in English military reckoning. The lethal combination of longbow and infantry had its reinforcement at Crécy and Agincourt, and the idea that the sailing ship could be a tremendously formidable weapon of war persisted too.

Functional and successful as the cog had proved itself to be, neither civilian nor military ship designers were willing to leave it at that. Mediterranean shipwrights in the years after Sluys began, for the first time, to build their ships with internal skeletons, nailing the carvel planking of the outer hulls to it. The efficient use of labour and timber of such a construction combined to make the technique dominant. Cogs constructed in this way were known in the Mediterranean as *cochas*. Vessels increased in size to allow larger cargoes and still more military freeboard, and soon immense sailing ships with multiple masts began appearing in northern waters in the quest for English wool. These behemoths, known as carracks, dwarfed the cog, just as the cog had loomed over the war galley. The English King Henry V is perhaps better known for his appreciation of the longbow than his respect for the large sailing warship, but he invested heavily in naval technology. Planning for an invasion of France, Henry poured considerable resources into

> '...behold the threaden sails,
> Borne with the invisible and creeping wind,
> Draw the huge bottoms through the furrow'd sea,
> Breasting the lofty surge:
> O, do but think
> You stand upon the ravage and behold
> A city on the inconstant billows dancing...
> — WILLIAM SHAKESPEARE, HENRY V

69

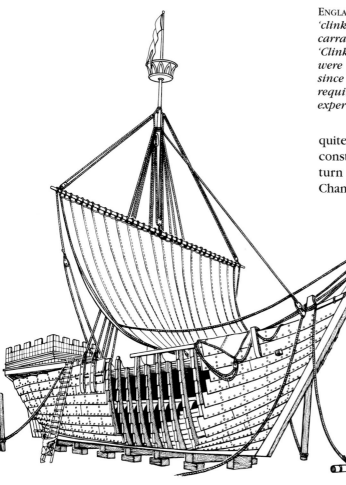

ENGLAND'S HENRY V *revived the earlier form of 'clinker' hull construction for the great war carracks he built for his struggle with France. 'Clinker' hulls such as employed in this cog were tremendously flexible, and also strong since their strakes overlapped, but they did require a great amount of timber and expertise in their construction.*

quite successfully, and a sister-ship was under construction when Henry's war took a dramatic turn inland. No ships ever appeared in the Channel to challenge Henry's great behemoths, but the *Grace Dieu* burned accidentally in 1439.

Lepanto 1571:
Hour of the Galleass

Even as the sailing ship grew ever more dominant in northern waters, the galley would have its last, great moment of glory in a massive struggle on the sea. The Byzantine *Siphonophores* with their *siphons* of Greek fire had been able to damage enemy ships from a safe distance. In the century between Sluys and the Battle of Lepanto in 1571, it became apparent that a galley with a cannon could do the same. In the age of the ram, galleys had faced each other prow to prow, rushing against each other in the hope of either crushing in an enemy's bow or veering suddenly into the hull or oars of another foe. Like infantry in line, warships moved side by side towards the line of the enemy. In the sixteenth century, however, galleys added firepower to their previous asset of manoeuvrability.

By the late sixteenth century, cannon had achieved a degree of standardization, in the sense that the assorted products of the various foundries could be grouped into three rough categories. Light cannon – labelled in some reckonings as 'periers' – fired stone balls that shattered on impact, shattering both hulls and men. Cannon per se were the welterweight pieces, with longer barrels that trapped greater propulsive power out of their gunpowder and fired shot of iron or stone.

the construction of his own fleet of huge carracks, vessels able to counter the Genoese examples then employed in the Channel by the French. Accounts of the largest of them all, the *Grace Dieu* of 1418, were not believed, and rightly. The chroniclers of the time reported her size at 1400 gross tons while loaded; modern study of the surviving remnants of her hull indicate that she was, in fact, 2750 gross tons, nearly equivalent in size to Nelson's *Victory* more than 300 years later.

Henry's shipwrights, moreover, reverted to the older clinker style of hull for strength. The amount of timber required was apparently not a factor in the *Grace Dieu*'s construction, for she had a triple hull requiring complicated inner mortising to construct. The finished vessel was some 66m (218ft) in length. This monster put to sea in 1420,

PROOF AGAINST SHOT AND WORM, *the triple-laminated clinker hull of the* Grace Dieu *required the intricate mortising seen here. Such strength was perhaps required by the great size of the vessel. A section of her bulk has survived fire and the ages to provide the details of this reconstruction.*

The heavy artillery of the day was the culverin, 3m (10ft) long or more, firing imperfectly shaped balls of iron or stone that bounced around their loose barrels before flying towards the enemy with presumably devastating effect. A galley could generally carry one heavy culverin down its centreline, flanked by lighter guns, and fire it from range before closing to board, the enemy crew ideally thrown into disorder by the carnage caused by the cannon's fire.

The foremost navy of the time was the Venetian fleet, whose dominant design was the 'great galley' – pulled by up to four men on an oar or by men sitting on a bench with four oars. The galleys had civilian incarnations specialized to carry cargo in divided hulls. The military models featured cannon at the bow; the largest 'great cannon' on the ship's centreline, with smaller 'dragons' or 'drakes' to the sides. Venetian cannon were simple, functional, standardized and supremely lethal, the products of the Venetian *ghetto,* or 'foundry'. This area was the site of the most advanced and best-

AN ENGLISH BEHOMETH, *the great war carrack* Grace Dieu *was meant to smash anything the French could build or hire from the Mediterranean. Her triple hull would have given protection to English archers and cannoneers while her lofty forecastle loomed over the sides and deck of any other vessel she might encounter, offering a murderous field of fire.*

managed industrial plant in the Western world. Vats of boiling pitch and legions of workers in shifts had inspired the infernal visions of Dante Alighieri. As a maritime republic, Venice had many centuries of seafaring experience; the city's Arsenal had provided ships for war and trade throughout her history. Within the guarded walls of the Arsenal, trained specialists and standardized parts combined in the months before Lepanto to produce and fit out a huge fleet of over 100 galleys.

Facing the Venetians in the wars for the control of the Mediterranean were the galleys of the Ottoman Turks. Muslim admirals, such as the dreaded Barbarossa, favoured the *galiot*, a small, fast galley, well suited to hit-and-run attacks, scouting and commerce raiding. For set-piece naval engagements, the Ottomans built light galleys similar to the smaller Venetian models. These tended to be faster than the heavily armed galleys of the Spanish but slower than the Venetians vessels. The Turkish compound bow was powerful and handy in shipboard fighting.

Muslim galleys had a lower freeboard than their Christian counterparts. Turkish and Venetian ships lacked a fighting platform above the bow armament, as used by the Spanish and Italian powers, although the Turks favoured a high stern structure in their galleys, which could be used as a redoubt against boarders. The Turks also developed a ram for grappling, which the Venetians later copied. This device would hold the enemy ship against the attacker while boarding parties swarmed across onto the enemy deck. Both the Turkish and the Spanish navies favoured boarding combat more than the Venetians, especially as artillery improved. Naval combat had evolved to an initial discharge of cannon, the closing of range to grapple, and, finally, boarding and hand-to-hand fighting.

A New Weapons System

Faced with the very real threat of destruction in the forthcoming battle, the Venetian Republic added a new and innovative element to their preparations. By one recounting, six of the largest

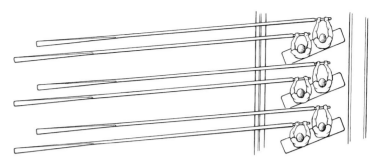

TWO MEN ON THE SAME ANGLED BENCH *pulled oars of different lengths in the type of rowing system known as a* zenzile, *which allowed more rowers and shorter, cheaper oars than the later 'stepped tier' system, in which men on vertically angled benched pulled together at a single massive oar.*

merchant galleys in the Venetian state-operated fleet stood by in one of the Arsenal's storage basins while the preparations for the impending battle reached a fever pitch. It occurred to some inspired soul that these huge vessels could be used to carry freight rather more lethal than their usual cargoes of silks and spices.

No other shipyard in the world could have effected so sudden and drastic a conversion. The traditional emphasis on bow armament shifted under the pressure of necessity. Workman equipped the six *galeazas* (large galleys), with specialized fighting structures at the bow, the stern and along the sides to hold the largest cannon available from the Republic's stockpiles. The resulting 'galleass' was quite literally a castle on the sea. At the bows of the ships, the high, protected forecastles bristled with cannon. These were balanced by similar armament in the substantial aftercastles. Nine or so periers, or full cannon, jutted out along each side – the guns and their carriages were mounted above, below or even among the oarsmen. On a lighter galley meant for speed and manoeuvre, such weaponry could never have been accommodated. With the creation of the galleass, however, the broadside was born.

Our detailed knowledge of the construction of the galleasses comes from specifications for later versions of these formidable hybrids. These were 49m (160ft) long and 12m (40ft) wide – twice as wide as the lighter galleys. Six men pulled each of the 76 heavy oars, and the decks were protected from boarding by the high freeboard, the long distance from the water to her deck being a difficult obstacle for an attacker to surmount. A galleass's battery probably contained five or so full cannon firing a ball weighing 50lb (22.7kg); two or three 25lb (11.3kg) balls; 23 lighter pieces of various sizes and shapes; and around 20 rail-mounted swivel guns, used to slaughter rowers and boarding parties. The heaviest Venetian galleasses could fire some 325lb (147.4kg) of shot in every salvo. Five standard galleys would have been required to carry a similar armament.

The new leviathans did require towing by their smaller counterparts to achieve any sort of speed of manoeuvre – but this was no problem in a large fleet of galleys; the wind could provide the same impetus it gave to Edward III's cogs at Sluys. Certainly on later examples, three huge lateen sails, each on its own mast, loomed above the deck. The exact size and armament of the six prototype galleasses at Lepanto is not known, but their performance is well documented. The Venetians were about to surprise the Turks.

The Strategic Situation

The westward expansion of the Ottoman Empire in the century following the fall of Constantinople in 1453 had given the Turkish galleys control of the eastern

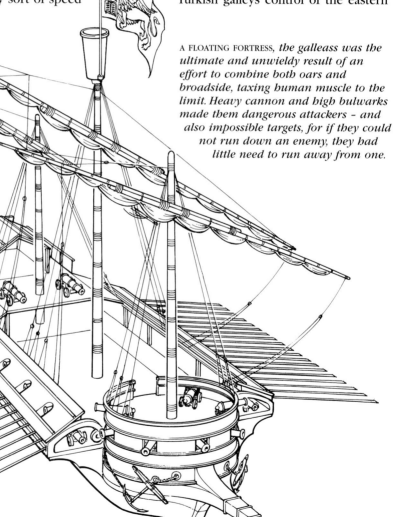

A FLOATING FORTRESS, *the galleass was the ultimate and unwieldy result of an effort to combine both oars and broadside, taxing human muscle to the limit. Heavy cannon and high bulwarks made them dangerous attackers - and also impossible targets, for if they could not run down an enemy, they had little need to run away from one.*

Mediterranean and the coastal waters around North Africa. By the middle of the sixteenth century, the Ottomans were threatening to take control in the waters of the western Mediterranean too. In 1571, the Venetians were in danger of losing the vital port and outpost of Cyprus when Pope Pius V proclaimed a crusade against the Turks. There was not much time to be lost in mobilizing the Christian response – a powerful Turkish fleet was poised to enter the Adriatic Sea.

The Pope himself rented 12 galleys and sent his own squadron to sea flying a papal flag. The dire nature of the situation in 1571 also spurred the other Christian powers to their utmost. The Venetians had abandoned their previous wars with the Turks or negotiated when financial or political advantage made the course seem advisable – but the Republic now faced a simple question of survival. The fleet the Venetians dispatched to Lepanto would be the largest in the Republic's history, and the best equipped. The urgent need for manpower prompted for the Venetians for the first time to fill the benches of their new galleys with convicts, promising freedom for victory, and to place men from territories subject to Venice among their crews.

Assisting them was a new and formidable Spanish fleet. Philip II had not squandered all his financial resources from the New World on the Dutch wars, and worsening relations with the English had prompted considerable naval expenditure. Spain also had a long Mediterranean coast and Philip was well aware that the Turks considered much of the Iberian Peninsula as Muslim territory to be reclaimed at the first opportunity. The Spanish ships were heavily built, though as a consequence were somewhat slow, and their marines well armoured and equipped with matchlock arquebuses.

Such was the extent of the Spanish involvement that the commander of the allied squadrons at Lepanto was none other than Philip's bastard brother, Don Juan of Austria. Although younger than his admirals at 34, Don Juan was a competent and decisive leader who had previous experience fighting Turkish raiders and understood the need to contest the apparent supremacy of the Ottoman fleet. Don Juan also understood the intangible elements of the struggle, making the most of the Pope's explicit support for the campaign. European armies had defeated invading Muslim forces in earlier centuries; the hope existed that the unvanquished Turkish fleet could now be halted in the name of God.

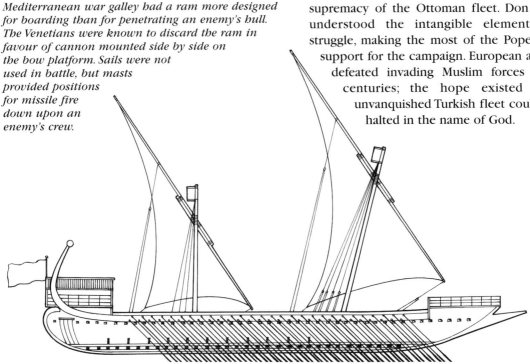

LAST OF A LONG LINE, *the final version of the Mediterranean war galley had a ram more designed for boarding than for penetrating an enemy's hull. The Venetians were known to discard the ram in favour of cannon mounted side by side on the bow platform. Sails were not used in battle, but masts provided positions for missile fire down upon an enemy's crew.*

Don Juan's piety had its own counterpart in the temperament of the Turkish grand admiral. Ali Pasha was an aggressive commander in his own right and with his admirals he was fully prepared to fight it out to the finish. Like Don Juan, Ali Pasha had risen to his command through royal favour, but his sub-commanders were all experienced men and the marines on board his vessels were the terror of Christian Europe. There was every reason to expect the success that had met the Preveza Campaign of 1538, when Turkish squadrons drove an earlier coalition Christian fleet from the vital straits in disorganized retreat.

The international situation had changed, however, in the period between the debacle of 1538 and the campaign of 1571. The Spanish could now pour resources from more than one continent into the struggle. The natural resources and wealth of the New World built Philip's hulls

THE BATTLE OF LEPANTO *(from the National Maritime Museum, Greenwich, London). A distinguishing feature of the great decisive naval battles in history – from Salamis through Lepanto, Trafalgar and Midway – has been the willingness of both sides to fight the issue out to a final and conclusive finish.*

and equipped his marines. Money, as ever in human history, proved a major component in military power. The Spanish military, moreover, was an instrument sharpened to a razor's edge by centuries of struggle against the Moors in Spain and on the African coast.

The Battle

As Ali Pasha methodically collected his forces in the Gulf of Patras on the western coast of Greece, the Christian fleet moved slowly eastwards, shadowed by light Turkish galleys. Don Juan's combined forces numbered possibly 240 vessels, carrying approximately 74,000 men in ships ranging from light *nefs* to the six huge Venetian galleases. The Turkish fleet numbered approximately 210 vessels with full complements totalling 75,000 men.

The Turkish confidence was high and the fleet was eager for combat. Two large fortresses with heavy cannon protected the inner portion of the Bay of Patras at its narrows as the Christian fleet approached on the morning of 7 October 1571. The outnumbered Turks still had the ability to refuse battle – the galleases were a new and unknown factor yet to be understood by their

Ottoman Janissary Archer (1570)

Taken and coverted, the original janissaries began life as Christian boys levied from the Ottoman Empire's Slavic territories. Kept celibate and strictly Muslim by Turkish officers, they constituted the elite of the Ottoman army and its most feared combat arm. This archer carries the dreaded and effective short composite bow, which was made famous in cavalry action but was equally handy and lethal in the crowded confines of combat at sea. His distinctive headgear identified his type and reputation to his opponents, while offering some measure of protection. The Turkish short bow was made of laminated wood and horn, which were held together by a glue that suffered from long exposure to moisture. Its range and power, if not its accuracy or rate of fire, was comparable pto the English longbow. Christian armour and arquebuses proved an effective counter.

intended targets. Instead, Ali Pasha and his subordinate admirals formed a line of battle in a position where the guns of the fortresses could not provide support.

Some of Don Juan's rear admirals urged withdrawal in the face of the Turkish offer of battle. Don Juan's answer was pungent: 'It is too late for counsel, it is now time for battle.' The Christians shifted from line astern to line abreast as the sun rose behind them, the light blinding the Turks. Making the signal to engage, Don Juan fired a gun and raised a large flag that had been blessed by the Pope. The Christian flagship was a light, fast vessel, the speed of which offered the commander safety and a chance to arrange and direct the battle as he fed the assorted squadrons and varieties of vessels into the developing battle.

Under the express order of Don Juan, the galleasses moved out in front of the main Christian formation, each under the tow of four of their smaller brethren. Behind these leviathans the Christian fleet moved forwards, ironically in the form of a crescent with its horns bent towards the advancing Turks. In the van were 12 galleys under the Genoese mercenary commander Andrea Doria, which moved out to the extreme flanks of the formation. The Turks smelled another victory, the cry going up that the Christians were already in disorder and retreat. The sun's further ascent revealed the awful truth of the size of the Christian fleet. Ali Pasha's own signal to engage now began what was intended by both sides to be a set piece, decisive battle.

Ali Pasha noted the six large vessels set out as the vanguard of the Christian line and chose to bypass them by ordering his three squadrons to divide and sail around the galleasses without engaging. The Turkish admiral's only other option would have been to turn his galleys' bows and cannon on the behemoths, but in so doing the Turks would have exposed their flanks to the cannon and rams of the Christian galleys, a risk Ali Pasha apparently considered prohibitive.

Long-range fire from the broadsides of the galleasses added to the disorder of the Turkish squadrons as they passed the behemoths. The situation became worse as the Christian line moved to engage before the Turkish fleet could

reform, and any hope of avoiding the terrible firepower of the galleasses proved vain as the lumbering monsters reversed direction and fell upon the Turkish rear. The ferocity of the fighting was appalling even by the standards of the day. The Christian order was simple: 'Fire not until the blood of thine opponent shall spatter thee.'

The Turkish efforts to reform were not assisted by the clouds of smoke resulting from both sides' cannon and from the arquebuses that Philip had purchased with his New World silver. The Turks were accurate and proficient archers, but matchlocks provided a counter to their arrows. Light artillery pieces on swivels, called *versos* or 'murderers', poured fire onto the Turkish decks.

Incendiary Weapons

If the *siphon* itself had perished with the fall of Byzantine Empire in 1453, other incendiary weapons had not. Both sides had men trained to throw clay pots filled with flaming oil, animal fat or quick lime to set the enemy decks ablaze or render them perilously slippery. Arms and cannon threw hollow iron balls filled with burning matter onto enemy vessels, and the flaming shower of sparks from the *bomba* marked the efforts of the Spanish vessels. The galleasses used their oars to wear ship as required to bring their stern, broadside or bow guns to bear on the targets offered, while the great height of their wooden sides rendered them practically immune to Turkish efforts to board them.

The goal of both fleets was to envelop the other, and fierce fighting raged on the flanks of each line. Gunpowder and thick armour began to make a difference in the Christians' favour. As the Turkish marines perished, another calamity befell their ships. The Christian slaves on the benches of the Turkish fleet began availing themselves of weapons dropped in the carnage and attacking their former masters. While the ships were so embroiled, they lost all propulsion and hope of manoeuvre or escape.

Still the Turks fought on. Ali Pasha's command squadron forced its way through to a cluster of Christian flagships in the centre of Don Juan's line. Even the commanders became involved in the fighting: a septuagenarian Venetian nobleman too

Battle of Lepanto

1571

Sea after sea, peninsula after peninsula fell to the advancing Ottoman Turkish Empire. With Greece and the coastal islands coming one by one under Turkish control, the next peninsula in line was Italy, the centre of Catholicism. The Pope and the Venetian Republic combined forces with Philip II of Spain, prudent enough in this instance to fight this battle well away from his own kingdom and possessions. The Turks had always been superb archers and by the time of the battle had become very good sailors in fast, deadly galleys. Venetian prototypical mass-production of ships and cannon combined in a powerful fleet. Spanish armour and arquebusiers countered traditional Turkish strengths, and the presence of a Papal fleet and the Pope's own proclamation of indulgence made for a furious battle that was an act of religious faith for both sides.

The Gulf of Lepanto is situated east of the Gulf of Corinth close to the Greek port of Patras, in a long channel of the Ionian Sea that separates the Peloponnese peninsula to the south from the Greek mainland to the north.

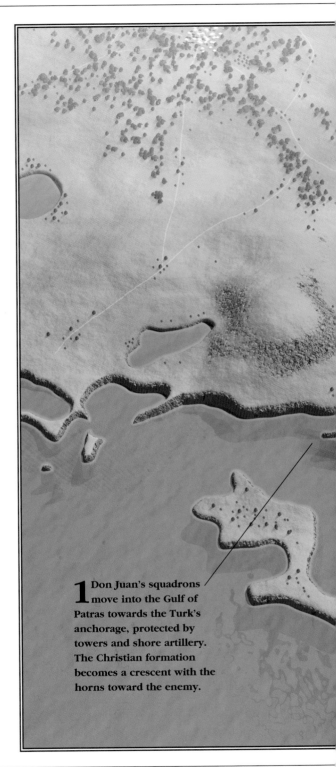

1 Don Juan's squadrons move into the Gulf of Patras towards the Turk's anchorage, protected by towers and shore artillery. The Christian formation becomes a crescent with the horns toward the enemy.

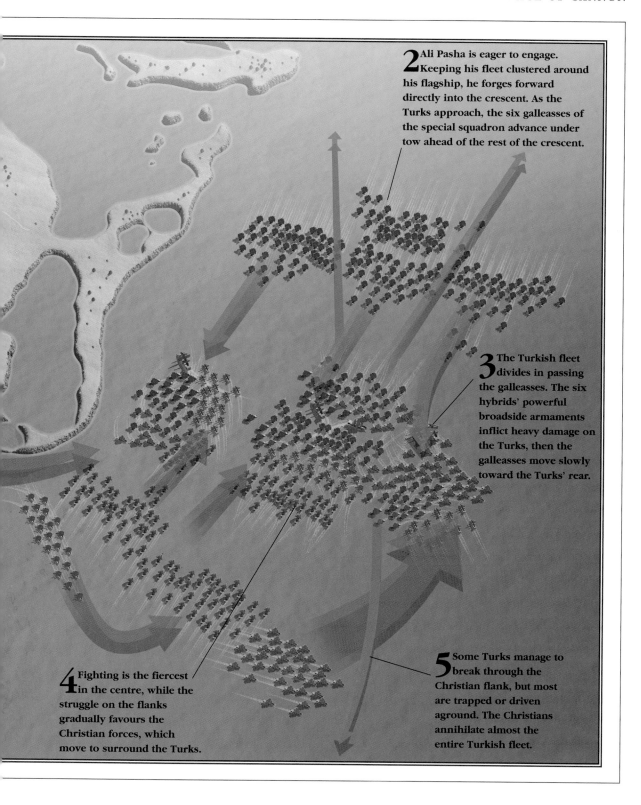

2 Ali Pasha is eager to engage. Keeping his fleet clustered around his flagship, he forges forward directly into the crescent. As the Turks approach, the six galleasses of the special squadron advance under tow ahead of the rest of the crescent.

3 The Turkish fleet divides in passing the galleasses. The six hybrids' powerful broadside armaments inflict heavy damage on the Turks, then the galleasses move slowly toward the Turks' rear.

4 Fighting is the fiercest in the centre, while the struggle on the flanks gradually favours the Christian forces, which move to surround the Turks.

5 Some Turks manage to break through the Christian flank, but most are trapped or driven aground. The Christians annihilate almost the entire Turkish fleet.

SHE WAS ALMOST SUCCESSFUL, *but a sharp turn and a sudden wave sank the* Mary Rose, *dooming her crew and Henry VIII's navy. This section of the vessel, though, was saved for history. Heavy guns low in the hull provided stability, but the high castles above her spar deck were enough to heel the galleon over sufficiently for water to flow into her gunports and sink her. Her successors would lack the top clutter and emulate her layered gun decks.*

weak to span his own crossbow picked off individual Turks from the masthead while Ali Pasha himself bent a bow in the final surge of the fighting.

When the day ended, 7700 Christians and 12 ships had sunk beneath the reddened waters of the gulf. By contrast, some 30,000 Turks had perished in the carnage and 170 galleys and lighter vessels of the Turkish fleet had been captured. Don Juan demonstrated his appreciation of the decisive impact of the new technology by awarding the unit prize for valour to the galleasses, for he and most of the other commanders credited them with the victory. The disaster made such an impression on the vanquished Turks that to this day it is known as the *Singin*, or crushing defeat. Once again, a new weapon, a new kind of ship, had prevailed against a previously unbeaten foe. The West's faith in technology had been amply vindicated at Lepanto.

The Armada 1588: Cannon and Flame

While the Catholic powers fought their great struggle in the Mediterranean, the inheritors of Henry V's English kingdom had not been idle. The legacy of *Grace Dieu* was manifest in name and size when King Henry VIII ordered the construction of the carracks *Henry Grace à Dieu* and her sisters *Peter Pomegranate* and *Mary Rose* in 1509. Naval preparations only increased in expense and urgency after Henry's break with Rome in 1533, when it became increasingly certain that the fleets of the Catholic powers would soon be turned against England.

Great Harry, as the fleet called Henry's new warship, carried a crew of 2000 and was fitted with lofty bow and sterncastles, and enough top-clutter for a Venetian observer to note that her magnificence was likely to keep her from putting to sea. Far above her deck, more swivels and 'murderers' pointed down to sweep enemy decks and masts - if, of course, the monster could get into action without turning turtle. Such, of course, was the sad fate of the *Mary Rose* when a French counteroffensive in 1545 led to battle in the Solent and she capsized and sank beneath the waves.

Ongoing analysis of the remains of the *Mary Rose* has lead to some revision in our understanding of English naval technology at the time of the Spanish Armada. The galley's shadow lay heavily over the builders of the *Mary Rose*, who went to great and unsatisfactory lengths to design her broadside batteries for forward fire;

'bowed' guns aimed as far ahead as their mounts permitted, at the cost of much reduced accuracy and ease of reloading. The idea was to match the galley's forward firepower, but the necessary obstructions to the rigging and bows of a sailing vessel proved prohibitive.

Fortunately, in action such expedients were solutions in search of a problem. The *Mary Rose* sank when she was caught by an unlucky gust of wind as she smartly wheeled to discharge the weight of her broadside into the French. It was this tactic that eventually made her sisters and the other large ships the bane of galley warfare in general.

The new direction of weapons and platform technology was something the Spanish themselves had already experienced - though they failed to take due note. At the Straits of Preveza in 1538, the dreaded Turkish admiral Barbarossa cut off and then surrounded the flagship of the Venetian squadron of Charles V's allied fleet. This 'Galleon of Venice' was the first of a new design that was meant to handle more easily than the ponderous carrack despite being heavier than its lighter descendant, the caravel. For all her superior manoeuvrability in a wind, however, a flat calm left the galleon apparently helpless, enabling the Turkish galleys to close in.

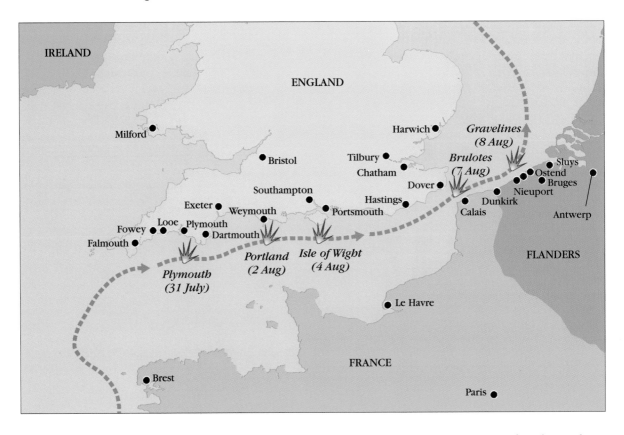

The result was completely unexpected. Alessandro Condalmiero, a scion of one of Venice's oldest naval families, kept his gunners at their ordnance, ricocheting the shot from his broadsides off the ocean into the circling Turks. Despite the loss of her mainmast and her abandonment by the rest of the Christian fleet, the galleon repulsed every Turkish attack with heavy loss of life. To those observers less obsessed with the classic tactics of the bows-on rush, it was clear that even a becalmed sailing ship had held her own against a fleet of galleys – and that firepower was the ultimate source of victory.

The loss of the *Mary Rose* had other lessons to offer. The lofty top-castles that had proved so fatal to the vessel would not appear in her descendants such as *Triumph*, the largest ship to take part in the Armada battles. Large, ship-killing guns in the hold remained a feature of English design – incidentally serving as effective ballast to counterbalance the sailing ships' heavy masts and upperworks.

Gun Carriages and Iron Cannon

In two areas of cannon design, the English, by going their own way, had travelled even further than the Venetians towards perfecting naval artillery. In a galley crammed with rowers rushing to attack, there was little room and less time to reload the battery – hence the 'single-shot' nature of the massive culverins and crude gun carriages that so many vessels of the Armada lugged into battle. Among the remains of *Mary Rose*, however, have been found some of the earliest examples of the four-wheeled gun carriage. It is hard to overstate how useful this innovation was – the very recoil of a muzzle-loading gun served to push the piece back within the shelter of the hull for swift reloading before ropes and tackles could easily send it forth again. Weapons designed to move inboard could be stowed behind sealed gunports in a seaway. In fact, the doctrine of the time called for the *Mary Rose*'s crew to close her lowest gunports before her turn; had they done so, they would have kept out the waters that flooded her. The Armada of 1588, by contrast, would carry cannon commandeered from land installations, or ancient pieces on two-wheeled sledge-style carriages. By all accounts, in the ensuing combat,

THIS EARLY BREECHLOADER *left an unwanted legacy to naval artillery development. Its wrought-iron construction lent strength to the barrel, but the hoops shrunk over the seams were not enough to prevent eruptions of gas when firing, nor were the wedges around the breech enough to prevent sparks and explosions. Its two-wheeled carriage fitted to a muzzle-loader made for very slow reloading – as the Armada's gunners discovered.*

the British would send forth three shots for every discharge of the Spanish cannon.

The other advantage the English possessed in the age of the cannon was metallurgical. The Italian gun makers had to import their ores in an age when heavy transport was slow and fantastically expensive. The English rejoiced in Cornish tin for bronze, the favoured gun metal of the day. Yet there is strong evidence that one of Henry VIII's most enlightened policies was to encourage the casting of iron cannon. From the 1540s onwards, there is evidence that English foundries were casting large numbers of iron cannon – at a cost one fifth that of bronze pieces.

The result was that more of the superior bronze cannon were available for the navy, with

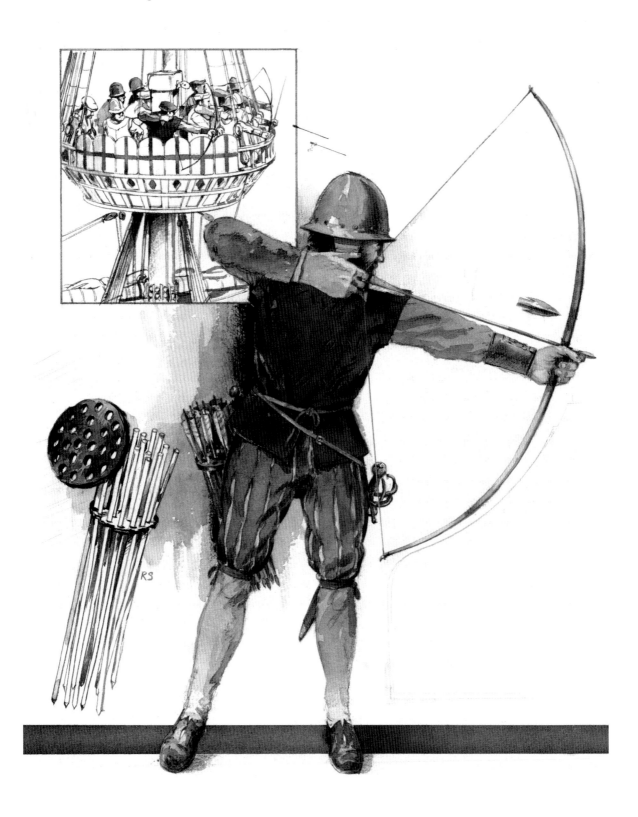

OPPOSITE: FROZEN IN TIME, one of Henry VIII's archers in the fighting top of Mary Rose left his bones and gear as testimony to the costs of the English Longbow's successful use in combat. A perforated quiver held arrows ready - a well-trained archer loosed his next arrow before the first one struck. Helmet, cutlass and leather jerkin offered protection from everything but the devouring sea. The stress on the tendons of his chest altered the configuration of the archer's ribcage - the result of the demands the heavy pull of his longbow made upon his upper body. Bone ends prevented wear from the bowstring.

the needs of raiders and traders met by the cheaper, but still functional, ordnance. Stone shot was desirable - the shattering effect of stone projectiles was more damaging than the neat, patchable holes made by iron cannon shot. Iron shot, however, was cheaper in terms of labour and production time and the English were soon following the Venetian precedent of standardizing bore and shot sizes. The English also appear to have stumbled on the great secret of black-powder artillery - that beyond a certain point, roughly 3m (10ft), there is nothing to be gained from a longer barrel. Consequently, shorter English cannon would have the same effect as the longer, heavier pieces mounted on some of the Armada's vessels.

The Spanish Solution

Given his acquaintance with the great sailing ships of Portugal, Philip II of Spain was under no illusion that the galleys which had won the day at Lepanto would be able to conquer England. Accordingly, the Armada would contain the Mediterranean world's best sailing vessels - augmented by still others begged, borrowed or stolen from Philip's subjects and trading partners. Nonetheless, the cutting edge of the fleet would still be the super-weapon of Lepanto. The galleasses Philip sent north against England had now been improved to the extent that they no longer required towing to get into action. With his usual methodical reckoning, Philip set a very limited objective for his fleet against England - one that they had every rational expectation of being met. All that was required of the Armada was for it to rendezvous with the 300 invasion craft and an additional 27,000 soldiers in the Netherlands. Once transported across the Channel, the Duke of

Parma's army would return England to Catholicism, putting paid to Queen Elizabeth's irksome support of rebellion in the Netherlands and piracy on the high seas.

It is also noteworthy that Philip's disadvantage in artillery had lacked neither notice nor attempts at rectification. Spanish ordnance experts had laboured over the years of Philip's reign to construct a cannon manufacturing industry almost from nothing - and from the outset they had attempted the same standardization of shot and bore that the English cultivated. Philip's gunners received scientifically calculated muzzle protractors to determine angles of elevation and range tables to determine the precise placement of shot.

Unfortunately for Philip's projections, however, a host of commandeered cannon brought in during the final collection of ships and armament undermined his attempts to standardize ammunition, while mathematical errors in his range tables rendered them worse than useless. Perhaps his ordnance experts can be forgiven - the great Galileo Galilei would fail to take air resistance into account when he prepared his own range tables decades after the Armada. But the results for Philips fleet in 1588 would be damaging.

Preparing for the Great Armada

On 25 May 1588, 40 warships and an additional 90 support craft, carrying 19,000 marines, set sail from Lisbon, headed for the English Channel. Philip's commander, the Duke of Medina Sidonia, had been chosen for command only because of the death of the Marquess de Santa Cruz that February. Medina Sidonia neither wanted the command nor had any opportunity to prepare for it. His quite justified forebodings of doom gradually solidified as it became clear that circumstances were already not as anticipated. Unfavourable winds greatly slowed the Armada's progress. Worse still, a great deal of the procured food had already spoiled. Medina Sidonia put into port on Spain's Atlantic coast while there was still time to do so and made what corrections he could before the fleet put to sea again in July.

For her part, Elizabeth had sought to preserve a fragile peace by avoiding any obvious preparations for war, but eventually the awful reality of the Armada and its destination could no longer be ignored. Elizabeth responded by appointing Charles Howard, Lord Effingham, as the Lord Admiral of English Navy. Elizabeth's money and military inheritance provided Howard with 40 of her own heaviest vessels, including the monster *Triumph*. Accompanying the navy proper were approximately 160 lighter craft, which served as the fleet's scouts, dispatch boats and victuallers. English efforts at supply were much more haphazard than Philip's careful plans, but Howard had this considerable advantage: a homeland that was close by and willing to help supply the demands of both men and cannon.

The English ended their own hasty preparations at Plymouth when a fleeing merchant vessel brought news of the approaching Spanish fleet on 29 July. Despite the size of the great Armada and the understandable terror it could be expected to exert, Howard's fleet set forth during the night of 30 July directly across the Spanish line of advance. Years of skirmishing and predation – the great privateer Sir Francis Drake was among Howard's commanders – had given the British ample confidence in their men, ships and guns.

First Clashes

In front of the British line of about a hundred ships lay Howard's own pinnace, *Disdain*, bearing the admiral's formal defiance to the Duke of Medina Sidonia in one last gesture of knightly formalities before the battle commenced in earnest. In his flagship *Ark Royal*, Howard had pragmatically seized the weather gauge, the wind bearing his

Medina Sidonia's San Martin *gave him no cause for complaint as his flagship: her deep hull carried substantial provisions, her armament could be worked in a sea. Inadequate planning, communication, and superior English ship-handling and cannon made the difference, leading to the Armada's failure.*

fleet and the smoke of their volleying guns directly into the Spanish crescent – the same formation that the Catholics had employed at Lepanto.

The Spanish line stretched over 3km (2 miles) from tip to tip. The triumph at Lepanto had another legacy for the Spanish, this one disastrous. Spanish manoeuvring demonstrated the unwillingness of the Spanish to expose their broadsides to the enemy, for fear of a ramming attack that would never come. Howard and his admirals had no such reservations and promptly exposed their broadsides and cannon to the Spanish, opening rapid fire at too long a range and inflicting little damage. The era of the sailing ship and the cannon was just beginning and neither side were certain of the best way to use their weapons or the platforms on which these weapons were based.

The initial cannonade failed to slow the Spanish advance towards their rendezvous with Parma. On the morning of 31 July, the Spanish captain Juan Martínez de Recalde tried a gambit of his own, letting his huge galleon *San Juan de Portugal* fall slightly behind the rest of the Spanish formation, where an English squadron hovered in hope of exactly such an opportunity. De Recalde, one of the best Spanish captains in one of their most powerful ships, had come to the conclusion that the Armada would never get to grips with the English unless it was with their own acquiescence. The ploy did not succeed, however. Recalde's armoured marines took losses without reply while the English plied *San Juan de Portugal* with cannon shot, ignoring the proffer of boarding combat.

Proof of inexperience on the part of the Spanish crews came early, as Spanish gunners with unsuitable equipment and poor training did their best to match the blizzard of English fire. *San Salvador* suddenly erupted into flame and smoke as her powder exploded. The galleasses proved their worth as combat tugs when they towed her to safety. The next calamity befell the *Rosario*, one of the largest and most valuable of the Armada galleons, who lost her bowsprit and then her

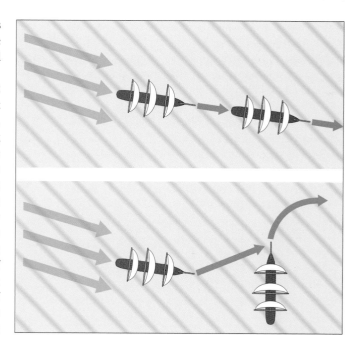

THE TERM WEATHER GAUGE *means that a vessel can attack or manoeuvre against an enemy with the advantage of the wind/tide in its favour, turning downwind or altering course at will during the attack, as shown in these illustrations.*

foremast in a collision and became uncontrollable. Spanish efforts to take her under tow while under fire proved unsuccessful. Soon *Rosario* fell into the clutches of Francis Drake. The only consolation for the Spanish was that their nemesis departed for a time as he scurried back to port with his prize.

With nothing proved other than both side's willingness to fight, Howard drew off, shadowing the Spanish and awaiting an opportunity while poised to prevent his own greatest fear – that the Spanish might descend on an English port and there establish a permanent beachhead for the coming invasion.

Clash of Titans

On 1 August 1588, the Spanish fleet finally had a chance to use the galleass as something other than a salvage vessel. *Triumph*, under Martin Frobisher, lay invitingly becalmed against the Portland Bill while five merchantmen sheltered in the galleon's lee. The Spanish galleasses bore down for the kill, precisely as they had when a Venetian flotilla had found the notorious Dutch pirate Carstens becalmed in the Mediterranean a few years before. The result was rather different. Target and prizes lay behind one of the most dangerous sandbars in the channel, the dreaded Shambles.

The Spanish found themselves warily manoeuvring in the ebbing tide while the *Triumph's* big culverins tossed iron at them. Eventually the Spanish drew off in frustration. Two days later, the galleasses would stalk a windless *Triumph* again, this time in more open water, only to have the wind freshen and the *Triumph* escape again in a hail of iron. The galleasses could not destroy what they could not catch.

More Firepower

The high rate of British fire forced Howard on 5 August to withdraw his fleet to Dover, where he sent forth a flurry of letters to London and nearby towns, pleading for powder and shot. The British had managed in the course of the fighting to damage this or that Spaniard – only to see their quarry drop back into the enveloping arms of the Spanish crescent and escape to make repairs. Something would have to disrupt the Spanish formation if the Armada's progress towards the rendezvous with Parma at Dunkirk was to be halted. Lighter Spanish pinnaces were already carrying a torrent of progress reports and messages from Medina Sidonia, urging the invasion squadron to make ready.

Straining all available resources, the frantic English officials of the Channel coast managed to refill the magazines of Howard's command, and

> *'This Armada was so completely crippled and scattered that my first duty to Your Majesty seemed to save it…. Ammunition and the best of our vessels were lacking, and experience had shown how little we could depend upon the ships that remained, the Queen's fleet being so superior to ours in this sort of fighting…'*
>
> — *DUKE OF MEDINA SIDONIA, LETTER TO PHILIP II*

with the Spanish so close to their object, a fleet of 55 ships that had been blockading the passage from Calais to Dover dropped down to augment the strength of the English fleet. By that time, the Armada had made its way up to Calais, a mere 40km (25 miles) from where the Duke of Parma was expected to have the invasion fleet in readiness. The French at Calais, comfortably Catholic, would sell food but not powder to the Armada; Medina Sidonia was prepared to take what supplies he could get.

Instead he received the worst possible news. The Duke of Parma finally replied that not so much as a barrel of beer was ready for the crossing. The same winds that had delayed the Armada's progress had delayed the messages from Spain and it would be another six days before the army in Flanders would be ready to sail across the Channel. Charles Howard had no idea of this state of affairs and no idea why the Armada stayed huddled in Calais for days, but he was too good a commander to let such an opportunity pass him by.

Flames in the Night

On 7 August 1588, eight condemned British supply ships, converted into fireships, bore down upon the anchored Spanish squadron. Just as the Spanish had most dreaded, their crews set their sails and escaped aft in boats as the fireships moved with tied rudders directly towards the Spanish anchorage.

Medina Sidonia had made provision for just such an attack, but forethought, once again, did not prove sufficient. Even as the Spanish ships stationed for the purpose made to grapple and

Spanish Soldier (1588)

Warrior in the wetlands, this light infantryman in the Duke of Parma's invasion force faced the swamps, the elements, and the Dutch in the course of Spain's long and, in the end, failed struggle to maintain supremacy over the Netherlands. A brass morion helmet, traditionally associated with Spain, protects his head and offers unit identification to his comrades and officers. A padded jerkin offers less protection and lighter weight than the traditional back-and-breastplate of the heavier troops. Next to his canteen dangle wooden cartridges with powder and ball to pour into the bore of his caliver, a lighter, musket-sized version of the more famous and much heavier arquebus. A long sword stands ready as his final recourse should the battle come to close quarters in a lack of ammunition or a chance to reload.

Battle of Gravelines

1588

With 'not so much as a barrel of beer' ready for the dash across the channel and onto England's nearly unfortified shore, the Duke of Medina Sidonia had no choice but grimly to keep the Armada in its crescent formation and resist English attacks while hoping that Parma could prepare the invasion fleet that the Armada was meant to escort to invasion and victory. Superior British firepower, maneuverability, and Lord Howard's care to maintain possession of the weather gauge did not allow Medina Sidonia to do more than survive. The amount of planning for the Armada's provision and armament was unprecedented, and in many respects reflected inadequate efforts to grasp the required complexities. With food running out, the Armada anchored in between Calais and a Spanish outpost at Gravelines and sought to buy provision. Lord Howard sent eight fireships into the Spanish anchorage, fatally scattering the Armada and sending it into a disintegrating transit around the British Isles to disaster off Ireland.

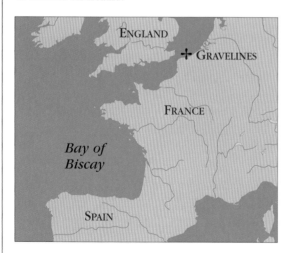

A lack of communication between the invasion fleet of the Duke of Parma and its escort, the Armada, under the Duke of Medina Sidonia prevented coordination, and forced a pause of which the British took fatal advantage.

5 Holed, and with severe damage to their tackle, the Spanish attempt to make repairs at sea and disengage, the order being to sail around the north of Scotland.

3 Medina Sidonia reforms the bulk of his fleet, losing only the galleass *San Martin*. The scattering of the fleet forces and prevailing winds force Medina Sidonia to abandon his mission.

4 The British do their best to detach and destroy individual units and form up for a fleet-wide cannonade.

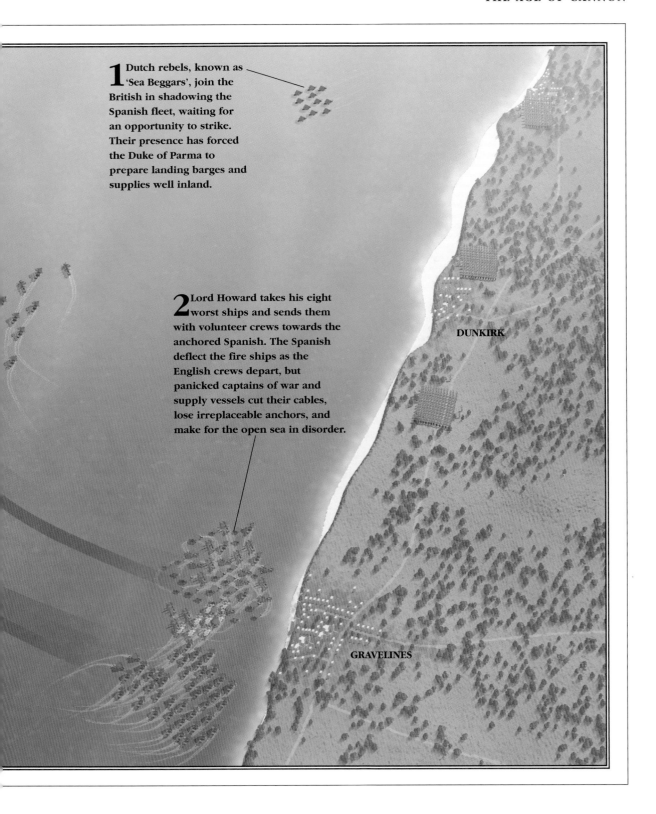

1 Dutch rebels, known as 'Sea Beggars', join the British in shadowing the Spanish fleet, waiting for an opportunity to strike. Their presence has forced the Duke of Parma to prepare landing barges and supplies well inland.

2 Lord Howard takes his eight worst ships and sends them with volunteer crews towards the anchored Spanish. The Spanish deflect the fire ships as the English crews depart, but panicked captains of war and supply vessels cut their cables, lose irreplaceable anchors, and make for the open sea in disorder.

DUNKIRK

GRAVELINES

tow off the flaming derelicts, the rest of the fleet was lapsing into a panic. A cable cut is an anchor lost, and as the Armada scattered, it lost the cohesion that had so far sustained it against English courage and cannon.

The following day's engagement, the Battle of Gravelines, began with Medina Sidonia and the fours ships under his direct command trying desperately, in rough seas and adverse winds, to regroup with the ships that had sailed off into the darkness of the night before. Howard finally closed the range until just outside the reach of Spanish grapnels and for a second time emptied the magazines of his fleet – this time to considerable effect. Medina Sidonia tried the desperate expedient of hanging one of his pusillanimous captains, but even that example was insufficient to recall his men to their duties and his ships to their stations.

'It came, it went, it was' was the inscription on one Dutch medal commemorating the disaster.

Dutch privateers known as the 'Sea Beggars' swarmed out from Dutch and Flemish ports and attacked individual Spanish vessels, in search of booty. Chaos and winds swept the surviving vessels past the Spanish army and around the coast of the British Isles; heavy storms and the lack of their anchors wrecked many of the Spanish vessels on the Irish coast as they tried to return home. In all, only 60 vessels out of 200 that had set forth returned to Spain, carrying a mere 4000 starving survivors of the 19,000 soldiers and sailors that Philip II had so confidently dispatched for the conquest of England.

Hansando 1592: Iron Turtles, Iron Cannon

Chained ships had fought at Sluys in 1340 and chained ships also fought on Lake Poyang in China just two decades later. In 1588, England had stood to perish from a seaborne assault until cannon, command and courage proved decisive. In 1592, less than four years after the passing of the

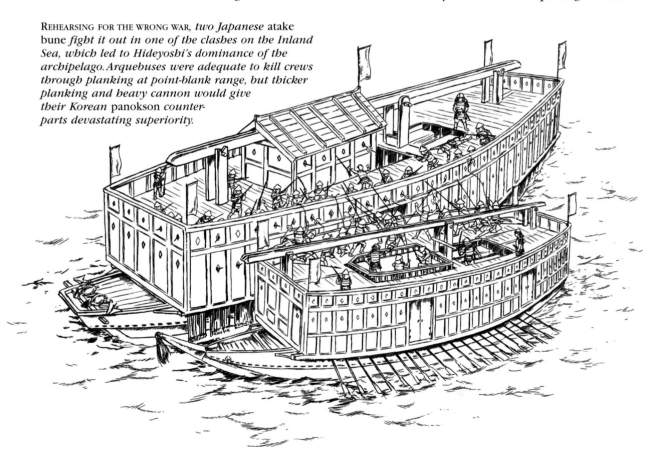

REHEARSING FOR THE WRONG WAR, *two Japanese* atake bune *fight it out in one of the clashes on the Inland Sea, which led to Hideyoshi's dominance of the archipelago. Arquebuses were adequate to kill crews through planking at point-blank range, but thicker planking and heavy cannon would give their Korean* panokson *counterparts devastating superiority.*

Armada, the endangered kingdom was Korea, the superlative army menacing it that of the great unifier of Japan, Toyotomi Hideyoshi. The differences in naval events and technology between Europe and Asia are less striking than the similarities. Identical objectives were met on both sides of the globe, with some telling differences and many astounding similarities.

By 1590, having made himself master of Japan, Hideyoshi correctly reasoned that the surging bellicosity which had forged Japan into a single, militarily powerful nation would need an external outlet, or risk tearing Japan apart once more. Korea was the obvious target. From centuries of trade, the Japanese were well aware of the quantity and quality of Korean iron manufacture, an industry that was very useful for a military society. The peninsula even resembled a set of stepping stones leading up into the soft underbelly of Ming China, which was already in the early stages of disintegration and collapse.

The decision to invade a kingdom and a vast empire had recent impetus. Hideyoshi was convinced that he had the technological weapons to prevail over both Korean resolve and the huge Ming Army. In 1542–43, a typhoon had forced a Chinese merchant junk to put into Kyushu. On board, the

SLAUGHTERING SAMURAI in Japan, and Koreans in Korea, Japanese ashigaru *like this example brought the full weight of the gunpowder revolution to Asia. His iron helmet was a version of a peasant's straw hat, providing protection against both missiles and the elements. He carried a cheaper version of the samurai sword, but his primary weapon was his matchlock arquebus, based on a Spanish design. He could fire three inaccurate shots a minute.*

Japanese found three Portuguese traders and, among their effects, two matchlock arquebuses. Upon learning of their existence and use, the local *daimyo* bought both the weapons and lessons in how to manufacture them and their ammunition. In an amazingly short time, the knowledge spread throughout Japan, and soon the Japanese *ashigaru*, or men-at-arms, possessed firepower previously undreamed of on the islands. The primitive *midfa*-style handguns of the Koreans and Chinese lacked the portability and rate of fire of the new European-style weapons, and Hideyoshi took care to have nearly every matchlock in Japan at hand for his planned invasion.

The robustness and ease of use of the arquebus had much to recommend it as a weapon for a nation bent on conquest. The Japanese favoured a lighter version than that employed by the Spanish conquistadors; a single individual with fairly rudimentary training could soon operate such a weapon to the limits of its accuracy and rate of fire. Either as an implied threat or as a gesture of romantic fair play, Toyotomi Hideyoshi had sent to Korea a single arquebus, along with his ultimatum, in 1591. Only a single provincial minister, Yu Seong-ryong, urged that the Koreans copy the weapon as the Japanese had done. That plea and Seong-ryong's frantic efforts to have the peninsula's defences repaired while there was yet time fell upon deaf ears. The bonds between the Confucian nobility and ruling caste and the Korean people were tenuous, and the king in Seoul did not care to listen to predictions of invasion and war so soon after a previous struggle that had left him a vassal of the Ming.

Pirates to Conquerors

It helped that Korea was hardly *terra incognita* to the Japanese. Pirates called *wako* had long enriched themselves by way of raids across the 200km (120 miles) of the Korean Strait, with the islands of Tsushima and Iki providing convenient bases. It was due to the severity of the *wako*'s depredations that Choe Mu-Seon had received government support for his own experiments into gunpowder in the fourteenth century. Korea was fortunate that the efforts of that particular inventor had not all fallen upon barren ground. Korean education had long emphasized both the technical and theoretical in study, and Korean craftsmen had centuries of practice in the crafts that would prove to be the peninsula's salvation.

As a result of the two Mongol invasions of Japan in 1274 and 1281, Hideyoshi knew that large armies could cross the Tsushima Strait even in river craft, which was fortunate given the relatively poor sea-keeping qualities of the Japanese junks that had for centuries fared from island to island in the sheltered waters of the Inland Sea. There had been large-scale landings in Korea before. A *wako* raid supported by 70 ships in 1555 had brushed aside Korean defenders and returned safely carrying much booty.

After a rejected bid to buy two European galleons from the Portuguese in 1585, Hideyoshi began his final preparations for the assault. On 23 May 1592, Japanese ships began landing the first detachments of what would eventually be around 158,000 men destined by Hideyoshi for the subjugation of Korea. The initial Japanese success was overwhelming. Two of Hideyoshi's best generals each led a part of the Japanese army along the coasts of the peninsula. Unskilled levies from the Korean peasantry fell by the thousands under the razor swords of the samurai. Armed only with flails and padded coats, Korean cavalry rode bravely forward into lethal volleys of musket fire from the *ashigaru*. Korean cities and fortresses collapsed so rapidly that the Chosun monarchy in Seoul barely had time to escape before their ancestral capital had fallen. By August 1592, the Japanese were the masters of

'The man trying to preserve his life will die, the man unafraid of death will live. Military doctrine says, if one defender of the homeland stands guard at a strong gateway, he can daunt the hearts of the enemy coming 10,000 strong....'

— YI SUN-SIN

their every objective in Korea, and their armies now gathered on the banks of the Yalu River to make the crossing into Manchuria.

The Overlooked Admiral

The Korean naval bases off the peninsula's southern coast had not been one of the Japanese objectives. There appeared to be no need to take the naval bases, particularly in light of the performance of two of Korea's four senior admirals. Park Hong, commander of the Eastern Gyeongsang fleet and entrusted with the defence of Pusan, fled his command at the first news of the Japanese landing, pausing in his flight only to order the destruction of his base and the 75 ships under his command. The commander of the Western Gyeongsang fleet, Won Kyun, fled with four of his ships as a personal escort while the rest of his squadron was utterly destroyed.

The third Korean admiral was named Yi Sun-Sin. As a boy, born in the same year as Francis Drake, Yi Sun Sin had done sufficiently well in the standardized Confucian exams to have his choice of careers, and had chosen the military. He made himself well acquainted with both the traditional Chinese military manuals and the deplorable state of Korea's armed forces and static defences. As a brilliant young officer, Yi Sun-Sin aroused the jealousy of more senior commanders. It was only due to the intervention of Yu Seong-ryong, the same minister whose warnings about the Japanese invasion of Korea had been so foolishly ignored, that Yi Sun-Sin had been saved from disgrace or execution. It was well that he did so, for in saving his life, Yu Seong-ryong saved Korea.

Yi Sun-Sin appreciated the strengths of the Korean Navy far more than the Japanese or, indeed, his own countrymen. One legacy of Choe Mu-Seon's experimentation had been the early

ADMIRAL YI SUN-SIN'S statue smiles down on the nation he preserved from annihilation by the Japanese. Repeatedly broken on false charges, displaced by palace intrigues, Yi Sun-Sin persevered, and went on to preserve both his fleet and country, using innovative ships and tactics to sever Japanese lines of communication. Yi's brilliance forced the invaders' retreat away from his shattered homeland.

utilization of Korea's iron industry in the construction of cannon, giving the Koreans the same advantage enjoyed by the English in the quantity of available arms. In 1592, the Korean Navy was ahead of even the English in possessing four standardized units of ordnance, designated (in order of size) by the first four characters in a standard reading text: 'yellow,' 'black,' 'heaven' and 'earth'. From some source or other, moreover, the Koreans had acquired or invented their own version of the four-wheeled gun carriage. Yi knew the capabilities of these guns and grimly proposed to use them in the defence of his homeland.

While Yu Seong-ryong was making his frantic pleas and preparations to resist the Japanese on land, Admiral Yi had been experimenting with a ship design he had garnered from his military reading. The existing capital unit of the Korean fleet was already very good. The *panokson* ('board-roofed ship') was a rectangular vessel with high wooden sides supporting a protecting wooden roof and command tower. The rectilinear construction gave the Korean war galley formidable armament at bow, stern and broadside. Korea's sailors were well acquainted with the preference of the Japanese for hand-to-hand combat, and the *panokson*'s high sides were constructed to prevent that possibility.

Panokson varied in size, with the largest around 35m (110ft) at the waterline and smaller versions around 15m (50ft) in length. Oarsmen rowing 'gondola style' worked on the deck below the *panokson*'s cannon. The crews totalled around 125 officers and men. Like the galleass, the *panokson* possessed limited sail power when not in combat. Also like the galleass, slow as it was, a properly handled *panokson* seldom had to run away from an enemy that it wished to fight. The Japanese had so far had no reason to run away from anything Korean.

Yi wanted something fast enough to catch and destroy its quarry, and thought he had found the answer. The Chinese military manuals contained references to a low, speedy oared junk called a 'covered swooper' (*meng chong*). The Chinese sheathed such vessels in fire-resistant moistened leather and intended them for ramming. Korean naval architects had experimented with a similar vessel in the fourteenth century. The idea of a cut-down, armoured *panokson* led Yi Sun-Sin to create perhaps the most powerful naval weapon of his day.

The Turtle Ship
Confusion still persists concerning the details of what Yi and his contemporaries labelled the *kobukson,* or 'turtle ship'. Much of this confusion can be avoided simply by reading the actual words of the ship's inventor. Multiple volumes of Yi Sun-Sin's war diary, which the admiral maintained until two days before his death, have been preserved. In addition to his own account, Yi's nephew produced another description of the vessels.

Most obviously, the 'turtle ships' were turtle-backed as a defence against boarding from above. Standing oarsmen and gunners could work side by side from the single rectangular upper deck that overhung the lower deck in which the crew had their quarters. It is conceivable that the turtle ships could have had a second deck for the guns exclusively, but the idea that fewer guns would hit more often at closer range argues for a single deck on a ship meant to close, ram and hole enemies at or just above their waterlines. Less top-clutter meant greater agility and a smaller target for an enemy's guns.

There is still much confusion over the 'ironclad' nature of the turtle back. Iron armour on the back of a turtle ship would have consisted of thin anti-incendiary plates, not heavy cannon-proof material that would have and did cause one putative replica to collapse under the unnecessary weight. The Japanese did not have cannon capable of firing down onto a turtle ship. Yi's nephew mentions another form of protection on the armoured backs of the vessels – spikes, concealed in the hope of impaling a boarder's foot. Another area of confusion persists, a consequence of defective eighteenth-century illustrations of the vessels. Both contemporary accounts agree that the cannon fired through 'dragon's heads' on the bows of the ships. The later illustrations place dragon figureheads of the type used on traditional 'dragon boat' racing sculls on the top of the turtle back, in a position from which not so much as a musket could have been fired. Yi and his nephew clearly meant that the entire front end of the ship took the form of a dragon's head, with the forward two or three bow guns firing from ports among the 'teeth' along the bow.

How the turtle ships executed their ramming attacks is another problem. Most modern reconstructions of the boats feature a flat face mask on the reverse-angled bows of the vessels. Such placement of a flat casting would never strike the enemy at all. Instead, the impact of a ramming attack would have been spread over the surface of the forward end beam, diluting the momentum of a ramming attack into uselessness

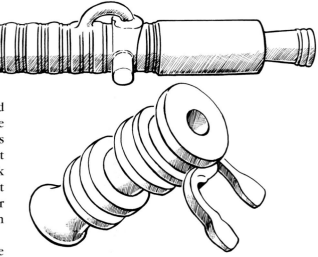

THEY HAD THE SAME USE *and a similar design to their European counterparts, but this Korean cannon and 'crouching tiger' mortar owed nothing to the Western analogues they roughly resembled. The trunnions on the Korean cannon allowed its elevation and depression on its wheeled truck carriage. The mortar's explosive bomb proved devastating against Japanese ships at anchor or drawn up on the shore during Yi Sun-Sin's onslaughts.*

against the side of the target's hull. In this instance, the eigtheenth-century illustrations are correct in their placement of an actual ram, another simple detail rendered accurately. They portray a second dragon's head projecting from the cutwater - a ram not at all unlike the proven model of the Ancient Greeks, notably the one dredged up from the sea floor at Athlit in 1980. Impact behind a narrow metallic wedge would break the timbers of the target's hull, as the historical records indicate. By a combination of ramming and cannon attack, for example, a turtle ship would severely maul the *Nihon Maru*, a tower ship originally built as a floating castle for Hideyoshi, at the Battle of Angolpo in 1592.

A Nation Saved

There is much to praise in Yi Sun-Sin's fighting techniques in addition to their technological innovation. Korea's saviour was a humane and compassionate man to whom refugees fled for assistance, bringing with them priceless knowledge of the location and intentions of their

Japanese tormentors. Yi augmented his own knowledge of the coast and tides by good relations with the coastal fisherman, acquiring by his courtesy a network of expert observers who helped him to track his fleet's objectives.

The paralysis of Korea's government under the Japanese onslaught extended to those still willing to obey its orders. It was not until Won Kyun and his four surviving ships entered his defensive area that Yi Sun-Sin secured authorization to sail forth against the invaders. If Hideyoshi was to consolidate his control of Korea and launch his invasion of China, he would need to control the seas in between his objectives and Japan. Yi's demonstrations that the Japanese did not, in fact, have such naval mastery were so swift and sanguinary that it took the Japanese a fatally long time to appreciate the lesson.

The admiral's first engagement with the Japanese came on 16 June 1592 off the island of Okpo. Yi's good relations with the local fishermen provided him with information about the location of a completely unprepared Japanese naval force that was then engaged primarily in loading loot. The egregious Won Kyun and his remnant squadron joined forces with Yi's fleet of 24 *panokson* and bore down on the invader. The Japanese made frantic efforts to man their ships and put to sea, but such was the quality of Korean cannon that there was no need for Yi's command to close to where the arquebuses of the scattered Japanese could injure his crews. Firing huge iron arrows wrapped in ignited tow, the Koreans methodically burned 50 or so of the Japanese ships and moved to their next objective before any warning could be sent. Such an incendiary device

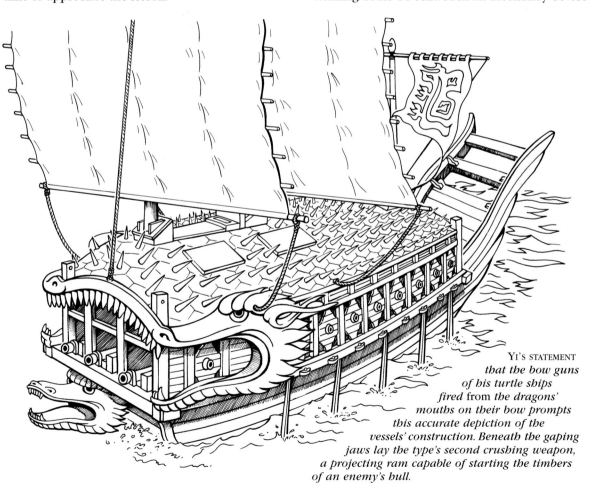

YI'S STATEMENT
*that the bow guns
of his turtle ships
fired from the dragons'
mouths on their bow prompts
this accurate depiction of the
vessels' construction. Beneath the gaping
jaws lay the type's second crushing weapon,
a projecting ram capable of starting the timbers
of an enemy's hull.*

Battle of Hansando
1592

After Yi Sun-Sin's fleet had destroyed three of theirs, the Japanese were aware that something had to be done about the defiant Korean admiral and his crews. Toyotomi Hideyoshi's orders were to consolidate his remaining naval assets and overwhelm the Koreans with sheer numbers – but arrogance on the part of the Japanese commanders continued to be a fatal flaw. Not deigning to wait for coming reinforcements, Wakizaka Yasuharu moved with nearly 40 heavy ships and 24 medium vessels toward the Island of Hansan, driving refugees before him. One of these informed Admiral Yi of the impending attack, towards which Yi brought the consolidated Korean fleet of over 100 vessels, including multiple examples of the devastating *kobukson* 'turtle ship.' A picket squadron of Korean vessels lured the aggressive Japanese into Yi's ambush, in which Japanese *élan* protracted a losing battle while Korean cannon and mortars wrought deadly havoc.

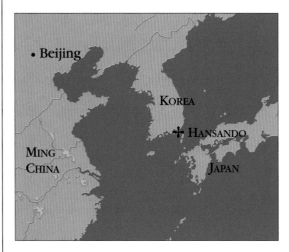

Too far from the sheltered inland sea, the traditional war galleys and junks of the Japanese found the coastal waters of the Korean peninsula less than hospitable. The islands and harbours of Korea provided secure bases for ships and a naval tradition more formidable and better led.

CHUNGMU

5 Yi completes the disaster with a devastating barrage of exploding shell from the open upper decks of his *panokson* ships in the line. Japanese survivors escape to the islands of the sound or in the few ships remaining.

2 Informed of the Japanese onset by Korean refugees, Yi notes Wakizaka's aggressiveness and arranges his fleet in a Lepanto-style crescent formation, into which damaged vessels can retreat and which can surround an attacking enemy.

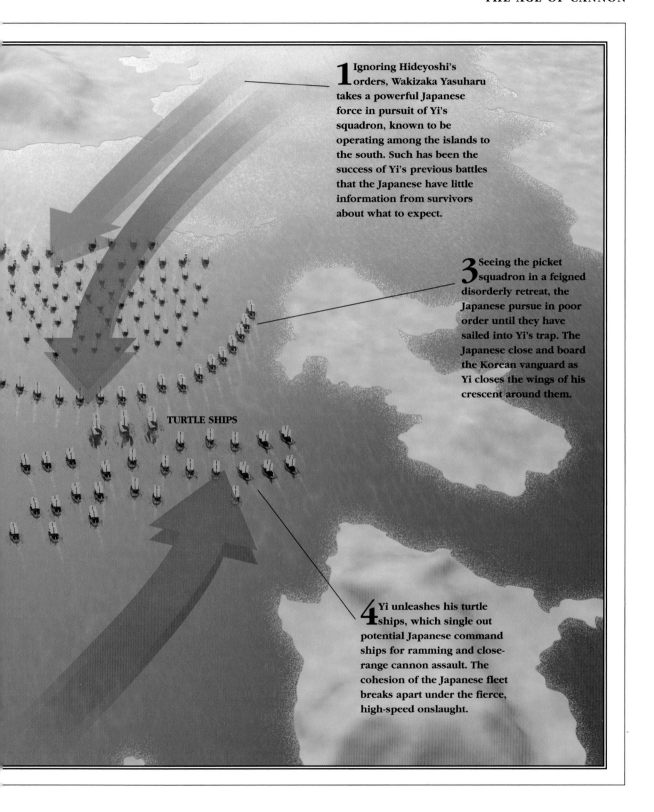

1 Ignoring Hideyoshi's orders, Wakizaka Yasuharu takes a powerful Japanese force in pursuit of Yi's squadron, known to be operating among the islands to the south. Such has been the success of Yi's previous battles that the Japanese have little information from survivors about what to expect.

3 Seeing the picket squadron in a feigned disorderly retreat, the Japanese pursue in poor order until they have sailed into Yi's trap. The Japanese close and board the Korean vanguard as Yi closes the wings of his crescent around them.

TURTLE SHIPS

4 Yi unleashes his turtle ships, which single out potential Japanese command ships for ramming and close-range cannon assault. The cohesion of the Japanese fleet breaks apart under the fierce, high-speed onslaught.

would have offered a considerable advantage both at Lepanto and at Gravelines.

On 8 July at Sacheon, the first prototype of the turtle ship joined Yi and his command to find a Japanese fleet loading still more loot, in a bay that was surrounded by high cliffs, from which plunging fire posed a threat to ships that the Koreans could not afford to lose. Yi accordingly turned fox instead of sea-wolf, his fleet appearing in the mouth of the bay and then making haste in disorder for the open sea. The surviving Japanese, who so far had no grounds for anything other than contempt for the Korean military, took the bait and gave chase. The Japanese suddenly found themselves in the arms of an inverted crescent, with the turtle ship playing the role of the galleasses by darting into the Japanese formation

and wreaking havoc with ram and cannon. For the next five weeks, Yi's force would scour the Korean coast, annihilating Japanese squadrons at Tangpo, where the turtle ship's attack resulted in the death of the Japanese commander, and Tanchangpo, where once again Yi's new warship tore into the Japanese flagship. Yi's tactic of a feigned retreat once again lured the rest of the Japanese into deeper water; the Koreans then suddenly reversed course and destroyed the invaders with their artillery.

Even without the turtle ship's 'decapitation strikes', the Japanese had been outbuilt. Their *atake bune* bore a superficial resemblance to the *panokson*, but with a telling difference. The Japanese *Ashigaru* arquebusiers had slaughtered Korean infantry in open land battles. Similarly, the Japanese had expected the lines of marksmen stationed along loopholes in the planked sides of their own capital ship to slaughter Koreans behind what they thought would be thin palisades on their vessels. Instead, the Japanese marksmen found their bullets unable to penetrate the Koreans' thicker bulwarks and the Korean cannon far outranged their matchlocks. Yi's victories were

EQUIPPED FOR BATTLE, *this smaller* panokson *packs a lethal mixture of protection and cannon. The large Korean 'earth' cannon could fire an iron ball or a large iron arrow wrapped in incendiary material into its target. Officers such as Yi Sun-Sin commanded from the central observation cupola. Japanese and Korean vessels were smaller and slower than their globe-spanning European contemporaries, but mounted a great deal of armament.*

the long-awaited vindication of Choe Mu-Seon's interest, two centuries previously, in the development of artillery.

The Battle

Yi's greatest victory over the Japanese came on 14 August 1592 at Hansan Island (Hansando in Korean). The Japanese had belatedly realized that Yi would need to be dealt with and Hideyoshi had thus given appropriate orders to his admirals. In complete ignorance of exactly what to expect and without waiting for reinforcements, Wakizaka Yasuharu set forth with 82 vessels, hoping to crush the Korean naval presence once and for all. Yi's squadron had by now grown to nearly 100 vessels, including at least two more turtle ships.

Yi had been manoeuvring warily in the fear of finding a Japanese land army in a position to damage his squadron. When a fleeing refugee informed him of the impending Japanese attack, Yi and his sailors got ready for the largest and most decisive of all their battles. Once again, Yi let the Japanese surge forward into the awaiting arms of his crescent, the Japanese as set upon his destruction as he had been upon theirs. Yi's men were justifiably confident in their commander and the admiral's sudden signal to cease backwatering and engage was obeyed with a fury that shattered the characteristic vigour of the Japanese.

The Battle of Hansando was a fierce, protracted struggle. Some of the Japanese managed to close and board a few of the Korean vessels, including, by their own accounts, one of the turtle ships, into which the samurai hacked with their swords. The Koreans by no means abandoned their artillery. In fact, the huge 'earth' guns of the *panakson* fired explosive shell for the first time in the conflict. The Japanese fleet was annihilated. Only a few of the ships managed to escape Yi's ensnarement.

> *'Captains of this fleet are expected to follow my orders exactly; if not, even the minor errors will not be pardoned, but will face the full punishment of military regulations.'*
>
> — *YI SUN-SIN*

Over the course of the next week, Yi defeated Yashuharu's reinforcements in detail, finding out at Angolpo that the Japanese had finally learned not to believe the feigned retreats. They lost their ships regardless when Yi closed with relays of bombarding ships and destroyed them where they lay. Yi did, however, allow the Japanese survivors to escape, in order to prevent them slaughtering helpless villagers on the shores of their anchorages.

Yi's victories bought Korea a space of five years in which Hideyoshi suspended his invasion. In the interim, the Japanese convinced Yi's jealous Chosun superiors that their greatest nemesis was, in fact, their pawn, prompting Yi's torture and his reduction to the ranks of the infantry. Won Kyun received command of Yi's fleet and promptly squandered it in an ambush where Japanese shore and sea missile fire managed to destroy even the fabled turtle ships. Returned in 1597 to command of what was left of the Korean Navy, Yi once more broke the Japanese fleet even as it tried to withdraw from Korea. In the course of the final battle, Yi Sun-Sin was mortally wounded. The admiral's last order was for a sailor to cover his body with a shield, so that his death would not discourage his men.

At sea, faith in technology found vindication not just once but time and time again, even if the form that it took differed over the passage of the years. Greek fire, the cog and the longbow, the galleass and the gun carriage all made the case for technological innovation in the West, while Yi and his turtle ships became an enduring legend in the nation that he helped to save. To a greater or lesser degree, innovation on board ships produced the idea that, in at least some venues, progress was possible. That idea - like the keel, the naval gun and the sailing ship - lingered on long after the Age of Cannon had passed.

CHAPTER 3

THE AGE OF SAIL

The period from the early seventeenth century to the 1780s was the true Age of Sail, in which the sailing warships became ever larger and more sophisticated. The maritime competition for supremacy, an open field at the start of the era, had been settled by the end in favour of Britain and her Royal Navy.

The loss of the Grand Armada in 1588 did not spell the beginning of the end for Spanish sea power. Her *Armada Real*, or Royal Navy, soon recovered its former numerical strength, if not its former arrogant self-confidence. Unlike her European adversaries, Spain, which was then united with Portugal, had a desperate need for a strong navy because of her vast, wealthy but vulnerable overseas empire. Her most significant adversary at sea was not the English but the king's former subjects in the Netherlands, where the United Provinces of the north had been fighting for decades against Spain.

Not only were the rebel Dutch building their commercial wealth at the expense of the Spanish and Portuguese, but Spain was having the worst of

A FIERCE BATTLE *took place between the English and their most dangerous adversary at sea, the Dutch, in August 1653, off the Dutch coast at Ter Heyde. Dutch admiral Maarten Tromp was killed at this battle.*

the fighting at sea as well. Having seemingly learnt nothing from the past, the Spanish were still trying to board enemy ships when it was gunnery that was now crucial. This was rammed home, once again, on 25 April 1607, when a Dutch fleet of 26 ships under Admiral Jacob van Heemskerck defeated and sunk a Spanish fleet off Gibraltar. Following this defeat, Spain was ready to sign, at the price of her true interests, the Twelve Years' Truce (1609–21) with the Dutch.

Imperial Spain Versus the Dutch: 1621–1639

Before the truce expired, the Spanish had to figure out a way to recover and then fight off the Dutch. Don Gaspar de Guzmán, Count-Duke of Olivares, thought he knew how. Spain was, like France, not a natural naval power and her most fearsome force was the army and not the navy. The Netherlands could be isolated by the army in Flanders, Olivares believed, its coast blockaded, its trade cut in the Channel by Spanish privateers and its economy ruined before the Spanish invaded its coastline.

Spain had to spread its limited naval forces thinly across the world to protect endless sea lanes and her sprawling empire from Dutch, French or English attack. The main Spanish fleet was the *Armada del Mar Océano*, or Atlantic Fleet, created to defend the all important sea lanes across the Atlantic. Without the silver of New Spain (Mexico), Spain's finances, and with them her ability to wage war, would collapse. By the early 1620s, following a belated construction programme begun in 1617, this fleet numbered 46 vessels. The main naval base, Cadiz, housed 23

A CAST IRON CANNON ON BROAD wooden wheels, which allowed it to roll across the wooden decks. Alongside it is the equipment used for its handling under fire, including smaller tools to clean touch holes for ignition of the shot.

vessels and another 18 galleons were stationed at Gibraltar. The Spanish had spent 2.6 million ducats on building some 24 galleons. By 1638, Spanish naval power had never been more impressive.

Truce or not, the Dutch had rounded the Cape of the Horn (Tierra del Fuego) in May 1615 with six warships under Admiral Joris van Speilbergen and routed, with the loss of two Spanish vessels, Admiral Rodrigo de Mendoza's *Armada del Mar Sur* (Southern Pacific Fleet). Fleeing into Callao, Mendoza left the intrepid Dutch to plunder much of the Pacific coast of Spanish America. To prevent similar disasters in the Atlantic, the Spanish rebuilt their Convoy Fleet (*Armada de la Guardia*) specifically to protect the annual silver fleets (*Flotas*) that sailed from Vera Cruz via Havanna to Cadiz with Mexican silver. The Windward Fleet (*Armada de Barlovento*) was created under Admiral Fadrique de Toledo and stationed at Havana or Cadiz, depending on need, to clear out the pirates that infested the West Indies and threatened Spanish lines of communications. Yet demands linked to another war with France, which broke out in 1635, depleted both forces.

These were still essentially defensive measures that left the Dutch free to

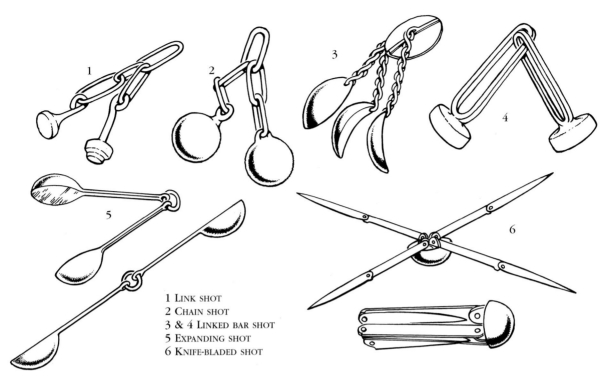

1 LINK SHOT
2 CHAIN SHOT
3 & 4 LINKED BAR SHOT
5 EXPANDING SHOT
6 KNIFE-BLADED SHOT

IN ADDITION TO SOLID SHOT OR SHRAPNEL, *designed respectively to sink the vessel or kill its crews, these chain shots were primarily for cutting beams and masts or to shred sails to pieces.*

grow ever stronger based on their near monopoly on trade with the Baltic. Without the timber from this trade, the Dutch ships would rot; without its naval stores (tar, pitch, rope and hemp), the Dutch Navy would deteriorate; and without Polish grain, its inhabitants would starve. Olivares therefore laid plans in 1626 to cooperate with Poland to build up a joint fleet, with bases either at Riga or Danzig, to prey on Dutch shipping. Plans for a naval base at Weimar or Stralsund were plotted until 1630, when Sweden's entry into the Thirty Years' War put paid to these plans.

Olivares was a bold global strategist who was willing to gamble for high stakes. If the Dutch western connection through the Channel could be cut, it would ruin them as much as if their Baltic lifeline were severed. In 1621, Olivares allocated 20,000 ducats to the improvement of Dunkirk and the building of 20 galleons there. The plan was to have 40 galleons at Dunkirk by January 1636. This

was possible since the Spanish shipyards, despite shortages of money and skilled labour, were building 50 vessels per year during the 1620s and 1630s. Operating from Dunkirk, Spanish privateers took a heavy and steady toll on Dutch shipping and on the North Sea fisheries, hitting the Dutch in their pockets – their most vulnerable point.

The Downs 1638: Spain's Final Gamble

By 1638, the Dutch – isolated and hopelessly divided – seemed ripe for the plucking. Olivares planned to crush the Dutch in a pincer between Cardinal Infante's regulars in Belgium, advancing north of the Meuse-Rhine, and an amphibious landing on the Holland coast. Using Dunkirk as a base for this invasion fleet, the Spanish would send 20,000 men in specially built barges with blunt ends, shallow draughts, 12 guns and a capacity to carry 150 musketeers. Orders were issued for the already overstretched yards to begin mass producing the landing barges. Through their agents, the Dutch soon learnt what Olivares was planning and they laid siege to Dunkirk – the lynchpin of all the Count-Duke's schemes for total victory. Olivares' plan may have been bold but it

Battle of the Downs

1638

This most important of sea battles signalled the ascendancy of the Dutch as the world's greatest naval power, yet it has often been overlooked. Dutch Admiral Maarten Tromp managed, despite overwhelming odds, to defeat the Spanish fleet off the French coast. Admiral de Oquendo fled with his ships for the dubious safety of Spain's former enemy, England, at the Downs. After waiting for reinforcements, and realizing that the Spanish would not come out to give battle, Tromp attacked on 21 October. Firing quick rounds and coming in close for a kill, his crews trusted in their audacity against an inexperienced enemy. The Spanish ships were raked with shot, and Tromp then unleashed his fireships with devastating results. The *Santa Theresa*, flagship of Admiral de Hoces, exploded, taking both the admiral and his crew to the bottom of the sea. Oquendo managed to escape with the remains of his fleet and delivered some, though not all, of the promised troops to the Cardinal-Infante's army in Flanders.

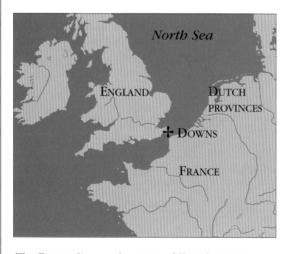

The Downs lies on the coast of Kent between Walmer castle and the strategic port of Dover in the southeastern extremity of England, facing the Channel and France.

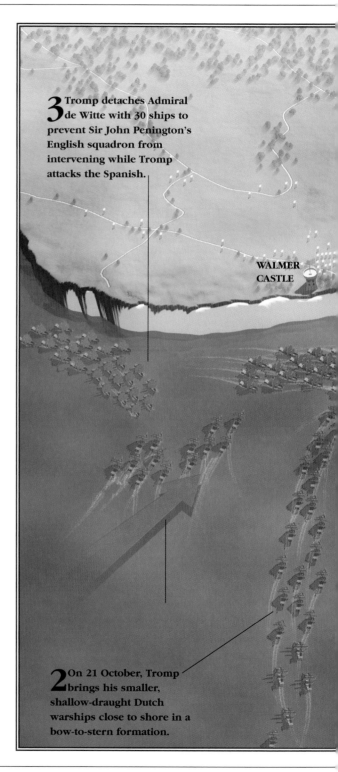

3 Tromp detaches Admiral de Witte with 30 ships to prevent Sir John Penington's English squadron from intervening while Tromp attacks the Spanish.

WALMER CASTLE

2 On 21 October, Tromp brings his smaller, shallow-draught Dutch warships close to shore in a bow-to-stern formation.

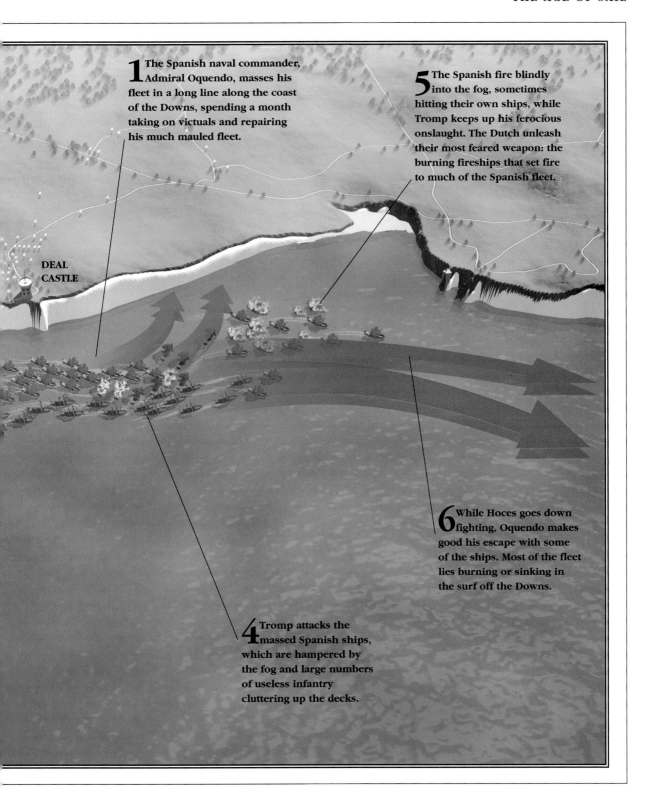

1 The Spanish naval commander, Admiral Oquendo, masses his fleet in a long line along the coast of the Downs, spending a month taking on victuals and repairing his much mauled fleet.

5 The Spanish fire blindly into the fog, sometimes hitting their own ships, while Tromp keeps up his ferocious onslaught. The Dutch unleash their most feared weapon: the burning fireships that set fire to much of the Spanish fleet.

DEAL CASTLE

6 While Hoces goes down fighting, Oquendo makes good his escape with some of the ships. Most of the fleet lies burning or sinking in the surf off the Downs.

4 Tromp attacks the massed Spanish ships, which are hampered by the fog and large numbers of useless infantry cluttering up the decks.

was overly dependent on that single Channel port and it overestimated Spain's sea power. Both errors were to prove fatal.

In July 1639, Olivares concentrated the largest Armada since 1588 under the command of Admiral Antonio de Oquendo. This was a far from ideal choice since the Dutch had worsted him back in 1631 and he was up against an old sea dog, the Lieutenant Admiral of Holland, Maarten Tromp. Tromp had crushed the Spanish at Gravelines in 1588, and he now proceeded to blockade Dunkirk.

Again Olivares' plans were on a grand scale. Oquendo's great Armada would sweep up the Channel, defeat the Dutch Navy, relieve Dunkirk and prepare the way for an invasion of Holland. A fleet of 24 galleons assembled at Cadiz under Oquendo, while 63 vessels gathered under Vice Admiral Lope de Hoces at Corunna. A total of 30 transports (including 7 hired English ships) were to carry 8500 troops to Flanders. This Armada was numerically smaller than the one in 1588 (in both ships and men). But the Spanish had learnt the bitter lessons of that tragic year: their galleons had proper gunports, trained crews well able to use their guns and, above all, plenty of artillery. The galleons were faster, better equipped and more heavily gunned than in any previous Spanish fleet. Oquendo set sail on 6 September.

Dutch cruisers spotted this vast Armada of 77 warships and 55 transports just off Selsey Bill in the western approaches of the Channel. The signal was given to prepare for battle. Tromp had only 17 vessels but did not hesitate to attack. The Spanish Armada held good order, waiting to fire until the Dutch were close enough. With superior numbers and a favourable wind, Oquendo was sure he would win. The Spanish fought with customary fervour and at the mouth of the Somme managed to surround the Dutch. However, a number of Spanish ships, including Oquendo's flagship *Santiago,* were badly damaged by Dutch fire. Conscious that his fleet's first priority was to protect the Spanish troops, Oquendo signalled his captains to retreat. The fleet sailed northwards and took refuge at the anchorage of the Downs on the English coast.

Though theoretically neutral, the pro-Dutch English played extremely reluctant hosts to their guests, who were charged through the nose for supplies. The hesitant and self-doubting Oquendo meanwhile agonized over whether to remain while his ships were repaired – giving the Dutch time to grow stronger – or to make a run for Dunkirk. Tromp made better use of his time. Dutch naval reinforcements, both warships and armed merchantmen, were pouring in and when he had more than 100 vessels, Tromp decided to attack. He detached 30 ships under Admiral Witte de With to keep Admiral Sir John Penington's hovering English fleet at bay, and on 21 October gave the signal to attack.

A descending fog gave Tromp's battle line, sailing bow to stern, good cover as it came upon the enemy, taking the Spanish by surprise. The Dutch had small, compact warships but good artillery and crews to handle the guns. Generally, the Dutch relied on aggressive close-quarter fighting, sometimes boarding, and the liberal, deadly use of fireships. Given the Spanish superiority in weight, in the height of ships' sides, in artillery and, above all, in armed crews, Tromp decided to keep a prudent distance. He had 96 warships and 12 fireships. His own flagship, *Aemelia,* had a mere 46 guns. Like sheep in a pen, the Spanish vessels huddled around Oquendo's *Santiago* and the Portuguese flagship *Santa Theresa* as the Dutch sea wolves bore down. The thick fog made it difficult to distinguish friend from foe and many a Spanish ship fired into the massed ranks of their own fleet. The Dutch moved closer, firing at close range and raking the crowded Spanish decks with deadly shot. The *Santiago* was so riddled with shot that it looked, the Dutch joked, like a colander.

Tromp now played his ace. Against a disorganized and unnerved enemy whose commander had lost control over his large fleet, the Dutch unleashed the dreaded fireships. These wreaked havoc within the tightly massed ranks of the enemy. Among their victims was the *Santa Theresa,* which caught fire and blew up with all men on board, including Admiral Hoces.

Oquendo fled with whatever ships he could muster, including the *Santiago,* to the Belgian coast. It was Spain's last throw of the dice and the gamble had failed. Spain's once mighty navy was a shadow of its former self and the Dutch, thanks to Tromp and his intrepid Dutchmen, now ruled the waves.

The Dutch Navy

It was probably just as well for the Dutch that they were able to crush Spain as early as they did. The British were to prove a far greater menace to Dutch naval supremacy over the next four decades. Even more so than Britain, the Dutch depended on naval power to defend their far-flung imperial and economic interests. As a consequence, both the West and East Indies Companies developed regional navies to protect Dutch trading interests in the West Indies, Africa and the East Indies (modernday Indonesia). The Dutch East India Company (VOC) alone could muster some 200 large ships as well as 15,000 sailors.

Despite their natural aptitude and dependence on the sea, the Dutch proved rebellious sailors. In 1652, there was a mutiny in Amsterdam over the sailors' share of captured Spanish coin; and in

THE BATTLE OF THE DOWNS *in 1638 proved a far more decisive turning point for the eclipse of Spanish sea power than the demise of the Armada half a century earlier. This etching shows the climax of the battle as the shattered Spanish forces sink.*

1665, Admiral Johan Evertsen was almost lynched by rebellious sailors for his part in the defeat at Lowestoft. The officers proved little better. In October 1639, Admiral Maarten Tromp had to decline an invitation from English Admiral Sir John Penington since 'he had a great many clownish boors amongst his captains'. Most Dutch naval officers were merchant navy captains and lacked the polish of their aristocratic English counterparts.

The motto in the Dutch Navy was to treat the crews 'as men ashore and donkeys on board'. The 'donkeys' were kept in check with flaying whips and rope-ends, or by keel hauling, ducking from the yard arm or, in severe cases, by having their hands nailed to the main mast. For mutiny, murder or sodomy, there was only one punishment: death. In the latter case, the culprits were sown into bags and thrown overboard. The increasingly affluent Dutch grew less keen to take seaman's work at whatever the pay, leaving the Dutch navies to be manned by Germans and Scandinavians known as *Ostlanders*. These men proved to make good and obedient sailors, who marvelled at twice-weekly rations of meat and the relatively high pay. The differences in conditions between crewmen and officers could be huge. While the crews were often reduced to starvation rations, one Scotsman was struck by the 12 delicious dishes served at the captain's table of a Dutch ship in 1680. Yet both De Ruyters and Tromp were popular with their men, who called them endearingly *Bestevaer*, or grandpa.

Compared to other navies, particularly the French, the Dutch were renowned for their spick-and-span ships and well paid, contented crews. As often as possible, the Dutch Navy issued fresh fruit and vegetables to the crews – especially oranges and apples – although they had not caught on to the scurvy-beating qualities of lime juice. Nonetheless, sailing with a Dutch sailing ship was not a pleasant experience. The cheese-paring

> *'The English are about to attack a mountain of gold; we are about to attack a mountain of iron'.*
> — DUTCH COMMENT ON OUTBREAK OF WAR WITH ENGLAND IN 1652

directors of the VOC, for example, failed to issue their crews with winter clothing. The reasoning was that the 'donkeys' were going to the tropics and hardly needed hardly any thick clothes! No wonder sailors mutinied, drank like animals and spent their hard-earned money in the 'music halls' (brothels) of Amsterdam.

The Evolution of the Galleon

During the seventeenth century, the Dutch and the English in particular had brought the galleon to its evolutionary peak. Galleons were constructed with carvel planking for smooth, fast propulsion and the ends of the deck beams passed through the side planking for strength. Added strength was provided by vertical battens outside the hull and by stout fore-and-aft planks called 'rubbing stakes' since they protected the hull from friction when going alongside other ships. Galleons were built three-masted for greater stability and improved steering, with a lateen sail on the mizzen mast and large square sails on the main and fore masts. By adding length to the masts, allowing larger sails, propulsion could be almost doubled. With a straight, slim, low hull shape and a beak-head projecting forward from the stern below the bowspit, speed was further improved.

The English were the master ship builders of the early seventeenth century, as epitomized by Phineas Phett's masterpiece – the 100-gun *Sovereign of the Seas,* weighing 1500 gross tons. Ironically the ship could be used against the Dutch in 1652 only after reducing her to two decks. To the practical, hard-nosed Dutch, this was a further vindication of their view that prestige ships were not worth the expense. They believed that English

OPPOSITE: IN THIS PAINTING *from 1883 by John S. Lucas, the victor of the Downs, van Tromp, ponders on the problems of his complex command and the increasing need for professionalization of the Dutch Navy.*

ships were too narrowly built, carried too many guns and became unstable as a consequence. Dutch vessels were built for maximum cargo capacity, stability and speed under sail with broad, flat bottoms and solid hulls. Yet in battle the English artillery superiority could prove decisive against their lighter, poorly armed Dutch rivals. In 1658, the Dutch introduced staysails to the main mast, then another two staysails and a system whereby topmasts could be lowered, then stored or housed in heavy weather. This was a major improvement, but it was not until some time later that a practical 'jib' was introduced on either Dutch or English ships.

During the course of the century, the shape of the galleon changed considerably, becoming ever more streamlined and losing its earlier barrel-shaped form, while the decks lost their upward curve from the waist to the stern. The formerly high forecastles eventually became almost horizontal in shape. The long thrusting beak-head was shortened and eventually ended up with an ornamental figurehead at the end. Incredibly, all

navies maintained the primitive *whipstaff* until around 1710, when it was replaced by rope, pulleys and a strong wooden wheel, thereby improving steering considerably.

The galleon was not the only ship to develop over the period. The light, frigate-like *pinnaces*, with less than 50 gross tons deadweight, carried three masts with square sails like the galleon, but could use oars as well. From the primitive *pinnace* evolved the frigate – a single-deck warship rigged with three masts for speed and carrying between 28 and 32 guns. The frigate was the first warship to use a jib. One size below the frigate came the 18-gun, single-deck, two-mast sloop – or *corvette*, in French. It too had a jib and a topgallant sail to each mast. Even smaller than the sloop, but with two masts and three sails, came the 'snow'. By the eighteenth century, all three types were known as brigs-of-war.

In the Mediterranean, the corsairs were forced to redesign their galleys to stay in business. Retaining the lateen sailing rig mounted on three short masts, the *chebeck (xebec)* mounted guns

THE NORTH AFRICAN *Barbary* chebeck (xebec) *combined lateen sails and a sleek designed hull for sailing prowess with oars. The hull was sturdy enough, unlike the galley, for a large number of guns.*

SOVEREIGN OF THE SEAS, FROM THE STERN: *The pretentions of the name reflect Britain's quest for supremacy at sea against her continental rivals, and the heavy hardwood carvings covered with gilt only reinforced her Dutch nickname of the 'Gilded Devil'.*

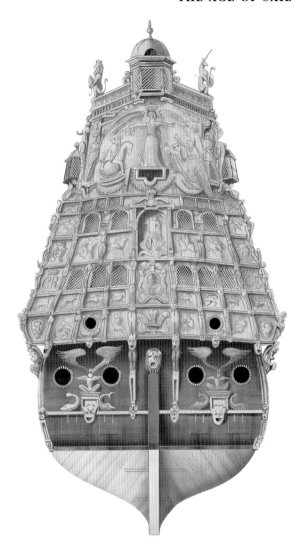

along the sides. Rowers had benches between the gunports and manned the guns in battle. The *chebeck* proved a roaring success and the Baltic powers later modified these combination vessels for battle there.

The Anglo-Dutch Wars: 1652–1672

By the middle of the seventeenth century, England and the United Provinces of the Netherlands were Europe's major 'Maritime Powers' and the most powerful Protestant powers. They were also fierce commercial and maritime rivals, fighting three wars for control of the world's trade and oceans.

England held most of the trump cards in the coming wars. Lying astride the Dutch lines of communication, England was also windward of the Netherlands with the prevailing westerly in their favour. The British could therefore cut Dutch trade links and could sail out and form up for battle more quickly than their continental rival. Furthermore, the British Navy was purpose-built for service in the Narrow Seas and the ships armed with heavy and numerous guns. By contrast, the Dutch had no regular, standing navy at the outbreak of war in 1652 and relied heavily on converted merchantmen. The main role of the Dutch warships was to protect and escort merchant ships, not do battle with large warships. Here the Dutch Estates Generals had placed profit and politics ahead of sound strategy. As a consequence, Dutch vessels were dismasted, holed and shattered faster and more often during the wars than the English ships.

Furthermore, the seven provinces of the Netherlands were hardly 'united'. The navy was controlled by three or four separate admiralties – the most important being those of Holland, Zealand and Friesland – meaning that there was no centralized authority, as there was in Britain, to control and direct the navy. Even worse was the division between supporters of the Prince *Stadthouder* and the Estates Generals. Thus Maarten Tromp and his son, Cornelis Tromp, were 'royalists' or Orangists, while De Ruyter and Witte de With were parliamentarians. The Dutch Navy was split right down the middle, much to the detriment of its efficiency in battle.

In 1653, the Dutch fleet was defeated by the English at Scheveningen, losing not only 11 ships and 4000 sailors but also their commander Maarten Tromp. Oliver Cromwell, however, was reluctant to fight a fellow Protestant power when Catholic Spain offered a more lucrative target, and peace negotiations to end the First Anglo-Dutch War were concluded the following year. The Dutch now began to build stronger, sturdier and more heavily gunned warships that would be able to stand up to the English broadsides. By April 1665, the Dutch

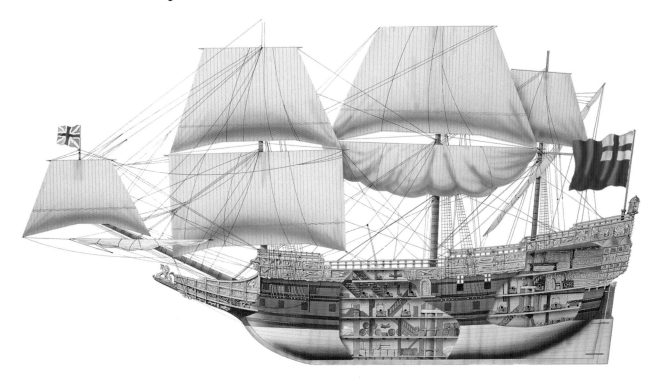

had four 'first rate' warships carrying 70 or more guns. The English, however, were determined to keep pace in the arms race and built a further eight. As a rule, the Dutch ships remained smaller and less well armed than their rivals. Thus Cornelis Tromp's flagship was a mere 600 gross tons deadweight and carried only 54 guns.

It was no wonder, then, that the Dutch lost 17 ships and were badly mauled at Lowestoft in June 1665. The defeat was in part due to the inexperience of the Dutch commander, Admiral Baron Jacob van Obdam, who had been appointed because he was a staunch supporter of the Dutch parliament. The Dutch secured a narrow victory over the English in the Four Day Battle (4–8 June), though even this was marred by the politically motivated removal of Cornelis Tromp from command, and they were then defeated on 4 August 1666 in the St James's Day Battle.

Medway, 1667: Humiliation of the English Navy

Fortunately for the Dutch, the situation was little better on the English side. Although Charles II had managed to unite the country following his

SOVEREIGN OF THE SEAS, CUT-AWAY VIEW: *With her 1500 gross tons and 100 bronze cannons, the flagship of Britain's Royal Navy was truly the sovereign of the home seas. Here she is shown with the cut-through to reveal the decks and interiors of the vast hull.*

restoration in 1660, parliamentary grants proved stingy and the English Navy deteriorated rapidly in quality and quantity. By contrast, the Dutch ship-building programme peaked in 1665 and the Dutch Navy was ever more ready for battle. The Grand Pensioner of the Dutch republic, Johan de Witt, intended to force the English to sign a favourable peace treaty and he knew this could be achieved only by a mighty knock-out blow to the Royal Navy.

On 1 June 1667, an English agent in Holland reported that a large Dutch war fleet had massed at Texel, ready for an attack on England. The Dutch fleet set sail on 4 June under Admiral Michiel de Ruyter with 51 large warships, 3 frigates, 6 armed yachts and 14 fireships. Three days later, the fleet reached the mouth of the Thames and a war council was held aboard De Ruyter's 90-gun flagship the *Zeven Provincien* (Seven Provinces). It was decided here that Admiral Baron William van

Ghent was to take a squadron up the Thames all the way to the naval station at Deptford, while Vice-Admiral van Schram was to keep an eye on the Straits of Dover. Van Ghent raided up the Thames and then returned, with London in uproar, to rejoin the rest of the fleet.

The proconsul in the fleet, Cornelis de Witt, consulted with De Ruyter and decided to raid up the Medway. It was only on 10 June that the English finally sent Prince Rupert to Gravesend and Lord Albemarle to Chatham to organize their respective defences. Meanwhile, Van Ghent ordered his firebrand commander, a Rotterdammer by the name of Captain Jan van Brakel of the *Vrede* (Fury) to attack the incomplete and poorly manned battery at Sheerness.

Van Brakel attacked in the afternoon on 10 June, sending the seven artillerists stationed there fleeing for their lives, and Dutch forces occupied Sheerness, raising the flag of the Dutch Republic on English soil. On 11 June, Lord Albermarle finally arrived at Chatham while the Dutch, led by Van Brakel, sacked villages on the Isle of Sheppey. De Witt then had Van Brakel arrested for plundering.

By this point, Dutch yachts had reached the Musselbank at the mouth of the Medway. Admiral Van Ghent, in command, sent Captain Thomas Tobiaszoon with three frigates, two yachts and two fireships to attack the English upriver. Tobiaszoon left Sheerness and spent much of the day moving the English block ship *Adam and Eve* out of the way so that Van Ghent's fleet could get past.

The following day, Sheerness was evacuated by the Dutch, who sacked the place and broke the embankments, flooding much of Sheppey. Tobiaszoon attacked at 6 a.m. with the incoming tide, but was held by the chain across the Gillingham reach and by the two English batteries on either shore. The Dutch fleet was now spread out in a long, vulnerable thin line from the chain across the Gillingham reach all the way to the Musselbank, unable to fire abreast. Van Brakel was released by De Witt after volunteering to run past

June 1666: *the fiercely fought Four Days Battle, in which the Dutch won, by the narrowest of margins, a great victory sealed by the abandonment of the* Royal Prince *shown here.*

the English with the *Vrede*, drawing their fire and distracting attention from the Dutch fireship attack on the chain at Gillingham, which was covered by the 44-gun *Unity*. As the *Vrede* came alongside the *Unity*, Van Brakel stormed aboard, encountering little resistance. The Dutch fireships broke the chain and set fire to the English ship *Mathias,* which promptly exploded. Van Brakel then stormed and captured the *Charles V.*

Once the chain had been broken, the Dutch were able to proceed unhindered upriver. As the Dutch bore down on the 'first rate' ship *Royal Charles* – half rigged, manned by unarmed sailors and carrying only 32 guns – the demoralized crew fled for their lives. Ghent and De Witt held a war council on board the captured English flagship. They decided that De Ruyter should join them for the final assault on 13 June. The tide had turned and the Dutch celebrated their stunning and audacious success with ginever and beer. De Ruyter arrived later that day with the main fleet.

Lord Albemarle did not remain inactive. He ordered three warships – *Royal James*, *Royal Oak* and *Loyal London* – to be moved and grounded on the southern river shore at Upnor bank. To prevent their capture, the English bored holes in their sides and erected three batteries to cover the dockyards and the upper reaches of the Medway with 10 heavy guns and 50 smaller guns.

Early on the morning of 13 June, five Dutch fireships arrived at the Gillingham reach. With a strong northeasterly wind, the Dutch needed only to wait for the tide to turn before attacking. By the time the tide did turn at noon, however, the wind had died down, slowing the Dutch advance and giving the English time to set their defences in order. Not until 2 p.m. did the Dutch vessels reach Upnor castle, and they suffered badly from the

ENTITLED *DUTCH ATTACK ON THE MEDWAY, 9–14 June 1667*, this painting by Pieter van den Velde was completed soon after the battle to celebrate the Dutch victory. A line of Dutch ships is visible in the background. To the right of the picture in the foreground is the captured *Royal Charles, in starboard-quarter view. The royal coat of arms is visible on the stern.*

ADMIRAL MICHIEL DE RUYTER *(1607-76), the greatest Dutch naval commander of his generation and the architect of the Medway raid in June 1667.*

English crossfire in the process. Nonetheless, the Dutch fireships did their deadly work against the grounded warships. The English crews scurried for safety on shore, leaving their commander, Captain Archibald Douglas, to die on the burning warships. Having lost 50 men and used up their reserve of fireships, the Dutch broke off their attack, opting not to push up the Medway to confront the 16 English warships holed up below Rochester bridge. On 14 June, the Dutch began to tow the *Royal Charles* out to sea.

Aftermath

In London, the Medway raid set off a panic. Three days later, the news of the raid reached Holland and was met with jubilation. A month later, the English signed the unfavourable Peace of Breda, bringing an end to the Second Anglo-Dutch War.

Charles II thirsted for revenge and, primed with secret French subsidies, England joined France in attacking the Netherlands in early 1672. While the Dutch staved off Louis XIV's 150,000-strong invasion army, Admiral De Ruyter headed a defensive campaign in Dutch home waters, where his shallow-draught vessels proved both faster and more manoeuvrable than the large, heavy allied warships. Despite being outnumbered, De Ruyter defeated a strong Anglo-French fleet at Solebay on 6 June 1672. In June 1673, De Ruyter routed the Allied fleets yet again in the two naval battles of Schooneveld off the Dutch coast, and in February 1674 the English sued for peace.

The Witt brothers were savagely murdered by an Amsterdam mob during the 1672 crisis and the *Stadthouder*, Prince William of Orange, seized power. At the invitation of the English parliament, in 1688, he gathered 500 vessels at Hellevoetsluis to escort 21,000 troops to invade England and unseat the Catholic King James II. In November 1688, this Dutch Armada – four times the size of the Spanish one – sailed unopposed by the Royal Navy through the Dover Straits and landed in Devon. William marched on London and was proclaimed King William III the following year, thereby forging an Anglo-Dutch alliance that would lead to the defeat of the French King Louis XIV by 1713.

The Rise and Fall of Louis XIV's Great Navy: 1661–92

A gambling man, if asked in 1661 to predict who would take over the mantle of Dutch naval supremacy – England or France – would probably have settled for the latter. France had many times the population, resources, tax income and financial clout of the smaller island kingdom. Compared to the apparent chaos of parliamentary politics, France was a soundly autocratic state, in which Louis XIV and his talented ministers made

Battle of the Medway

1667

The Dutch fleet under the command of Admiral de Ruyter reached the mouth of the Thames on 7 June with the intention of raiding up the Medway River and forcing England to sue for peace. Three days later, the Dutch attacked Sheerness, clearing the way for the fleet to sail up the Medway. The English responded by placing blocking ships, a chain and two gun batteries at the mouth of the river at Gillingham to keep the enemy away from the main English naval base. The Dutch used fireships to smash their way through the English defences on 12 June, burning several ships in the process and capturing the pride of the Royal Navy - the *Royal Charles* - intact. The following day, the Dutch sailed further up river, but in the face of increasingly heavy English battery fire progress was slow. Another three English vessels were either sunk or captured before the Dutch withdrew to home waters. The raid was a major military and political success for the Dutch and the English signed a peace agreement on Dutch terms in July 1667.

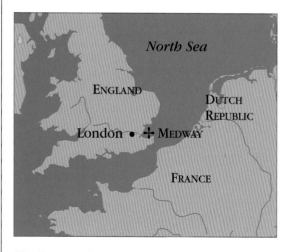

The River Medway lies at the outer mouth of the River Thames, just 40 kilometres (25 miles) from London. The British naval dockyards at Chatham were based a short way up the Medway.

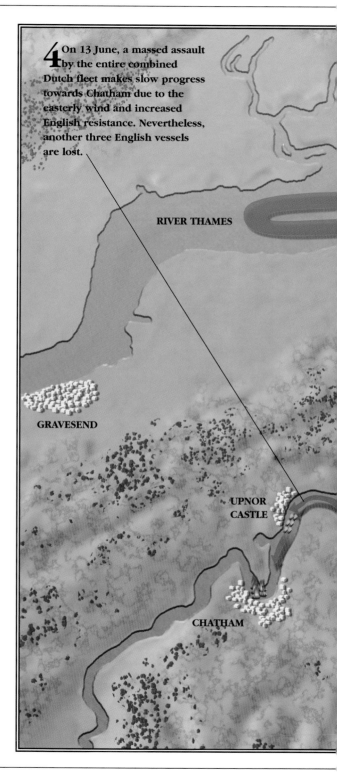

4 On 13 June, a massed assault by the entire combined Dutch fleet makes slow progress towards Chatham due to the easterly wind and increased English resistance. Nevertheless, another three English vessels are lost.

RIVER THAMES

GRAVESEND

UPNOR CASTLE

CHATHAM

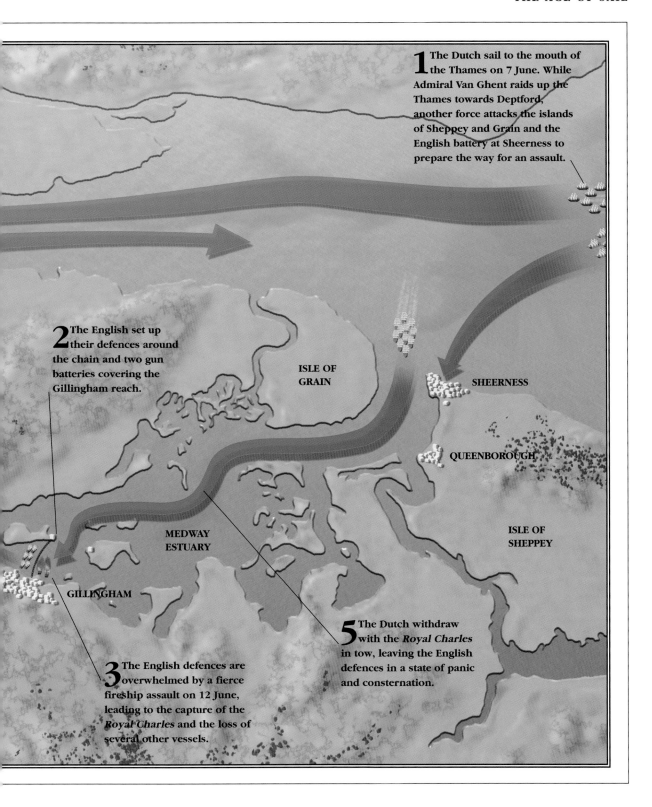

1 The Dutch sail to the mouth of the Thames on 7 June. While Admiral Van Ghent raids up the Thames towards Deptford, another force attacks the islands of Sheppey and Grain and the English battery at Sheerness to prepare the way for an assault.

2 The English set up their defences around the chain and two gun batteries covering the Gillingham reach.

ISLE OF GRAIN

SHEERNESS

QUEENBOROUGH

MEDWAY ESTUARY

ISLE OF SHEPPEY

GILLINGHAM

5 The Dutch withdraw with the *Royal Charles* in tow, leaving the English defences in a state of panic and consternation.

3 The English defences are overwhelmed by a fierce fireship assault on 12 June, leading to the capture of the *Royal Charles* and the loss of several other vessels.

all the important decisions. However, France did not have a strong maritime tradition – maritime matters were the concern of regions such as Brittany, Normandy or Provence, but not the nation as a whole. Dutch prosperity depended on naval supremacy and England's very survival, as shown in 1588, was dependent on its navy. No such urgency existed for the continental-minded and self-sufficient French. Like Spain, France was torn between the need for a strong army to dominate in Europe and a strong navy to challenge the growing monopoly of the maritime powers in overseas trade and the race for colonies. Furthermore, and again like Spain, it was not clear where she should build a strong fleet. France had interests in the Atlantic, the Channel, the Caribbean and in the Mediterranean. These geographic, economic and social obstacles to naval power were to prove fatal for French as well as Spanish sea power from 1650 onwards.

Armand du Plessis, better known as Cardinal Richelieu, was not only the creator of the rigid centralized French state but had a good stab at making the French into a great naval power. In 1626, he took the title *Grand Maître, Chef et Surintendant* (Grandmaster, Chief and Superintendant) of the navy in order to unite under one administration the four separate admiralties of France, Guyenne, Brittany and Provence. The results of the Cardinal's efforts – despite domestic troubles and war with Spain and Austria – were impressive. As Grand Admiral of France and Commander of the Mediterranean Galley Fleet, Richelieu gave France a first-class navy that numbered, when reviewed en masse outside Toulon in 1642, 65 ships of the line and 22 galleys. These latter vessels were stationed at Marseilles and Toulon.

Richelieu appointed Henri de Sourdis, Archbishop of Bordeaux, as Grand Admiral of France; if a cardinal could run France, Richelieu argued, then why not have an archbishop as head of the navy? Sourdis proved an inspired choice, capturing the Spanish-occupied Lerin islands off the Provence coast in 1637 and sinking 14 Spanish vessels when trying to escape from Fuentanabia the following year. His flagship, *La Couronne*, was 2000 gross tons – 500 more than the Charles I's great *Sovereign of the Seas*.

France's hour of naval glory proved fleeting. France was a continental-minded nation, and Richelieu had problems finding sailors and resorted to force and threats to man his ships. Officers were in even more short supply and nobles, who did not want to be cajoled like fishermen or sailors, preferred a career in the army. Furthermore, France's overseas colonies were limited in territory, population and wealth compared to Spain's and, as a consequence, the merchant navy remained weak. Most of France's trade was carried in Dutch or foreign ships, despite – or, more probably, because of – Richelieu's fanatical mercantile restrictions.

Colbert's Reforms

Under his successor Cardinal Mazarin, the navy that Richelieu had so painstakingly built up from scratch was left to rot in port – despite the self-evident need for a strong naval force. When, in September 1661, Louis XIV appointed Jean Baptiste Colbert as Minister of the Navy, he was shocked to find, all told, only 20 ships left in the entire 'navy': nine battleships, three frigates and a handful of galleys. Backed by Louis, the new minister set out to create, with his characteristic ruthlessness and single-minded determination, an entirely new Royal Navy for France. Harnessing the enormous potential resources of France, Colbert unleashed the largest naval building programme in Europe's history, constructing between 1665–70 no less than 65 battleships, including the largest ships afloat – the massive three-deck French ships of the line. Neither England nor the United Provinces could match these production levels. When Colbert died in 1683 from overwork and sheer exhaustion (he was also minister of finance, trade and colonies) the French Navy was the largest in the world. It numbered a staggering 112 battleships, 25 frigates, 7 fireships, 16 corvettes, 20 fly-boats, and 40 galleys. It amounted to around 250 ships in total – some 45 vessels more than the British Royal Navy could muster.

Although Colbert had the ambition to make France, despite her lack of a naval tradition, into a maritime power, he soon realized that he could not hope to match the merchant navies or the

Swedish Seaman (1630)

Sunk during her maiden voyage in May 1628 the Swedish flagship Wasa *went down with a small skeleton crew. The ship was raised in 1961 intact and with a handful of unfortunates onboard. One of these was used to reconstruct a sailor from the period, on which our figure here is based.*

The sailor's clothes gives a clue to the poverty of the typical seventeenth century sailor and the fact that proper naval uniforms were not introduced until the following century. He is wearing clothes similar to those of workman on land: a coarse grey cap with matching trousers, jacket and socks with a simple shirt and leather shoes. Not much to face the rigours of the North Sea and Baltic Sea during wartime.

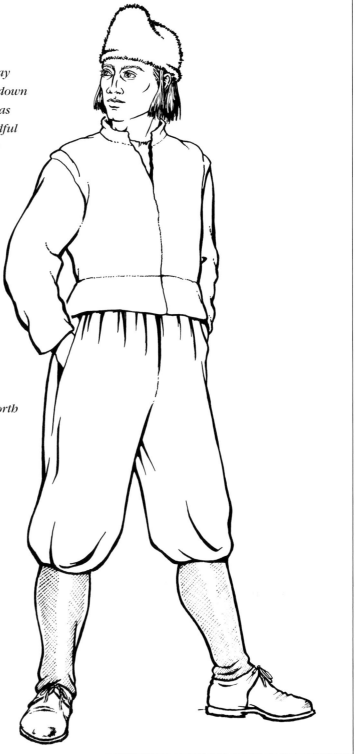

levels of trade of the more-established maritime powers. Nor could France sustain such a pace of production or naval expansion forever. There was a chronic shortage of naval stores, timber, sailors and, again, officers.

Nonetheless, the results were spectacular. How were they achieved? Firstly, he retained the patronage and close interest of the king by encouraging Louis to view his navy as a symbol of royal glory and power. Secondly, Colbert increased his own bureaucratic power until he had full control over the navy, promoting his own cousins Michel and Francois Bégon to key posts in the administration. Thirdly, he created *Intendants* to inspect ships and bases and to control the fleets under his command. He also sent spies to Holland and England, to find designs for ships and bribe the men that could build them. These men trained the French carpenters who went on to become the finest naval designers and engineers in Europe. By 1715, it was the Dutch and English who were spying on the French – a good measure of Colbert's success.

But much was directed towards sheer volume. Colbert wanted quick results but not at the expense of quality. His shipyards mapped out where the best timber was found closest to rivers, and produced an abundance of ships to a high standard with good sailing abilities. These ships were well built, if somewhat over decorated and gaudy in typical French style. The arsenals, with their rope-yards, sailmaking shops, dockyards, sawmills and foundries, were developed into seventeeth-century 'factories' of impressive scale and production levels.

The French Navy was constantly short of experienced sailors and combat-ready crews. Recruitment of both had been impaired badly by Louis' ill-advised decision, in 1685, to revoke the Edict of Nantes, leading to 200,000 French Protestants, or Huguenots, fleeing France. Ironically, their skills strengthened France's enemies. To help ensure a good supply of sailors, Colbert abolished the notorious press gangs and

THE BATTLE OF SOLEBAY *(Southwold Bay) on 28 May 1672 saw the Dutch see off the combined Anglo-French fleet, although they suffered heavy losses.*

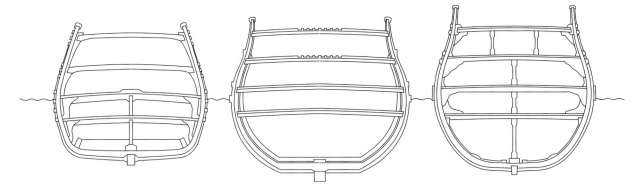

replaced these with more effective, although equally unpopular, registers of 'classes' – the precursor of enlistment.

The French Navy at War

It was one thing to build, administer and run a peacetime navy, but quite another to take it to war. As long as the other maritime powers were at each other's throats, Louis' navy could hold its own. At the Battle of Sole Bay in 1672, a combined Anglo-French Fleet with some 78 English and 30 French ships of the line made a poor show of themselves against Admiral De Ruyter's 75 ships of the line. In January 1676, the French took their revenge on De Ruyter. A large French fleet under the old ex-pirate and seadog Admiral Abraham Duquesne encountered the Dutch admiral off the northern coast of Sicily, by the Lipari Islands. At the Battle of Agosta, the Dutch lost five ships and, more significantly, Admiral De Ruyter was killed. His death signalled the end of the golden era of Dutch naval supremacy.

By 1688, Louis had the strongest navy in the world in terms of the number of its ships and seemed on the cusp of taking over Holland's maritime mantle. The French Navy had a total of 189 vessels, including 118 battleships and 19 frigates, and a string of good admirals and well-protected bases. From 1683, the Naval Academy at Brest had been turning out professional officers.

GUN DECKS: *This illustration shows, from bottom up, the orlop deck (below the water line), the lower gun deck with the heaviest pieces, the middle gun deck above, the upper gun deck and, finally, the quarterdeck with the fewest and lightest pieces.*

COMPARE AND CONTRAST: *Dutch ship design (left), with square, broad bottoms; the English design (centre) had a deeper draught and a round bottom; and the French design (right) with fewer gun decks and the lower gun deck at a higher level than the English.*

But it was all deceptive. That same year, William III ousted James II in England and France faced the combined might of the Maritime Powers. Her navy was not strong enough for such a challenge. France lacked the resources for a long naval war and Dunkirk had been overlooked, with fatal consequences, as a naval base. The lack of a major base in the Channel would cripple France.

France's greatest admiral, Anne Hilaron de Cotentin, comte de Tourville, led a fleet of

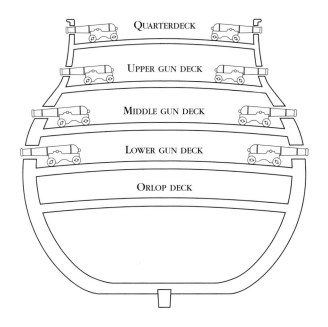

QUARTERDECK

UPPER GUN DECK

MIDDLE GUN DECK

LOWER GUN DECK

ORLOP DECK

The terminology of navigational direction: From port beam (on right), port bow, dead ahead, starboard bow, starboard beam (left), starboard quarter, dead astern, port quarter.

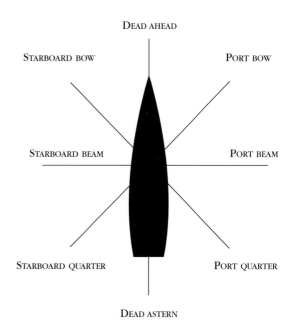

DEAD AHEAD

STARBOARD BOW

PORT BOW

STARBOARD BEAM

PORT BEAM

STARBOARD QUARTER

PORT QUARTER

DEAD ASTERN

78 battleships to victory over an allied Anglo-Dutch fleet of 57 ships at Beachy Head in July 1690. Two years later, Tourville made a serious error at Barfleur when he attacked an allied fleet of 98 ships of the line and 7100 guns with only 44 ships of his own and a mere 3100 guns. The battle was a draw after 12 hours, but Tourville lost some 12 vessels in a related action at La Hogue while escaping.

Although the French would not admit that La Hogue was a major turning point, or even a defeat, the French Navy declined steadily thereafter. By 1715, Louis XIV's Grand Navy was a mere shadow of its former self and the French had reverted to commerce raiding and operating privateers out of Brest and Dunkirk. During the first half of the eighteenth century, French naval endeavours, like those of Spain's before them, inevitably ended in disaster and humiliation. Only after 1756 was the French Navy to recover its honour by defeating the British.

Britain's Wars against the Bourbon Powers, 1713–1783

The first half of the eighteenth century saw the rise of the professional naval officer and the standardized ship of the line backed by a system of ports, docks and arsenals. The finest example of this new professional navy was that of Britain's Royal Navy, followed closely by the Bourbon powers of Spain and France.

When Philip V ascended the throne in 1700 as the first of the Bourbon dynasty in Spain, the country barely had a functioning navy. By 1714, however, the Spanish had created their own centralized Royal Navy, the *Armada Real.* Three years later, José Patino was appointed Intendant General of the Armada Real. Patino proved to be a Spanish version of Colbert as he rebuilt Spain's dwindling naval power and established *astilleros* (shipyards) and arsenals across the far-flung Spanish empire. The Atlantic bases were at Ferrol and Corunna in Galicia while the Mediterranean

Fleet was based at Cartagena. British ambassador Sir Benjamin Keene, who kept a close and wary eye on Patino's energetic work, noted that the *Armada Real* was short of crews, officers, money and real sea experience, despite the quality of its ships. When Patino died in office in 1736 – from sheer exhaustion like Colbert – the *Armada Real* numbered 36 ships of the line, 9 frigates and 16 smaller craft. This was an impressive-enough number on paper, but having built such a strong navy the Spanish were loath to put their ships and crews to the test for fear of losing them in battle with the British. After Patino, the Spanish Navy declined for lack of patronage and money.

The Spanish, as they had feared, were worsted by the battle-hardened and experienced British Royal Navy in the War of Jenkin's Ear (1739–48). Despite having begun the war with 46 ships of the line, there was an urgent need for new ships and crews by the time the Marqués de la Ensenada took charge in 1746. During his stewardship (1746–54), some 20 million pesos were spent on modernizing Spanish yards, building ships and acquiring materials. The most efficient yard was the Havana arsenal, which built 50 ships of the line during the century, including the largest sailing ship of the era: the four-deck, 136-gun *Santissima Trinidad,* launched in March 1763.

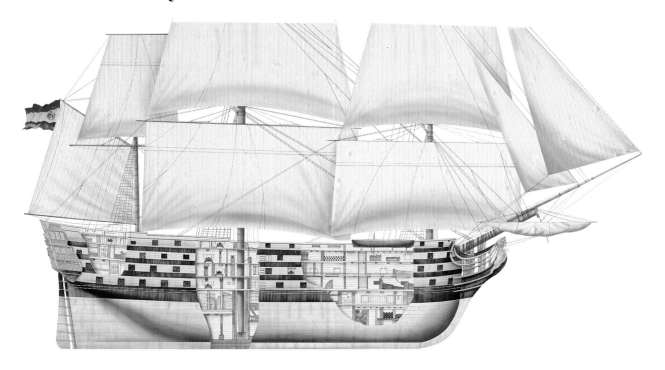

THE LARGEST SHIP AFLOAT, *the Spanish* Santissima Trinidad *(1763–1805) with 136 guns was more than a match for anything the British could mobilize, including the famous* Victory.

Ensenada appointed Jorge Juan as Master Builder and sent him to England to learn the fine art of English ship construction. Juan spent a year in England learning his trade, spying out new secret designs and luring some 60 well-rewarded English ship-builders to work in the new Spanish yards. Spain had only 18 ships of the line and 15 lesser craft in 1751, facing the 100 ships and 180 lesser craft of the Royal Navy. By 1760, they had again 47 ships of the line and 21 frigates, although they were badly beaten again in 1762, when they sided with France against the British.

The Spanish proved as good as, or even better than, their British foes when it came to designing and building ships – even if they were not so successful when it came to sailing or fighting in them. It took a staggering 3000 trees to build a 'third rate' warship of 74 guns; the devastation wrought to Spain's remaining forests was thought well worth the price. But most timber was, in fact, imported from the hardwood forests of Central America. Teak and mahogany, though lighter than English oak, were stronger and even more durable, giving Spanish ships a longer lease of life. The warship *La Africa* was built in 1752, for example, but sailed on until 1809.

The Ship of the Line

There was a remarkable similarity in the designs and methods used by European navies to build their battleships. To stabilize the vessels, they were built 'tumbledown' with narrowing upper decks so that the superstructure had a low centre of gravity. Further stability was gained by placing the heaviest guns on the lower decks – but if the sea was too rough, as it was at the Quiberon Bay in 1759, a ship could lose much of its firepower because the lower gunports would need to be shut to avoid flooding. The catchphrase of the era was firepower. The *Santissima Trinidad* carried 30 massive 32lb (14.5kg) guns, each able to penetrate 60cm (2ft) of solid oak at 1000m (3300ft). A single broadside from a three-deck warship would send half a ton of metal into its opponent with devastating results. As tall as a five-storey building, such a ship was an awesome sight when under sail and a terrifying one in battle when the lieutenant in charge of a division of gun crews would order his men to 'fire as you bear'. Whatever the damage wrought by the guns on the opposing ships, their own crews would need to be careful not to be crushed by their recoil, and their roar left many men permanently deaf.

Impressive or not, the ship of the line held few comforts, even for the officers. Across the aft end of the ship on the quarter deck lay the captain's 'great cabin'. Glass casement windows across the full width of the stern gave the captain light and fresh air, which was denied to his men. He kept his few belongings inside the cushioned locker settees on the sides and had a dinner table seated for his eight most senior officers. Below his cabin was the ward room – a narrow space running down the centre of the ship, closed off by the bulkhead. It was lined with the senior officers' 'cabins' – small compartments with portable wooden or even canvas sides. A door on each side led to the quarter galleries – narrow passages built along the side of the hull, providing the officers with their 'privies'. Stern windows provided their cramped quarters with some light and air.

The junior officers, chaplain and marine officers were housed below the ward room on the lower deck. Aloft on the same deck, some of the crew had their meagre living quarters among the guns and stores. Next down lay the orlop, below the water line, where light and air were both rare. One part of the orlop housed the purser and his stores while in the other the surgeon and his mates plied their grisly trade in battle. The main deck housed the carpenter, blacksmith, and armourer's stores and workshops in a jumbled space shared with the capstan and livestock pens. Whatever little space was left over provided quarters of sorts for some of the remaining crew, who made the most of the space by sleeping in hammocks and eating off tables lowered from the ceiling at mealtimes. At the fore end lay the brick-floored galley, where vast copper vats were used for cooking. Above this space, somewhat inappropriately, lay the sick bay. This was made even less salubrious by the proximity of the crews' privy overhanging the sides of the beak's head. No wonder that captains, especially the British ones, were obsessed with keeping their ships clean and tidy. They did this by pumping the bilges, replacing the shingle ballast as often as possible and scrubbing the decks with vinegar. Much of the stench was masked by the ever present and overpowering odour of the Stockholm tar used on most British vessels.

Sailors '...behave like wild boars; they rob and steal, drink and go whoring so shamelessly that it seems to be no disgrace with them...' thereby necessitating rule by '...a rod of iron...'

— Dutch East India Company document, 1677

Navies of the Eighteenth Century

We have seen the state of the Spanish *Armada Real*. The Dutch were in far worse shape during the eighteenth century, with a navy that was only a sad shadow of its former self. Allied with Britain, the neutral Netherlands neglected her navy, which fell from 86 ships of the line in 1700 to 25 ships of the line 60 years later and just 11 by 1775. Her ports silted up and there was no money or men to clear them. The Zuider Zee became so shallow that larger warships had to be towed in a mobile dock out to the North Sea proper.

Even at Texel there was a risk that larger warships would run aground. The Dutch continued to maintain the second largest merchant navy in the world, but depended on foreign crews and officers to man her ships, while the once pristine conditions on board also declined. The new naval base at Den Helder opposite Texel Island was completed only in 1812, but by then there was little left of the Dutch Navy following the bloodlettings of the previous

20 years. Although a new naval college (*Zeemanscollege*) was founded in 1748, the Dutch were forced to relearn the basics of shipbuilding from their English rivals.

The French were not in much better shape than the Dutch. Here one has to wonder how, during the first half of the century, the French Navy was able to offer any resistance whatsoever to their vastly superior British foe. There was nothing wrong with their ships. In fact, these were often far superior to the British ones, combining as they did a deep draught with a strong, narrow-built hull and guns placed on two decks, rather than three like the British, which gave added stability in a rough sea and greater accuracy during heavy seas.

A SCHEMATIC STANDARDIZED *view of a sailing warship of the seventeenth and eighteenth centuries – when there were no major innovations, except for placing fore and main topsails (top part) and the jib sails with an extended bowsprit.*

French vessels were also more comfortable for the crews. Larger hatches allowed more air and light to reach down into the holds of the ships, and spacious decks lessened crowding during battle. French ships, facing a superior enemy, were built for speed and evasion with streamlined, thinner hulls and plenty of sails. No wonder many British captains were keen to transfer their ensign to a captured French or Spanish ship.

British Naval Superiority

Much of the British Royal Navy's superiority over the French Navy was down to simple resources, logistics, supplies, facilities and organization. Portsmouth and Plymouth became the Royal Navy's main ports and dockyards, replacing Deptford and Chatham, which had silted up. Increasingly, Plymouth was the more important as it served as the home base for the Western Fleet used to blockade the French Navy at Brest. The British increased the number of dry docks from 16

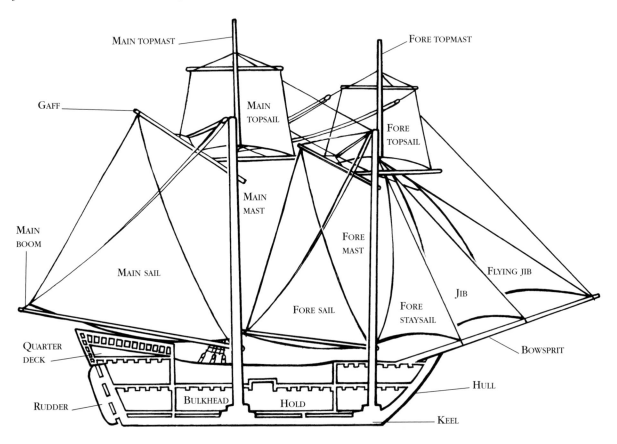

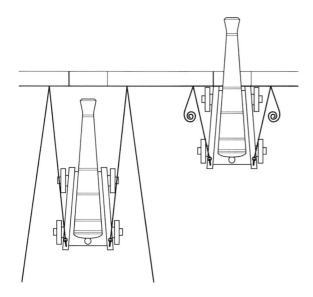

GUN POSITIONS: *Made of Baltic (Russian) hemp, ropes were used to haul the guns from the gun port to load, and once loaded the gun was hauled by rope into the fire position at the gun port and secured fast.*

significantly. The cost of feeding 48,000 sailors was £943,000 in 1710, but by 1758 that sum could feed 70,000 sailors, thanks to the new victualling system. The French by contrast persisted with their old wasteful system, which broke down almost entirely in 1757–8.

The new victualling system ensured regular and plentiful supplies of fresh fruits, vegetables and meats for the British fleet even when at sea and by 1756 had removed the scourge of scurvy in the Royal Navy. Here, at least, the culinary minded French kept pace and even grew fresh greens in large potted vats onboard. Yet typhus was still a great killer in both navies during the middle of the century.

The French fleet was similarly inferior in the quantity and more especially the quality of its cannons. French foundries were smaller, technologically backward and used inferior metals and methods to manufacture guns that were

to 24, reducing costs and the time used for repairs and maintenance. By contrast, the French had not renewed the yards bequeathed by Colbert in the previous century. As a consequence, the French had only four naval dry docks in 1750 and no private dry docks whatsoever. Of these, one was abandoned and the remaining three functioned poorly. Only in 1756 was the first properly functioning dry dock opened. The French also lacked these facilities overseas, whereas by 1739 the British had dry docks at Gibraltar, Mahan and Antigua. The French were therefore forced to strip down their ships on land – a dangerous and time-consuming exercise. The British had also invented a lighter and frictionless block, the Taylor block, which saved on topweight and manpower for ships. The Taylor block was introduced on French ships only in 1795.

The Victualling Board had been set up to reform the supply system for the Royal Navy and from the Deptford depot it began to cut costs

GUNS ON THE THREE *lower, middle and upper gun decks, as shown. On the lower, the gun is being prepared to fire; at the middle, the gun has been hauled backed; and on the upper gun deck, the piece is ready to fire.*

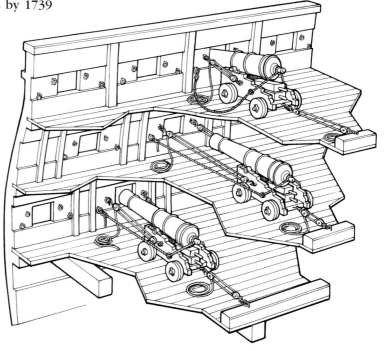

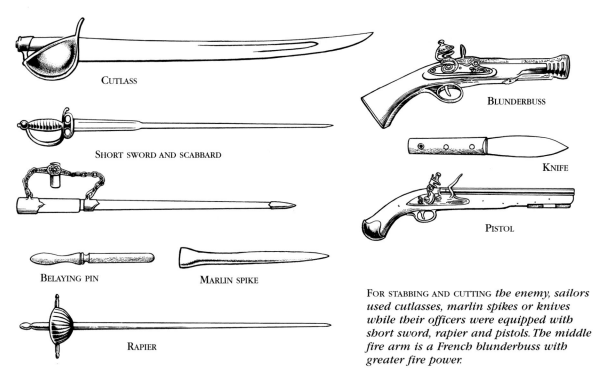

CUTLASS

SHORT SWORD AND SCABBARD

BELAYING PIN

MARLIN SPIKE

RAPIER

BLUNDERBUSS

KNIFE

PISTOL

For stabbing and cutting the enemy, sailors used cutlasses, marlin spikes or knives while their officers were equipped with short sword, rapier and pistols. The middle fire arm is a French blunderbuss with greater fire power.

brittle and apt to overheat and explode. The French crews could not trust their guns like the British, who could shoot double loads at a far greater rate since they knew their guns would bear the strain. Yet the French had developed by the 1750s the method of boring a hole through a solid piece of metal, which improved the sturdiness and loading capacity of the guns.

It was also a question of organization. British Vice Admiral Thomas Smith introduced a system of divisions headed by lieutenants, and this was generally adopted, to great effect, throughout the Royal Navy in 1759. The lieutenants forged these divisions into effective and deadly gun crews, in which each man was known to his officer and was part of a close-knit unit.

Much has been made of the draconian discipline and insubordination in the Royal Navy due to the fame of the *Bounty* incident. But, in fact, discipline in the navy was less severe than in the army, where flogging for minor offences was common. In fact, more disciplinary problems were due to fractious officers than mutinous crews, and most sailors equated weak or soft captains with chaos and catastrophe. A good ship was a tightly run ship headed by a paternalistic but stern captain.

The Warship In Battle

In battle, the captain would command from the quarter deck with two midshipmen to carry messages and orders from him to the ship's master at the wheel. The boatswain's party would handle the sails during the battle and carry out emergency repairs to the rigging. On the gun deck, only a minimal amount of the highly volatile and dangerous black powder would be stored near the guns for fear of explosions. Cartridges, vulnerable to damp, were filled only at the last minute. Gunner's mates were busy during battle in the handling chamber above the powder magazine, loading these cartridges and placing them in leather cases. These passed through double doors that were hung with wet baize to keep out deadly hot sparks. Experienced crews would keep the transit of powder to an absolute minimum to reduce the risk of explosion. Meanwhile, the carpenters were kept busy with the arduous work of plugging and repairing leaks below the waterline.

The French and Spanish have often been accused of aiming high with their guns to dismast their enemy's ships and having a penchant for boarding. This only really holds true of their privateers, who were greedy for goods. In fact, their naval crews emulated the British but with less success in terms of speed and accuracy of fire. In addition to inexperience and often poorer guns, the French built longer, lighter vessels that proved more vulnerable targets to British fire.

Discipline and good guns go a long way to explaining the deadly superiority of British fire. At the Battle of Finisterre in 1747, the British commander, the legendary Admiral Sir George Anson, believed his fleet's rapid and accurate rate of fire secured the victory. The French admitted that the British 'guns were handled as if these were muskets'. Statistics bear this out. In 1758, for example, HMS *Monmouth* engaged the *Foydrant* off Cartagena in a one-to-one battle with the weight of fire, unusually, 2.6 to 1 in favour of the French. Yet five Frenchmen were killed in the deadly struggle to every one British sailor killed.

In 1715, Britain had the strongest navy in Europe, but it was largely confined to European waters, where 124 British ships of the line faced 60 French and only 6 Spanish ships of the line. Over the next half century, the Royal Navy became, like the Spanish, a truly worldwide force with bases in the Mediterranean and Caribbean Seas.

Admiral Sir George Byng introduced the tactic of the running battle in a general chase against the Spanish fleet during the Battle of Passaro in 1718. Although a major breakthrough in naval tactics, it could only be contemplated using good ships with experienced crews. During the War of Jenkin's Ear, the British performance was not as good. An Allied Bourbon fleet fought off the British at Toulon, and the expedition against Cartagena in 1740 was a spectacular failure. But the French performed even worse. They were defeated by the British at Cape Finisterre twice in 1747, the first time by Anson and the other by Rear-Admiral Edward Hawke. Hawke was to prove something of a nemesis for the French Navy.

Once the war was over, there was a spate of changes on both sides. While building 90–100-gun ships, the British introduced the renowned 74-gun ship of the line - a fast cruiser rather than real battleship - which was to remain the navy's backbone until Trafalgar. It was a costly mistake on the part of the Bourbon powers not to emulate the British in building strong, large battleships, although they soon realized and reversed the error.

TYPES OF BOARDING AXES (EIGHTEENTH CENTURY): *When boarding an enemy ship, the crews would use various axes (as shown) to beat or cut the enemy - with devastating results.*

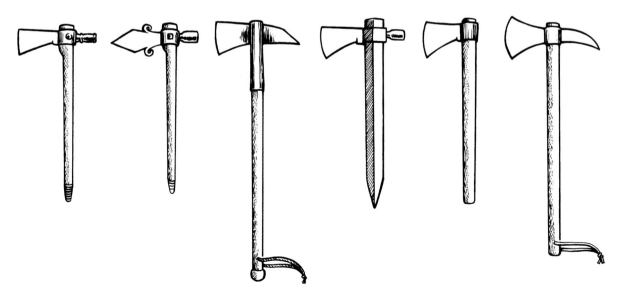

The new conflict, which broke out in 1756, began well enough for the French. The talented Admiral Marquis de la Gallissonière got the better of Admiral Sir John Byng at the Battle of Menorca on 20 May 1757. By retreating back to Gibraltar, Byng allowed Menorca with its vital base of Port Mahon to fall to the French. Byng was court-martialled for 'failing to do his utmost' to relieve the island and was shot *'pour encourager les autres'* ('to encourage the others'), as Voltaire so wryly put it.

Quiberon Bay, 1759: Storms and Audacity

The French opted for a bold but dangerously complicated invasion scheme intended to defeat the British with one blow. Depending as it did on troops and ships making a series of rendezvous in scattered ports, the plan was vulnerable to practical problems and began to unravel with alarming speed when Admiral de la Clue's Toulon

A PORTRAIT OF ADMIRAL SIR EDWARD HAWKE *(1705-81), the victor of Quiberon Bay. He was the greatest British naval commander prior to Nelson.*

fleet was defeated at Gibraltar on 18 August 1759. The defeat left the Brest Fleet under Hubert de Brienne, Comte de Conflans, to rendezvous with the invading army at Morbihan, where it was blockaded by the British. The invasion depended on a fleet that was both inexperienced and lacked self-confidence. Out of a complement of 750 men on the 80-gun *Orient* – the flagship of the first division commander Chevalier de Guébriant – only 30 were experienced sailors. The second division with 8 ships of the line was commanded by Chevalier de Beauffremont in the 80-gun *Tonnant*. The third division was under the command of Marquis Saint-André du Verger in the 80-gun *Formidable*. When the battle commenced, the brunt of the British assault would fall on Verger's squadron while Beauffremont's actions, based on his low opinion of Conflan's abilities, would doom the French Navy to its worst ever defeat.

The gale that blew Hawke off his station at Brest allowed Conflans to slip out of port and head toward Morbihan with his 21 ships of the line and five frigates. He sailed for Scotland at the first opportunity, as ordered by the Admiralty. Guessing that this was the intention, Hawke sailed for Belle Isle, where he intended to pounce on the French fleet. By the evening of 19 November, Conflans was 115km (70 miles) southwest of the island with a strong wind blowing and a sea rising at an alarming rate. He altered course northwards for Morbihan and began to take in his sails.

By daybreak the following day, Commodore Duff, Hawke's subordinate, had sighted Conflans and prudently retreated out to sea. Conflans ordered a general chase just as a gale blew up but reversed his order when he sighted the rest of Hawke's fleet. Conflans now headed back into Quiberon Bay, the bay formed by the long, protruding arm of the Quiberon Peninsula, the islands of Houat and Houedic, and the perilous Cardinal Rocks at the southern end of the reef. With its rocks and shoals, the bay forms a most dangerous and uncongenial battle site for two sailing fleets, especially in such unfavourable

conditions. Conflans was gambling that the British would not dare to follow him inside the treacherous bay during a gale. If they did so, then he would at least have the advantage by keeping inshore while the pursuing British would face the perilous Cardinals on their leeside. The orders of the Royal Navy stated quite clearly that an admiral should anchor and ride out the storm before giving battle, not least because the fleet would lose the use of its lower gun decks and the snipers in the rigging in the stormy seas.

It was unfortunate for Conflans that Hawke, as shown at Finisterre in 1747, was both bold and unconventional. Like Tromp or Nelson, Hawke was willing to risk all to defeat and destroy the enemy. As a consequence, Hawke's fleet entered the bay at around 2.30 p.m. just as Conflans' flagship, the 80-gun *Soleil Royale*, rounded the Cardinals. The French rear was immediately engaged in a running battle with the British. The French were shocked at the sheer audacity of Hawke's fleet, willing to risk running aground in the shallow bay or being dashed against the rocks by the stormy weather. Conflans ordered his fleet to turn about to support the rear, but Beauffremont, for reasons best known to himself, chose to ignore the order.

Deadly Melee

Hawke's 100-gun flagship, the *Royal George*, bore down on the 70-gun *Superbe* and sank it with a single, massive broadside at the waterline. It sank with all hands, spreading panic among the French ships. Captain Kersaint, in charge of the 74-gun *Thésée*, did not fancy sharing the *Superbe's* fate and ordered his lower gun ports opened. Unfortunately a sudden fierce squall rolled *Thésée* to leeward and water poured in. Both French and British onlookers were appalled as the ship sunk like a stone. The British Admiral Keppel ordered out the longboats to pick up survivors. By this point, both sides had begun to appreciate that the greatest enemy was the sea itself. Aboard the *Royal George,* the chaplain noted that, out of 100 shots

Battle of Quiberon Bay

1759

Quiberon Bay is a shallow, rocky and dangerous stretch of water and a far from ideal spot for a sea battle. But having shadowed the French to the bay where their commander Admiral Marquis de Conflans hoped to find sanctuary, Admiral Hawke overlooked the obvious dangers, made far worse by a oncoming gale, to signal his captains to 'Go at them!' The French were shocked that their enemy would be so bold as to fight them inside the bay in a gale and shock turned to panic when Hawke's flagship sunk the *Superbe* with a single broadside. The *Thésée* sunk like a stone in the foaming waves when her captain ordered the lower gun ports opened in order to fire back at the British with her heaviest guns, allowing water to flood the ship. The battle raged on with intense ferocity for another three hours. The French plans to land in Scotland were defeated and France went on lose the Seven Years' War.

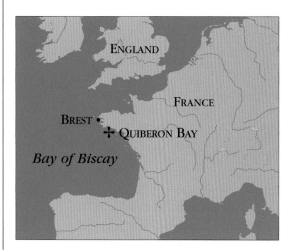

Quiberon Bay lies on the French western or Biscay coast near the port of St Nazaire. The passage into the bay can be treacherous in poor weather, with dangerous rocks and shoals.

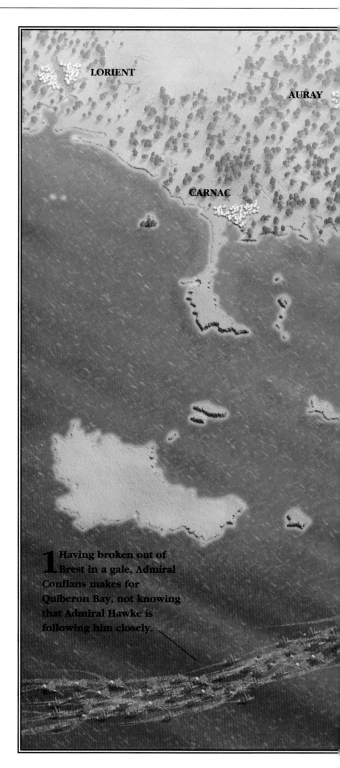

LORIENT

AURAY

CARNAC

1 Having broken out of Brest in a gale, Admiral Conflans makes for Quiberon Bay, not knowing that Admiral Hawke is following him closely.

5 The following day at dawn, Conflans finds himself surrounded on all sides by British ships, and burns his flagship, Soleil Royal. Part of his fleet flees up the shallow Vilaine River.

VANNES

3 Hawke's flagship sinks the Superbe with a single, massive well-aimed broadside and then turns on the Thésée, which is flooded and sinks when she opens her lower gun ports.

2 The battle begins during a storm on 20 November, when Hawke takes the risk of losing his heavy guns and fighting in the treacherous, shallow waters of the bay.

4 The confused battle rages on until well into the afternoon with mounting French losses. Several French vessels have to strike their colours. By 5 p.m., the battle comes to an end due to bad weather and growing darkness.

fired by the French ships, only 40 actually hit the intended target, a sure sign that the enemy was gripped by panic. Undirected bravery of the type shown by Kersaint and the *Thésée* would prove no match for the discipline and experience of the British crews.

At 4 p.m., the *Formidable*, which as the rear squadron flagship had borne the brunt of the British attack, hauled down its flag. Both the division commander and the ship's commander, who happened to be brothers, had been killed in the fierce battle. The 74-gun *Héros* had also been battered by the British broadsides and was now forced to strike its colours. Meanwhile, the easterly gale carried the French fleet ever further eastwards. Conflans signalled for his battered fleet to make it out to the open sea and escape as well as it could. But his signals were again poorly followed; it was now around 5 p.m. and the light had begun to fade.

First light on the morning of 21 November revealed that Hawke had managed to keep his fleet organized and safely anchored overnight. Conflans was not so fortunate. Finding the *Royal Soleil* surrounded on all sides by British vessels, Conflans ordered the cables cut, and the flagship was deliberately run aground and set alight to keep it out of enemy hands. Two French ships had sunk, one had burnt, one was captured and one was wrecked. Beauffremont and eight ships of the line escaped to Rochefort and another five ships managed to flee across the bar into the shallow Vilaine River. The British did not dare to follow this time, but another French ship was wrecked in the process. On 24 November, a captured French officer admitted that there had been 'great valour on the right; ignorance and total confusion in the centre; and poor manoeuvres on the left'. The catastrophic defeat at Quiberon Bay ensured not only that there would no invasion of Scotland but also that France would ultimately lose her North American empire.

French Revenge

The French thirsted for revenge at the first opportunity after 1763, and the instrument of this righteous revenge would be a revived navy. The new young king, Louis XVI, was obsessed with

avenging the defeat and reviving the French navy. For once, there would be money both to build ships and to recruit experienced sailors and train cadets and officers.

When, in August 1776, the Americans rebelled against the British, the French were soon on hand

QUIBERON BAY *in 1759 was as dramatic a battle as this later oil painting made it out to be, but the swell and weather was far worse than depicted.*

to cause problems for their old enemy. The much improved French Navy fought the British to a standstill at Ushant on 27 July 1778, and in the Indian Ocean Admiral Pierre Suffren wreaked havoc with British shipping, capturing the vital Trincomalee naval base in Ceylon and preventing a British occupation of the Cape.

The greatest moment came when Admiral Comte de Grasse defeated the British at the Virginia Capes on 5 September 1781. Shortly afterwards, the isolated British army at Yorktown was forced to surrender, leading to the humiliating loss of the American colonies. France had avenged the defeat at Quiberon Bay.

Russia and Sweden's Struggle for Supremacy: 1705–90

With its brackish waters, indented shoreline and lack of tides, the Baltic is more of a vast inland lake than a real ocean, making for difficult sailing and

RUSSIA HAD ONLY ONE SEAPORT, *Archangel, on the White (Northern) Sea, when Tsar Peter launched his first fleet in 1693, on the great Donets river at Voronezh. Two decades later, the Imperial Russian Navy dominated the Baltic.*

navigation conditions. A semi-Arctic climate imposes yet further restrictions upon sailing fleets and their use. It took all the iron will and determination of Tsar Peter the Great to found the Russian Navy in 1705 with the naval base at Kronstadt, on the Gulf of Finland. To outflank Swedish defences in Finland, Peter built a powerful galley fleet to combine with his new Europeanized army in amphibious operations.

Galleys were cheap and easy to mass produce, could easily be manned by sailors and did not require experienced naval officers to command them. Furthermore in the Baltic, like the Mediterranean Sea, the winds were often fickle and the oar was often superior to the sail. The Petrine galley measured 40m (130ft) in length, 7m (23ft) in width, had a shallow draft of only 1.5m (5ft) and was equipped with 2–4 heavy guns and 18 lighter mounted guns. With a crew of 90 sailors and 200 troops manning 24 pairs of oars, the galley could make a speed of five knots, weather and sea permitting. The hold had enough room for 30 horses, although the crew had to sleep on shore during the night. The effort expended on the galley fleet was vindicated when the Russians defeated a Swedish fleet at Gangut (Hangö Head) in August 1714, paving the way for an outright Russian occupation of Finland.

Less than five years later, Peter gathered a massive galley fleet in the Åland archipelago. His aim was to capture the Swedish capital of Stockholm. The Swedish sailing fleet would be unable to pursue the shallow-drafted galleys and would be immobilized by the lack of wind power. Numbering almost 270 vessels, including 40 ships of the line and 123 galleys, the Russian fleet set sail in late July 1719 with 26,000 troops on board. The aim was to land near Stockholm with one corps while the rest of the fleet laid waste to the long easterly Swedish coastline. The coastal raids ravaged the towns and settlements, leaving thousands of Swedes without homes. However, the great fear for the Swedes was that the capital could be reached via the narrow and shallow Stäket Sound. To prevent this, the Swedes placed a floating artillery *pråm* (battery deck) at the northern exit of the Stäket Sound and three heavily armed galleys in the middle passage. At the eastern entry to Stäket, where the Russians were expected, the Swedes built defensive works mounted by stakes and a gun battery, and manned by 500 troops. On 13 August 1719, 7000 Russian troops landed as expected at Stäket but were halted and driven back by a stout Swedish defence. This may have saved Stockholm, but the Russians captured the Baltic provinces with their ports at Riga, Reval, Pernau and Viborg, in addition to Kronstadt.

The Decline of the Baltic Fleet

When Peter died in 1725, Russia had a fleet numbering 34 ships of the line, 9 frigates, hundreds of galleys, sloops, gunboats and some 25,000 experienced men, and was the strongest naval power in the Baltic. Under the next six rulers, the Baltic Fleet was allowed to deteriorate to the point where it was weaker than the Danish Navy, despite Russia's status as a European Great Power. Compared to the army, the Baltic Fleet played a very minor role during the Seven Years War - where it was, ironically, Sweden and Russia who allied against Frederick's Prussia. This war showed that the key role for navies in the Baltic was not maritime at all but amphibious; coastal flotillas needed to cooperate closely with the army and, in turn, both services needed to collaborate

closely with the navy. If that coordination could be perfected, amphibious operations could be of great value. In the Baltic, the navies were operating close to the coastlines and under the direct operational controls of the admiralties in the capitals. This stifled initiative and independence in the naval officers, even admirals, to the detriment of the operational efficiency and combat potential of the Baltic navies. The Russians and Swedes, in their coming war, would show a fatal obsession with linear battle formations and theoretical operational procedures at a time when the British and French navies were revolutionizing naval warfare in the west. Russian and Swedish naval officers lacked combat experience, self-confidence and professional *esprit de corps* when compared to their Western counterparts.

Sweden had a few inherent advantages that were to give her the edge in naval warfare against Russia. After 1721, Sweden became a maritime trading nation in her own right with a considerable merchant fleet that could provide a useful pool of experienced sailors in time of war. Furthermore, Sweden, unlike her Russian foe, never allowed her sailing ships to deteriorate – even at the nadir of Sweden's military misfortunes in the 1740s, the building and repair of battleships were maintained. Having been at the receiving end of an attack by Russian galleys in 1719, the Swedes also built up a respectable flotilla of galleys based at the naval fortress of Sveaborg in Finland and at Stockholm. The Swedish Admiralty at Karlskrona

A RUSSIAN GALLEY OF 1719 CAMPAIGN: *these big beasts were 40m (130ft) in length, 7m (23ft) abreast and 1.5m (5ft) deep, and included 25 pairs of oars, 2-4 guns, 90 crew and 200 soldiers. They could make five knots by oar.*

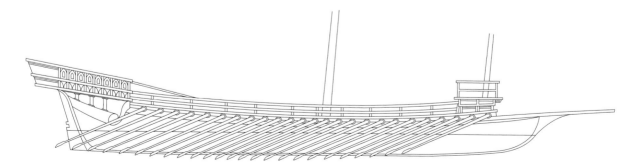

was also turning out a larger number of professionally trained naval cadets and encouraging their cadets, as well as their officers, to join the Western navies for experience.

The Russian Navy staged a remarkable recovery under the rule of Catherine II, who sought to establish Russian hegemony over the Black Sea. Although she had no practical knowledge or hands-on experience of naval matters like Peter I, Catherine had a sound grasp of strategy and was just as ruthless in pursuing her aim of expanding Russia to the west and south. The full extent of Russia's naval recovery and new-found power was demonstrated in 1769–1770, when a fleet was sent, with some British assistance, to the Mediterranean. The expedition was a great success since the Russian Fleet managed to defeat and sink most of the superior Turkish Navy in a single battle at Chesme on 8 July 1770. There were rich pickings for Russia in the south, but the real danger lay in the northwest with Russia's old enemy, Sweden.

Skärgårdsflottan: Sweden's Secret Weapon

One of Catherine's few and most damaging mistakes was to allow her talented and ruthless

cousin, Gustavus III, to take absolute power in Sweden in August 1772. He was to prove a formidable enemy, both to Russia and to her ally, Denmark–Norway. The king worked hard to rebuild the Swedish Navy in order to assist the new coastal fleet to take Zealand and force Denmark to cede Norway to Sweden. With Norway in his grasp, the king hoped to expand Sweden's maritime trade and power yet further.

The building of a *skärgårdsflotta*, or coastal fleet, had been underway since the disastrous 1741–43 war against Russia – when the lack of just such a fleet had enabled Russia to take Finland a second time. While the Karlskrona Admiralty wanted large ships of the line, the government back in Stockholm pushed for a strong coastal fleet. This fleet was to be under the command of the Army, with majors in charge of ships. Rejecting the Mediterranean-style galley, the Swedes sought something that could combine sails and oars with a large number of guns. The typical galley was poorly armed, weak in structure and used too many sailors and oarsmen. Sweden, with Finland, had barely 2 million inhabitants, which severely limited the pool of manpower for the coastal fleet.

SWEDISH GUNBOAT: *The* Udemaa *was a revolutionary design, with the guns stored amidships when moving. In battle, these could be rolled and placed into the fire position, combining the function of gunboat and galley.*

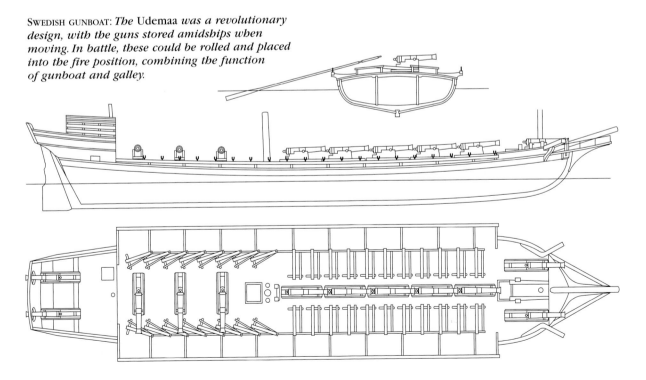

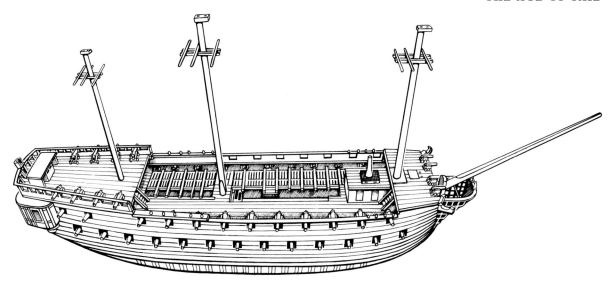

CHAPMAN'S VASA was purpose-built for supporting a Swedish amphibious landing on Zealand, but the enemy in 1788 was Russia not Denmark.

Luckily, the Swedes had an outstanding ship designer and architect in Fredrik Henrik af Chapman – the son of an immigrant British naval engineer. Chapman designed a special 'coastal frigate' (*skärgårdsfregatt*) that could sail or be rowed underway but which had the same number of guns as a frigate. It was far superior to the galley in most aspects and would wreak havoc on the Russian galleys at Svensksund. It was most vulnerable while underway – when it could not fire its guns – but it had huge potential.

Chapman, now Chief Naval Engineer, designed three types of coastal frigates of varying size and artillery strength. The smallest Pojama-class galley was least interesting from a design point of view. The Udema-class galley was designed such that its guns were stowed away amidships on the gundeck while the vessel was underway and rolled into place only when it was prepared for battle. The other two lighter classes, Turuma and Hemmema, were more conventional 'coastal frigates' without the stowing capacity.

With the King's enthusiastic backing, these new ships were mass produced with amazing speed and cost efficiency. All of the new coastal ships combined a low silhouette with high firepower for such small vessels, good manoeuvrability, and fairly good sailing performance, offering relatively high speeds when propelled by oars. In battle, they could be used for supporting fire or landing troops. Their only

drawback was the need for a naval escort when underway, their low radius of action and dependence on transport ships for supplies. With 14 benches for oars, the galley had a crew of 48–60 men, not counting troops. It was armed with several 18lb (8kg) and 24 (11kg) guns. Thanks to another of Chapman's ingenious innovations, these guns had an unobstructed field of fire since the upper parts of the stern and helm was detachable. In this, Chapman was about two centuries ahead of his time.

Gustav III's Great Naval Gamble

In Swedish maritime strategy, the coastal flotilla was seen as an offensive weapon to be used for amphibious warfare against either Denmark or Russia. King Gustavus had realized that in Baltic naval warfare it was vital to seize the initiative at the outset of hostilities by taking or neutralizing the enemy's main fleet and operational bases. While the Swedish sailing fleet, under the command of his brother Duke Charles, kept the Russian Baltic squadron at bay, Gustavus would use the coastal fleet to land 30,000 troops near Oranienbaum. He then planned to march on and capture St Petersburg. Like other later invaders of Russia, Gustavus had not planned for a long war

Battle of Svensksund

1790

Svensksund was the greatest naval defeat in Russian history prior to Tsushima in 1905, yet it remains curiously uncelebrated in Sweden. Under the personal command of King Gustavus III of Sweden, the 250-strong Swedish coastal flotilla occupied a strong defensive position along the northern edge of the bay. Underestimating his enemy's strength and leadership, the Russian commander Charles von Nassau-Siegen signalled his 150 vessels to make a frontal assault. As his ships advanced, they sailed into the trap the Swedes had laid for them, coming under heavy enfilading fire from their flanks. In the confusion, the Russian vessels drifted ever deeper into the Swedish trap until they could no longer move or manoeuvre properly and were shot to pieces. Nassau-Siegen finally admitted defeat, but the signalled retreat could not be executed. The Russians lost 7400–9500 men and almost 90 vessels were either sunk or captured.

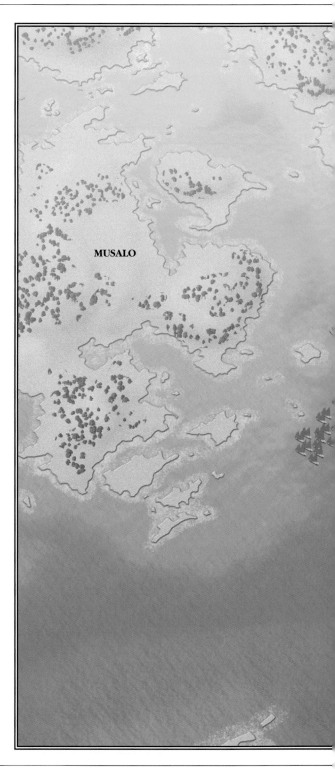

MUSALO

Svensksund, or 'Swedish Sound', is situated in the eastern part of the Finnish archipelago south of the towns of Kotka and Fredrikshamn (Hamina) and due west of Viborg (Vyborg/Vipuri).

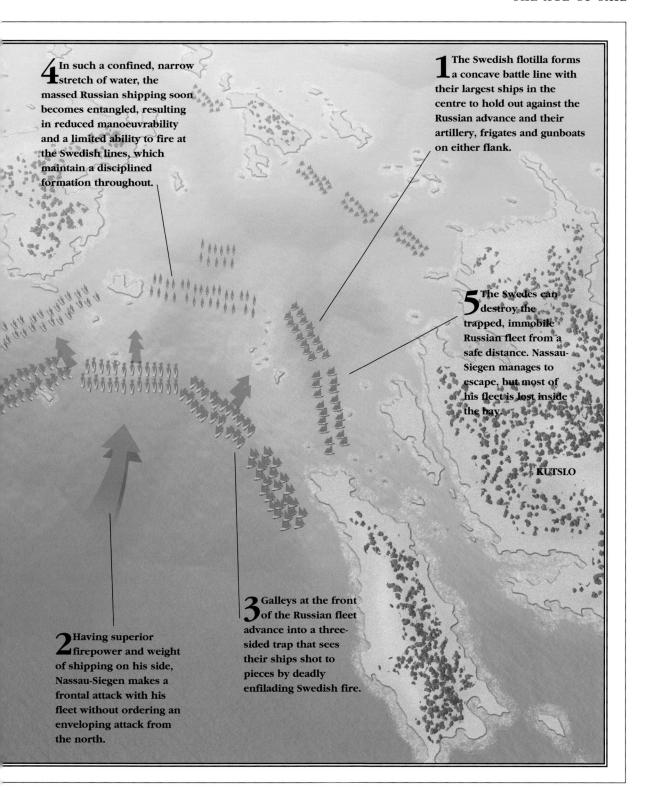

4 In such a confined, narrow stretch of water, the massed Russian shipping soon becomes entangled, resulting in reduced manoeuvrability and a limited ability to fire at the Swedish lines, which maintain a disciplined formation throughout.

1 The Swedish flotilla forms a concave battle line with their largest ships in the centre to hold out against the Russian advance and their artillery, frigates and gunboats on either flank.

5 The Swedes can destroy the trapped, immobile Russian fleet from a safe distance. Nassau-Siegen manages to escape, but most of his fleet is lost inside the bay.

KUTSLO

2 Having superior firepower and weight of shipping on his side, Nassau-Siegen makes a frontal attack with his fleet without ordering an enveloping attack from the north.

3 Galleys at the front of the Russian fleet advance into a three-sided trap that sees their ships shot to pieces by deadly enfilading Swedish fire.

against such a huge foe, and Sweden did not have the resources.

Gustavus' boldly optimistic plan hinged on a very crucial assumption: that the Swedish Navy was superior to the Russian Navy both with respect to quantity and quality. This was not the case. The officers, especially the admirals, of the Imperial Russian Navy were both professional and competent. In Admiral Samuel Grieg, recruited from the Royal Navy in 1764, the Empress had a tough Scottish professional who knew his business and would put paid, as commander of the Russian Kronstadt squadron, to the Swedish king's entire scheme at Hogland in July 1788. His replacement, Admiral Vasily Chichagov, was an experienced but cautious Russian naval officer whose hesitancy would cost Russia dearly at Viborg in early July 1790. But the officers in general were good, as were the crews once they had been 'seasoned' onboard for a while.

In terms of quantity, the odds were not in Sweden's favour either. The Swedish Navy, based in the Baltic base of Karlskrona, numbered 26 ships of the line, 12 large and four smaller frigates (two of which were based at Sveaborg). The Russian Fleet, most of which was based in the Baltic at Reval, Viborg and Kronstadt, numbered 41 ships of the line with 6 under construction and 25 frigates. Four of the Russian ships of the line numbered over 100 guns, nine were between 72 and 80 guns, and the rest were 66 guns. This reflected a basic fact that made the Russian Baltic Fleet superior to the Swedish: it was designed for a proper sea battle and for cruising into the Mediterranean. Furthermore, the Russian ships were better armed, sturdier vessels and in 1788 most were brand new. By contrast, the Swedish ships of the line were flimsier, smaller, lacking covered upper decks, and having high gun decks and shallow draughts. In a sea battle, these weaknesses could be fatal.

What could be seen as a weakness for a conventional sailing fleet can be explained by keeping in mind one fact: Swedish naval strategy was amphibious and not naval like Russia's or Denmark's. The Swedish ships of the line and frigates were built to support a landing on Zealand or the Russian Baltic coast with their shallow sandy beaches. They stood high in the water with high gun decks and a shallow draught in order to fire broadsides in support of troop landings, even in contrary winds. Hence the low buildings atop the decks that struck many foreign observers as so odd. Chapman believed that large ships of the line were only for show. As a consequence, Swedish ships of the line were small compared to Western European versions while the frigates were unusually large. Again this was deliberate since it would make coordination with the coastal or army flotilla and the army units smoother and easier.

> *'All the horrors of war filled these moments: the sea and the shores covered in thick smoke, only lit by the occasional fire, the waters filled with wreckage and floating bodies, the rocks...shaking from the thunder of the warships' fire...'*
>
> — SWEDISH POET OXENSTIERNA, BATTLE OF VIBORG 3 JULY 1790

The Russo-Swedish War: 1788–1790

Admiral Greig fought the Swedish Navy to a standstill at Hogland on 17 July 1788. The war that Gustavus intended to be a swift, amphibious romp to St Petersburg became a war of attrition that would drag on for another two years. In the summer of 1790, Gustavus took personal charge of the Swedish coastal fleet, determined to wrest back the initiative and momentum lost two years earlier. He sought to threaten St Petersburg and force the Russian army in Karelia to retreat from the Finnish border by attacking Viborg. Instead, he managed

OPPOSITE: FREDRIK HENRIK AF CHAPMAN *was Sweden's naval architect in chief and the creator of Sweden's naval renaissance of the Gustavian Age (1771-1809). He was of British descent.*

through his rashness to trap the entire Swedish Navy in the narrow sound of Viborg, where it seemed that his only choice was to surrender to Chichagov's superior fleet. Surrender would mean handing over 21 ships of the line, 12 frigates and 174 coastal craft. The capture of Gustavus and Duke Charles would have rendered Sweden leaderless in the middle of a war.

Such an outcome was unthinkable. Early on the morning of 3 July, Gustavus ordered his fleet to break through the Russian lines. Taken by surprise, Chichagov moved at a snail's pace to plug the gap and allowed his quarry to escape. The commanders of the Russian coastal fleet, Rear Admiral Prince Charles von Nassau-Siegen and his

deputy Count Chevalier Giulio Litta, were infuriated and vowed to recapture their Swedish foe. They would get their opportunity only a few days later at Svensksund.

Svensksund, 1790: the Swedish Navy's Finest Hour

If Chichagov's caution had lost Russia a chance to capture the Swedish king and his entire navy at Viborg, it was Nassau-Siegen's lack of foresight and underestimation of the enemy that would cost Russia dear in the next battle. Had the enemy been led by anyone other the Swedish king himself, the prince's calculation would probably have been correct. But Gustavus III was a bold adventurer like Nassau-Siegen and was willing to risk everything on a single battle if it gave him the opportunity to win all – or at least to deliver the Russians enough of a setback that they would grant him peace with honour. He called a halt to the fleet's retreat along

A DETAIL FROM THE PAINTING *'Battle at Svensksund' by artist Johan Tietrich Schoultz (1754–1807), held in the National Museum of Fine Arts in Stockholm, showing the second battle (9 July 1789).*

the Finnish coastline and arrayed its ships – including over 50 fresh vessels – at Svensksund.

The 'Swedish Sound' was a natural harbour with shallow waters surrounded by islands on three sides – ideal waters for a battle between coastal ships. Placing his heaviest ships, including 16 galleys, in the centre, Gustavus placed his 99-gun sloops and 55-gun gunboats on the flanks. He hoped, once he had blocked off the northern approaches to the battle site, that Nassau-Siegen would snap at the bait and make a frontal assault. It was only when the German prince got inside the bay that he realized that the flanks would shoot his advancing ships to pieces.

Nassau-Siegen took the bait. His fleet was numerically inferior but his ships were larger, had more guns and larger crews and seemed sure of victory. Some of the more cautious officers pointed out that the bay was shallow and narrow and that they would be faced with enfilading fire. Many of

his officers wanted a diversionary attack from the north. His crews were tired and the fleet was a composite of different ships hastily assembled for war. But the Prince was sure of victory.

On the morning of 9 July, the signal was given for the Russian flotilla to begin the frontal assault on the concave Swedish line. Unfortunately, the lead was taken by the galleys of the Count Chevalier Giulio Litta, presenting a large target for the Swedish guns. Litta's galleys were unable to answer the Swedish fire that raked the long, vulnerable vessels with shot, leaving a trail of destruction and death on the decks. The vessels that followed fared no better as they crowded into one another and were given a hot reception from the Swedish gunners. The further they rowed into the Swedish lines, the worse the confusion became and the harder it was for the commanders to control their vessels, with more ships being put out of commission. It did not help that a fresh southerly breeze blew them deeper inside the bay, where the entangled body of ships was now being shot to pieces from three sides simultaneously.

It turned into a confused and bloody massacre. Fires broke out in the Russian powder magazines, the gunners could not see or elevate their guns to answer the Swedes, and the decks were running red with blood and dying men. Even now, Nassau-Siegen could not admit that he had walked right into a deadly trap that was slowly but surely destroying his embattled fleet. His brave officers and men paid for the prince's pride with their blood. Hour after hour, the Russian crews bled, died and stood their ground as the Swedish fire ploughed relentlessly into their sides, sails and decks. Finally Nassau-Siegen signalled the fleet to retreat, but it took another three agonizing hours for the survivors to escape.

Carnage

When it was all over, the scale of the carnage dampened the euphoria among the Swedes. Burning, tilting and sinking were over 50 vessels. Some 34 vessels could be saved, but between 7400 and 10,000 Russians sailors and officers lay dead on their ships and in the water. Swedish losses amounted to no more than 4 ships and 300 men. The war had ended at a stroke.

CHAPTER 4

THE NINETEENTH CENTURY

The period from about 1780 to 1880 saw a series of remarkable transformations in naval warfare. It began with the last glorious burst of the age of sail, as Great Britain won control of the world's oceans in the course of the wars of the French Revolution and the Napoleonic Wars (1793–1815). An extraordinary series of innovations followed, in large part as other nations tried to find ways around British naval dominance, but also as European imperialism made it desirable to use navies in new ways.

By 1880, the sail had effectively been abandoned as a means of propulsion in naval warfare, replaced by steam power. The armament of naval vessels had been transformed by the invention of the explosive shell, reliable rifled guns and, even more decisively, the gun turret. And the warship itself was far less subject to injury, not only because rigging and spars were no

A 1790 PAINTING *of the Glorious First of June, by the artist Philippe-Jacques de Loutherbourg, shows the two flagships,* Queen Charlotte *and* Montagne, *closely engaged, and catches the spirit of the action.*

longer available as targets, but because the vessels were ironclad or even constructed of iron – the first steel-built ships appeared on the seas in 1880. Accompanying these developments of the physical sinews of war was a growing professionalism in the major navies, with much greater emphasis on trained gunnery and the creation of the career naval sailor, who moved from ship to ship instead of being paid off at the end of a ship's commission.

Ships of the Late Eighteenth Century

All navies of the late eighteenth century included vessels in a variety of sizes. Smaller ships such as corvettes and frigates carried messages and passed signals. Frigates, well-armed ships that mounted 30–40 guns, also frequently cruised independently to protect shipping from pirates and privateers. The key element for fleet actions, however, was the 'ships of the line' – strong warships that mounted a heavy armament of guns. These vessels had two or three gundecks (the Spanish ship *Santissima Trinidad* had four), bringing as many guns as possible to bear against the enemy. Such

ships had to be massively reinforced to bear the weight of the guns and their recoil, a process that led to heavier and heavier ships as nations tried to surpass each other within the existing technology of the time.

By the 1780s, a ship of the line was reckoned to need at least 64 guns, but by 1805 the standard was 74. By 1830, a first-rate ship of the line was a massive floating battery with 80 heavy guns. A good example of a ship of the line of around 1800 is the *Victory*, Nelson's flagship at the Battle of Trafalgar, which is still preserved in Portsmouth Harbour. The *Victory* was a massive, heavily constructed vessel even by the standards of the time, 69m (227ft) long and displacing 3500 gross tons. By 1805, she mounted 104 guns – 30 that fired 32lb (15kg) shot, 28 24-pounders (11kg), 44 12-pounders (5kg), and two 68lb (31kg) carronades, short guns that could fire very heavy shot inaccurately for short distances.

Even a vessel with as many teeth as the *Victory* was not normally a ship-sinker, however. The goal was to capture enemy ships rather than destroy them. Before the development of the explosive shell, a ship's most common ammunition was solid shot. Shot could pierce hulls, but left neat round holes that were relatively easy to patch. The main damage was usually to the vessel's masts and spars, and of course to the personnel on deck.

IN 1800, A SHIP might carry long cannon, short stubby carronades, or cannonades (a cross between the two). Guns were carefully tied in place - a loose cannon on deck could inflict massive damage.

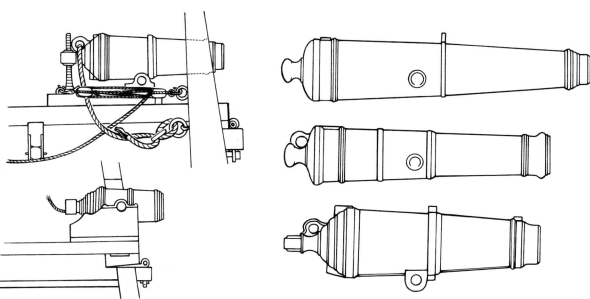

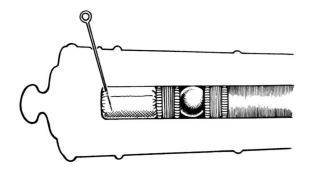

To load, a bag of gunpowder *and then a shot were rammed up the barrel. Then a spike in the touchhole pierced the bag, so that the powder would explode on firing.*

The ideal battle tactic was to manoeuvre in order to fire a complete broadside down the relatively unprotected bow or stern of the enemy vessel. Not only was the enemy unable to respond, since almost all guns were mounted on the sides of the ship, but this raking shot could clear the enemy's deck, causing bloody carnage. A ship that

had been thoroughly raked was often rendered unmanoeuvrable, making surrender necessary. Alternatively, it was still common to take a ship by boarding, preferably after thinning the enemy's ship with broadsides. A ship's guns could also fire grape or case shot, effective in clearing a deck. Chain shot - a cannon ball that had been cut in half, the pieces then linked with a short chain - was especially effective against rigging.

Operation of the guns required a great deal of physical strength and coordinated activity by the gun crew. Naval vessels relied most heavily on cannon of various sizes, guns capable of hurling shot 1000m (3300ft) or more - though the use of

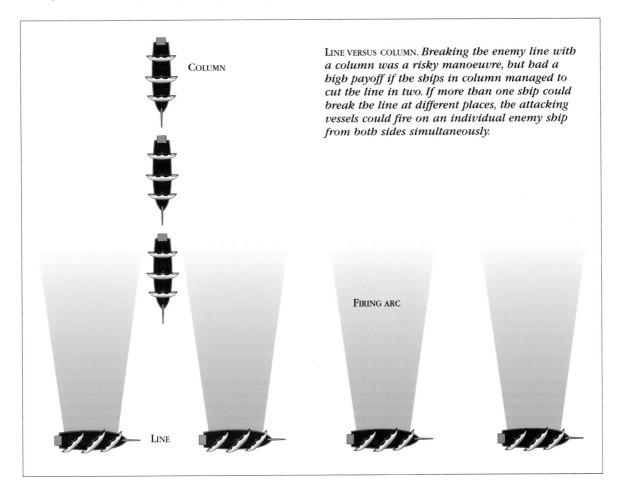

Column

Line versus column. *Breaking the enemy line with a column was a risky manoeuvre, but had a high payoff if the ships in column managed to cut the line in two. If more than one ship could break the line at different places, the attacking vessels could fire on an individual enemy ship from both sides simultaneously.*

Firing arc

Line

carronades also became common during the Napoleonic Wars. The guns were mounted on wooden carriages with small wheels; rope tackles controlled the recoil and brought the gun inboard for reloading – all guns of this period were muzzle-loaders. Guns were aimed by being heaved into position with a handspike.

Guns were only as good as their crews. There were no sights or other aids to aiming, and the massive clouds of black smoke that the guns bellowed out with each shot often completely obscured the enemy ship. Members of an untrained gun crew could easily be injured or killed by the recoil, and it was not uncommon for improperly loaded guns to burst on firing. Naval boards of the late eighteenth century did not impose any standard of training; the matter was left to each captain's initiative. Since gunpowder was expensive, the amount of practice using live fire was limited. In 1800, it was considered outstanding if a crew was able to fire three shots in five minutes. Only the British Royal Navy was consistently able to perform so well.

Revolutionary and Napoleonic France
Naval conflict at the turn of the nineteenth century was dominated by the long war between Great Britain and France, fought from 1793 to 1815 with only one short period of truce. Britain entered this conflict with two distinct advantages. First, the Royal Navy was in a state of high preparedness in 1793, following Spain's seizure of a British trading station at Nootka Sound in 1790. Spain eventually backed down from the ensuing confrontation, but the incident caused Britain to mobilize her fleet. Second, the French Revolution had wrought havoc in the French Navy. The ranks of its officers had been purged, and sailors had gone without pay for so long that many deserted or even mutinied.

When France declared war on Britain in February 1793, therefore, the Royal Navy was able to respond without delay. The British consolidated their advantage in August 1793, when French monarchists invited Admiral Hood to occupy Toulon, the port where nearly half the French Navy lay at anchor. Although land attacks forced Hood to withdraw after a few months, he destroyed 19 French ships and seized 18 others, damaging many more as he evacuated the port.

The Glorious First of June 1794: Bold Tactics
The first fleet engagement of the war came the following year. The surviving portion of the French fleet was stationed at Brest and at first showed little inclination to come out and fight the British. French morale was low; the French crews were poorly trained and many had mutinied at Quiberon Bay in 1793. Vice Admiral Morad de Galles was even imprisoned for his failure to impose discipline. Matters had improved thanks to administrative reforms and the leadership of Admiral Villaret-Joyeuse. But France remained at a severe disadvantage. After all, to train their crews, French captains had to put to sea and risk encountering British ships already worked up for action.

Nonetheless, in May 1794 the French government ordered the Brest fleet, comprising 26 ships of the line, into the Atlantic to protect a massive grain convoy of 117 merchant vessels sailing from America. On 28 May, they encountered a British fleet of 25 line-of-battle ships, commanded by the elderly and highly experienced Admiral Richard Howe. Howe had spent much of his career improving British naval tactics, discipline and signals. He now put his experience to good use in the ensuing engagement. The French tried to withdraw when they sighted Howe's fleet, but Howe maintained contact, capturing the last ship in the French line, *Révolutionnaire*, during the first day's action.

The fighting on the second day, 29 May, was a typical engagement in eighteenth-century style. The two fleets ran parallel to each other in line ahead, so that each line presented its broadside to the other. The gunnery match was destructive but inconclusive. Some of the French ships had to withdraw, but since several fresh French vessels arrived, the forces remained evenly matched.

The decisive action came on 1 June, when Howe decided to break the enemy line – a bold stroke that was possible only because of superior British training and even then it barely worked. The tactic had been carried out at the Battle of the Saintes in 1782 but was still regarded as highly

English 'Sea Dog' (1800)

In the early nineteenth century, it was still very common to take an enemy ship by boarding. First the approaching vessel would try to clear the decks as much as possible with cannon and sharpshooter fire from the fighting tops. When the ships met, the first moments were crucial: the aggressor had to get enough men onto the enemy deck to overwhelm resistance and perhaps even prevent a counter-boarding operation. Sailors were not usually trained in hand-to-hand fighting, but would board with any and all weapons available.

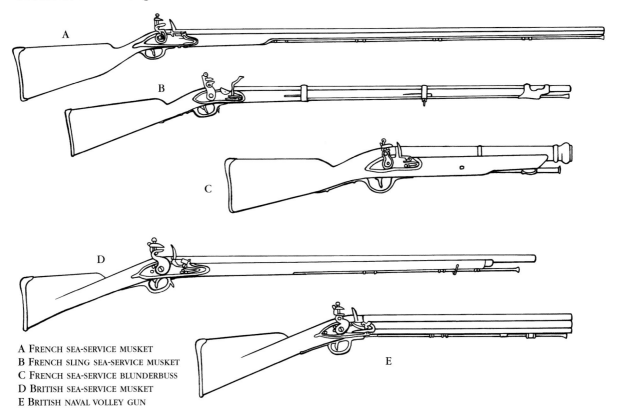

A FRENCH SEA-SERVICE MUSKET
B FRENCH SLING SEA-SERVICE MUSKET
C FRENCH SEA-SERVICE BLUNDERBUSS
D BRITISH SEA-SERVICE MUSKET
E BRITISH NAVAL VOLLEY GUN

MARINES PLAYED *an important part in nineteenth-century navies, both in naval battles and in amphibious operations. Often they were posted in the fighting tops with muskets to help clear the enemy deck.*

innovative and most admirals continued to prefer the line-ahead formation. The danger of running ships between the ships in the enemy's line as they proceeded in line were twofold. While approaching the enemy, the ships attempting the breakthrough were exposed to the full weight of the enemy's broadsides, without being able to respond. Their relatively unprotected bows would face the enemy, making it likely that they would be raked and suffer high casualties, as well as damage to masts and rigging that might leave them dead in the water. The attacking fleet would also suffer loss of cohesion, as its vessels would no longer be choreographed in fixed positions.

Only the fleet to windward (upwind) of its enemy could initiate such a manoeuvre, but on the whole British admirals preferred not to give up the windward advantage. So long as they were to

windward, they were less affected by artillery smoke, which the wind blew away from them and towards the enemy, and it was much easier to see signals. But a confident admiral might well undertake a breakthrough. If a ship did puncture the enemy line, it could fire both broadsides at the unprotected bows and sterns of the enemy ships while passing through. And once to the leeward, gunports on the lower deck could be kept open longer without waves breaking through, damaged ships could bear away to repair in greater safety, and disabled enemy ships would be driven to the leeward, where they could be further damaged or captured.

Breaking the Line

Howe turned his flagship, the *Queen Charlotte*, into the French line and signalled his captains to do likewise, to pierce the enemy line at several points. This bold action was possible because his fleet had a new system of signal flags that the admiral had devised himself. Many of the British crews and their captains were also disciplined enough to bear heavy enemy fire without sheering off, and the approach was made more bearable by the fact that the French gun crews were poorly trained. There were limits, however, to British discipline. Many of the captains did not carry out the signalled orders or sheered off before reaching the enemy. In the event, only the flagship and six other British ships of the line broke through.

As a result, instead of creating a new line ahead to leeward of the French line, the battle broke down into a general mêlée, a series of individual engagements in which all fleet control was lost. Some French ships had to fight on both sides simultaneously – a difficult manoeuvre because a single gun crew usually served two guns, one to port and one opposite it to starboard. The inexperienced French crews appear to have panicked, and less than half of their captains could be said to have performed well.

Admiral Villaret-Joyeuse finally broke off the engagement – which he was able to do since the British had not closed off his escape to leeward – and returned to Brest. Both sides suffered serious damage, but the British took six French ships of the line and sank a seventh, losing only one of their own vessels in exchange.

The result was a flawed, partial victory that the British public nonetheless hailed rapturously. By the end of the engagement, the 68-year-old Howe was exhausted, and his staff let the crippled French ships escape. Worse yet, they failed to intercept the grain convoy that the French had been mobilized to protect. Nonetheless, the Glorious First of June was a portent of things to come, as the more experienced Royal Navy proved able to outshoot the French and engage in riskier tactics.

An Expanding Conflict

In 1795, France conquered Holland, gaining control of the Dutch fleet. The following year, Spain made an alliance with France, changing sides

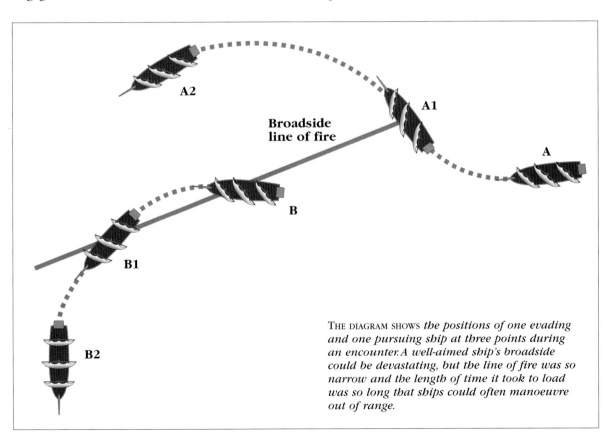

THE DIAGRAM SHOWS *the positions of one evading and one pursuing ship at three points during an encounter. A well-aimed ship's broadside could be devastating, but the line of fire was so narrow and the length of time it took to load was so long that ships could often manoeuvre out of range.*

French Gunnery Officer (1805)

The ship's gunner was a warrant officer, like the ship's master, surgeon, and bosun. Both the gunner and the bosun usually rose from the ranks of able seamen. The gunner served an apprenticeship as a gunner's mate for his responsible task, which included keeping the guns in good order and the gunpowder well-stored and dry, besides helping to train gun crews. Seafaring tradition allowed the gunner to sail with his wife, whose job aboard was to look after the younger midshipmen.

This officer wears the typical bicorne and revolutionary cockade. He carries a linstock – a stick with some lighted match cord impregnated with powder to make it burn slowly, wrapped around the end.

To fire the cannon, the officer blew on the lighted end to make it glow and thrust it into the touch hole on the barrel. Given the amount of loose gunpowder around, this was highly dangerous. It was replaced in the British Royal Navy with a flintlock firing mechanism.

in the conflict. These events left the British fleet badly outnumbered and the French greatly emboldened. The first tangible result was an attempted French invasion of Ireland – the disaffected and rebellious 'back door' to England – in December 1796. The French plan was to land 13,000 troops at Bantry Bay, with 17 ships of the line and 19 other warships protecting the transports at sea. The plan was ill-conceived, especially in its timing. The French fleet was scattered by December storms and poor weather prevented a landing in southern Ireland. Five French vessels were lost to the storms and the Royal Navy managed to captured another six of the storm-scattered survivors.

The failed invasion of Ireland may have encouraged Spain and France to combine their main fleets, the better to support a planned allied invasion of Britain. Early in 1797, the Spanish Admiral Don José de Córdoba duly set out from Cadiz with a fleet of 27 ships of the line, intending to join the French at Brest. A British fleet under the command of Admiral Sir John Jervis intercepted them off Cape St Vincent on 14 February. Despite being badly outnumbered (Jervis commanded only 15 ships of the line to Cordoba's 27), the British attacked.

Jervis's battle plan was simple although, as in the Glorious First of June, it was more ambitious than the previous generation's naval engagements: the British, in a single line ahead, pierced the Spanish line between its two divisions, intending to engage each division in turn. Jervis led the attack on the lee division. Instead of turning to assist their comrades, the ships of the Spanish weather division tried to escape behind the attacking British ships. They might have succeeded had Jervis's protégé, Commodore Horatio Nelson,

> *'Firstly you must always implicitly obey orders, without attempting to form any opinion of your own regarding their propriety. Secondly, you must consider every man your enemy who speaks ill of your king; and thirdly you must hate a Frenchman as you hate the devil.'*
>
> — HORATIO NELSON

not taken the initiative, tacking his ship *Captain* into the path of the advancing Spanish line; Nelson's friend Captain Collingwood followed close behind in the *Excellent*. Since Jervis had not signalled for his captains to act on their own initiative, Nelson's actions could have constituted a serious disciplinary offence. Fortunately, his gamble paid off. The Spaniards had to alter course, giving time for the rest of the British fleet to engage in a general mêlée.

Again, the British gun crews proved that they could fire more rapidly and accurately than their enemies. The Spanish ships were heavily armed – the *Santissima Trinidad* alone brought more than 130 guns into battle – but the speed of the British vessels compensated for the weight of Spanish firepower. Nor should the value of inspired leadership be underestimated. The decisive moment at Cape St Vincent came when Nelson took the initiative. And he then compounded his achievement by boarding and taking two Spanish ships of the line – Nelson's crew first boarded the 74-gun *San Nicolas* before crossing over her deck to board the 112-gun *San Josef*. This astonishing feat – hailed as 'Nelson's bridge' – has never been repeated in naval history.

The Battle of Cape St Vincent ended with the Spanish fleet driven back into Cadiz, having suffered heavy casualties and lost four of its ships to the British. On the whole, it was a much more important victory than the Glorious First of June, and Jervis was rewarded with an earldom, taking St Vincent as his title. The first Earl of St Vincent went on to serve as a superlative leader of the British Admiralty.

His unrelenting quest for naval efficiency did not prevent him from acting with deep humanity, working for the decent treatment of seamen and

Battle of Glorious First of June

1794

Howe, the British admiral, caught up with the French ships on the morning of 1 June. His plan was bold: to send his ships to pierce the French line individually and break through to their leeward, cutting off the French line of retreat. This would allow him to either scatter of destroy the French ships in a piecemeal fashion. However, he only partially succeeded – most of his captains misunderstood or ignored his signals. Howe's flagship, *Queen Charlotte*, and five other British vessels pierced the French line in a ragged attack, saved from serious damage by poor French gunnery. The battle became a confused mêlée, as ships engaged in individual duels. After some fierce exchanges, the French finally broke away, leaving seven captured and sunk ships behind. However, the British fleet was too badly damaged to pursue.

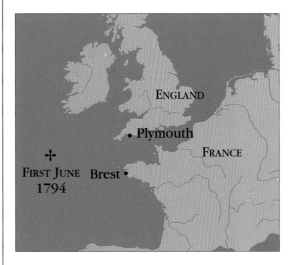

Admiral Howe chased the French Brest fleet into the open Atlantic, where it had been ordered to protect a grain convoy from America.

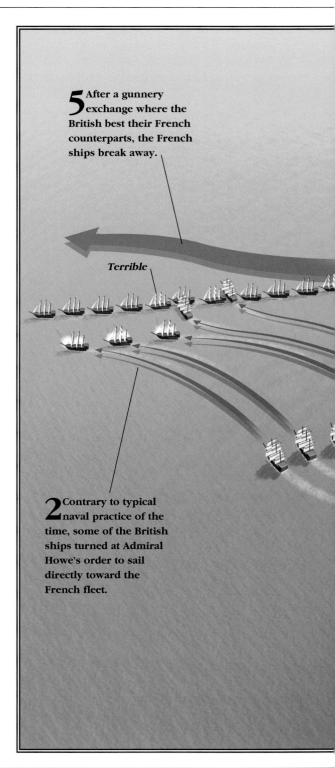

5 After a gunnery exchange where the British best their French counterparts, the French ships break away.

Terrible

2 Contrary to typical naval practice of the time, some of the British ships turned at Admiral Howe's order to sail directly toward the French fleet.

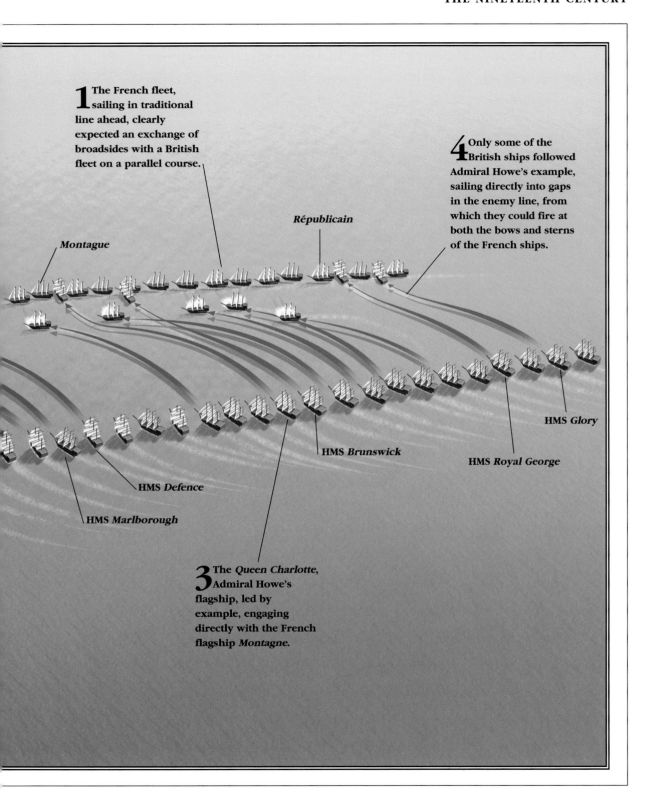

1 The French fleet, sailing in traditional line ahead, clearly expected an exchange of broadsides with a British fleet on a parallel course.

4 Only some of the British ships followed Admiral Howe's example, sailing directly into gaps in the enemy line, from which they could fire at both the bows and sterns of the French ships.

Montague

Républicain

HMS Glory

HMS Royal George

HMS Brunswick

HMS Defence

HMS Marlborough

3 The *Queen Charlotte*, Admiral Howe's flagship, led by example, engaging directly with the French flagship *Montagne*.

instituting health measures, including the supply of lime juice on board ship to prevent scurvy.

Blockade

In its wars with France, Britain's primary naval weapon was the blockade. British fleets were stationed year in and year out, guarding French, Dutch and Spanish harbours in a largely successful effort to strangle the French empire economically and to keep the Allied navies from taking to the sea. Blockade service was extremely wearing, both to ships and men, but provided constant training and must have caused great frustration to members of the French Navy, who knew that they would be set upon piecemeal if they tried to leave their harbours.

The third major sea battle of the 1790s developed out of this blockade. The Netherlands had been forced into alliance with France in 1795. The British responded to the new threat with a blockade; Admiral Sir Adam Duncan kept the

Dutch fleet shut up in harbour for two years, preventing it from setting out on a second planned invasion of Ireland.

In fact, the Dutch missed an opportunity to break out in 1797, during the great Nore and Spithead mutinies. Over 50,000 men aboard 113 ships of the British Channel fleet refused to obey orders, demanding improvements in pay and conditions. The conditions aboard the blockading squadrons could indeed be appalling, with poor and often spoiled food, delays in pay, and a fair leavening of unwilling sailors who had been taken and forced to serve by press gangs. Although regulations limited the amount of punishment a captain could mete out aboard, such rules were often ignored and a 'spit and polish' commander could make life hell for his sailors. The most notorious case was the mutiny on board HMS *Hermione* in 1797, when the crew killed their tyrannical captain Hugh Pigot and nine other officers before sailing their ship to Spain. The crews at Nore and Spithead did not take things so far. In fact, Admiral Duncan's reputation helped to settle the Spithead mutiny peacefully, while at Nore 36 ringleaders were hanged.

Fortunately for Britain, the Dutch were unaware that, for several weeks during the mutiny, only four British ships had been present to maintain the blockade. The British seamen

A DANISH GUNBOAT, 1801.
Gunboats were small oared craft that mounted one or two large guns, in the bow and stern. They were usually employed to protect harbors.

returned to duty in September, but Admiral Duncan soon had to withdraw from the blockade to refit. This time, the Dutch seized the opportunity to break out. As soon as the news of the Dutch departure reached England, however, Duncan set sail back to the Netherlands.

It was nearly sunset when the two fleets sighted one another off Camperdown on the Dutch coast on 11 October 1797. Duncan ordered an immediate engagement. Instead of ordering a line of battle, he set the ships under his command against the enemy in two rough columns. Both columns broke through the Dutch line and the superior British firepower once again did its work, this time engaging at close quarters. The two sides were fairly evenly matched, the British fleet having 14 ships of the line compared to 11 Dutch ships of the line, although the Dutch force did include more frigates. Nonetheless, Duncan managed to capture nine Dutch ships, including the flagship of Admiral De Winter.

Two points make this battle stand out in the history of naval warfare. The first is how rapidly and efficiently the British commanders carried out their admiral's order. Not only had the systems of signalling improved rapidly in the British fleets, but the captains were clearly subordinated and the crews sufficiently disciplined to undertake the risky manoeuvre successfully. The second point is the ever-increasing superiority in British gunnery, which was already clear by 1797. The more time that British crews spent at sea, the more their ship-handling and gunnery improved. Spanish, Dutch and French crews, however, were for the most part stuck in their harbours, and fell further and further behind the British standard.

For years, the Royal Navy blockaded the force that Napoleon had assembled for a great invasion of England, keeping the French ships bottled up in a few well-defended harbours around Boulogne, as well as blockading Brest and Toulon. During that time, the British not only kept the French from putting out to sea; they tried everything in their power to destroy French ships in their harbours. Some of the most gallant actions of the Napoleonic Wars were 'cutting-out' expeditions, when British sailors and marines rowed quietly into French harbours at night to board an enemy ship and steal her away. A classic example was the capture of the French corvette *La Chevrette* from Camaret Bay in 1801 from underneath the noses of the French and Spanish fleets. The British Admiralty even pioneered new weapons to attack the enemy ships at Boulogne, most notably Robert Fulton's floating mines and William Congreve's terrifying but erratic rockets. Increasingly, British admirals also attempted to lure the French out to sea. The most notable efforts to lure out the French fleet were made by Admiral Nelson.

The Nelson Touch

Horatio Nelson, a clergyman's son, began his naval career at the age of 12 as a midshipman; most naval officers of the period enjoyed a similar education at sea. Nelson was exceptional, however, in his ability to win the deep affection of subordinates, equals and superior officers alike – and perhaps most of all, of the British public. Nelson's promotion to rear admiral came shortly after the Battle of Cape St Vincent, where his dashing and innovative tactics had won him great admiration.

In 1797, Nelson attempted an amphibious assault on Tenerife; the operation not only failed but also cost him his right arm. The British public refused to blame him for the failure, however, and as soon as he had recovered Nelson returned to sea at the head of a squadron watching the French fleet at Toulon. The French planned an invasion of Egypt, intending to strike an economic blow against British shipping. As soon as a gale blew Nelson off his station, the French fleet sailed. Nelson set out in pursuit. Although he failed to intercept the invasion fleet in open water, he found the French ships anchored in Aboukir Bay at the mouth of the Nile late in the afternoon of 1 August 1798.

The ensuing Battle of the Nile displayed British seamanship, and Nelson's particular brilliance, better than any other engagement of the French-British wars. The French admiral, François Brueys, had placed his 13 ships of the line in what seemed to be an unassailable position. They were anchored in line, parallel to a line of shoals and further protected by gunboats and shore batteries. From that position, the French would be able to hurl an overwhelming artillery barrage if Nelson sailed by in line (the only obvious means of attack) with his 14 ships of the line.

The captain of HMS *Goliath* noted that the French were at single anchor and realized that there must be some open water between them and the shoals. Taking an enormous risk, *Goliath* moved around the head of the French line and into the shallow inshore waters, followed by several other ships. One ship, the *Culloden*, did in fact ground on the shoals, but the others began firing at the enemy. The French fleet was now caught between two fires, completely unable to manoeuvre. The British double line moved deliberately from ship to ship, with devastating results. The first three French ships in the line were demolished. The 120-gun *Orient* was powerful enough to beat off her attackers; unfortunately, some paint buckets on deck caught fire and the flames spread to the ship's magazine, causing her to blow up.

THE BATTLE OF COPENHAGEN, *2 April 1801, at which a British squadron under the command of Admiral Horatio Nelson destroyed the Danish fleet.*

OPPOSITE: ONE OF MANY *paintings of Admiral Horatio Nelson (1758–1805), Britain's most dashing and successful naval commander during the Napoleonic Wars. He enjoyed immense popularity, despite the irregularity of his personal life.*

By midnight, when the fighting ground to a halt from sheer exhaustion, all but three of the French ships of the line had surrendered. In the morning, two of the three ships escaped, while one ran aground. A total of nine French ships were taken, while two were destroyed, and Napoleon was stranded in Egypt. Nelson credited his success at Aboukir Bay to his captains, his 'band of brothers'. Certainly Nelson displayed here and elsewhere the crucial ability to lead his men while also allowing his officers freedom of initiative based on deep mutual understanding.

The Battle of Copenhagen 1801: Subduing the Northern Threat

In 1801, several northern European states, including Russia and Denmark, formed a coalition, the anti-British League of Armed Neutrality. Threatened by this initiative, the British

THIS PAINTING *of the Battle of Trafalgar (1805) shows clearly the immense destructive power of naval guns; the British ship to the right has reduced its French counterpart to a hulk.*

government sent Admiral Sir Hyde Parker to break it up, with Nelson as his second in command. The means they chose to carry out their mission was an attack on the Danish fleet in Copenhagen Harbour on 2 April 1801.

The great artillery contest that followed showed another face of naval warfare. Although ships of the line and frigates carried heavy armament, vessels did not typically attempt attacks where they were in close range of shore batteries. The batteries' plunging fire and heavy shot could pierce even the strongest vessel. Many fortresses were equipped with furnaces in which they could bring the shot to red-hot temperatures before

firing, setting enemy ships ablaze. Yet in the Battle of Copenhagen, Nelson led an assault against ships, fortresses and floating batteries.

Nelson had at his command 10 ships of the line and 31 smaller vessels. His plan was to attack a weak point he had spotted in the Danish defence, a key channel that did not have a fortress to guard it. Exploiting that weakness, Nelson was able to bring up mortar boats to a range at which they could bomb the city of Copenhagen itself. The British ships soon attracted very heavy fire from the Danish fleet. Seeing the stiff resistance, Admiral Parker signalled for Nelson to disengage. Nelson blithely disregarded the signal flags and proceeded with his business; legend relates that he held his telescope up to his blind eye saying, 'I really cannot see a signal'.

In the event, Nelson's bold move proved justified. In a three-hour gun fight, Nelson's force took 17 Danish ships of various classes, after which the Danish prince regent agreed to a truce. The battle was very costly, however. More than 2000 men died in the attack, with losses nearly equal between the two forces. Denmark withdrew from the League, but the British aggression was bitterly resented and Danish shipyards continued to build ships for France. A British fleet returned to Copenhagen in 1807, even though Denmark was a neutral state, bombarding it into submission. On that occasion, the British force burned all the Danish ships that they could not take. The outraged Danes responded with a guerrilla war against British shipping in the Baltic, which lasted from 1807 to 1814.

The Battle of Trafalgar: Nelson's Final Victory

In 1805, Napoleon prepared for yet another invasion of Britain. The French and Spanish fleets were still blockaded in their harbours, and the French Admiral Pierre-Charles Villeneuve was given the task of luring the British ships away so

that the transports of the invasion fleet could put to sea. For his part, Nelson maintained a distant blockade, hoping to lure the French out to fight.

The French fleet at Toulon put to sea on 30 March 1805, evading Nelson's blockading fleet. After freeing a Spanish squadron at Cadiz, they set off to the West Indies, with Nelson following close behind. The Allied invasion fleet did not put to sea, however, because of other contingents of the Royal Navy that were still on patrol in the Channel. The Allied fleet returned to Europe in July, fighting a British fleet under Admiral Sir Robert Calder off Cape Finisterre. The battle was not decisive; although the Spanish squadron took heavy damage, the rest of the Allied fleet escaped. Villeneuve reached Cadiz on 13 August 1805 and once again Nelson established a loose blockade. In terms of the overall naval situation, nothing had really changed.

In mid-September, Napoleon ordered his combined fleet to southern Italy. It was an ill-advised move since many of the Spanish crews were untrained, sickness was rife in the fleet and bad weather was on the way. Villeneuve was well

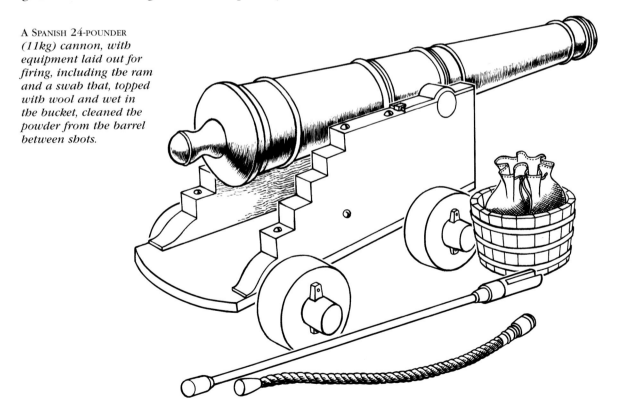

A Spanish 24-pounder (11kg) cannon, with equipment laid out for firing, including the ram and a swab that, topped with wool and wet in the bucket, cleaned the powder from the barrel between shots.

Battle of Copenhagen
1801

Admiral Sir Hyde Parker sent his second-in-command, Horatio Nelson, into Copenhagen harbour with 12 ships of the line that had relatively shallow draughts along with the smaller vessels in the fleet. Three British ships grounded while entering the harbour, but the remaining vessels anchored about 180m (200yd) from the Danish ships and batteries, where the two sides proceeded to fire broadsides at each other until each ship was disabled. In light of the heavy Danish resistance, Parker signaled a retreat, which Nelson disregarded. As superior gunnery disabled the Danish ships, British bomb ketches were able to approach the city. The battle ended when the Danes accepted an offer of truce. Copenhagen is often considered to be Nelson's hardest fought battle, surpassing even the intensive fighting at Trafalgar.

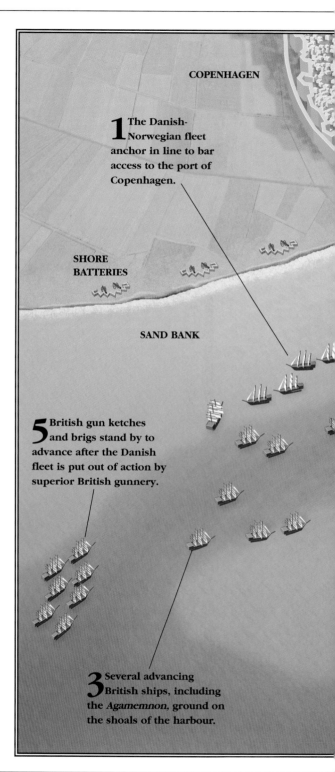

COPENHAGEN

1 The Danish-Norwegian fleet anchor in line to bar access to the port of Copenhagen.

SHORE BATTERIES

SAND BANK

5 British gun ketches and brigs stand by to advance after the Danish fleet is put out of action by superior British gunnery.

3 Several advancing British ships, including the *Agamemnon*, ground on the shoals of the harbour.

North Sea

DENMARK

✝ COPENHAGEN

ENGLAND

The result of failed diplomacy in Britain's attempt to break up the pro-French trading block of the League of Armed Neutrality, the battle of Copenhagen was an attack on the harbour of the capital of Denmark.

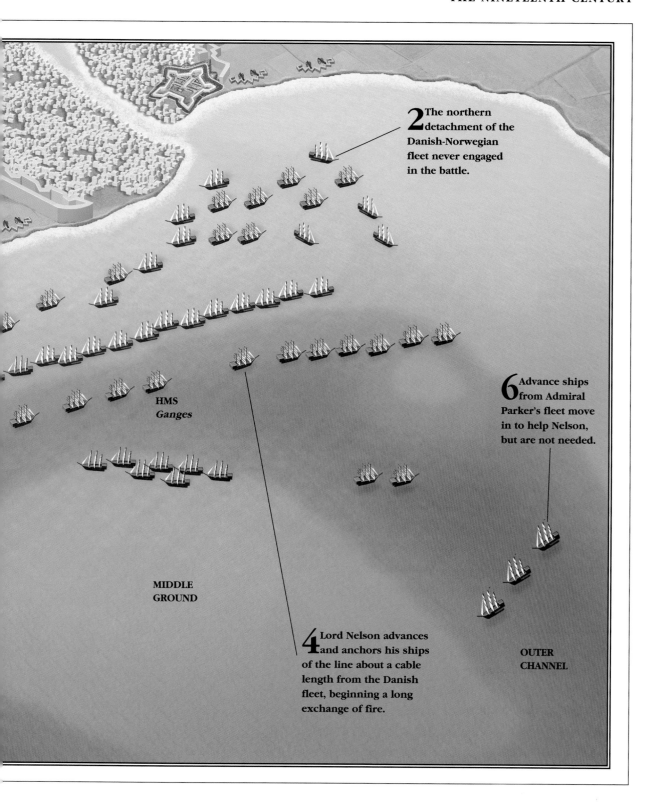

2 The northern detachment of the Danish-Norwegian fleet never engaged in the battle.

HMS *Ganges*

6 Advance ships from Admiral Parker's fleet move in to help Nelson, but are not needed.

MIDDLE GROUND

4 Lord Nelson advances and anchors his ships of the line about a cable length from the Danish fleet, beginning a long exchange of fire.

OUTER CHANNEL

aware of these dangers and gave the order to sail only because Napoleon had accused him of cowardice after his defeat at the Battle of the Nile. When the combined fleet broke out of Cadiz, Nelson was ready. The two fleets met off Cape Trafalgar on 21 October 1805, in what proved to be the last great fleet action of the age of sail.

The French admiral was doubtless taken aback by the speed at which the scattered British fleet received word that he was on the loose. In fact, Nelson had set up a relay of three ships between Cadiz and his own flagship 65km (40 miles) away. Using a system of 'distant signals' – balls, cones and other geometric shapes that could be made out from a much greater distance than flags – news of the fleet's departure from Cadiz reached Nelson in less than 10 minutes. Signals would not play a major role in the battle itself – other than Nelson's signal to his fleet before battle, 'England expects every man will do his duty'. The admiral had invited his captains to dinner the day before the action and talked his plan through with them, rather than relying on signals in the smoke and confusion of combat.

Thanks to their recent voyage to the West Indies, the Franco-Spanish fleet was probably better trained and prepared for battle than had been the case at Cape St Vincent, Camperdown or even the Nile. Nonetheless, Villeneuve did not want a decisive battle – or, indeed, any battle at all. As was usual in the Franco-British Wars, the French fleet accepted the leeward position when conflict became inevitable; their aim was to escape, rather than to bring the British to battle.

Battle is joined

On the morning of 21 October, Nelson's 27 ships of the line met their 33 counterparts of the Franco-Spanish fleet. Villeneuve placed his ships in line ahead, where the full weight of their broadsides could be brought to bear on the enemy. Nelson for his part had no intention of taking part in a traditional broadside-to-broadside artillery match. Instead, he divided the ships under his command into two columns, taking advantage of their windward position to sail towards the enemy. The first column, led by Admiral Collingwood in *Royal Sovereign*, was set to destroy the rear of the allied line. Nelson's flagship *Victory*, leading the second column, aimed to keep the Allied van occupied. Once again, the British fleet would sail directly

THIS CUT-AWAY SECTION *of the powerful British three-decker, HMS* Victory, *gives a sense of the complexity of a ship of the line, with three gun decks that were completely cleared before action.*

into the concentrated fire of the enemy line, which made it certain that at least the leaders of the columns would be badly cut up or even disabled. But Nelson surely counted on poorly trained French and Spanish crews and the heavy swell to keep British damage to a tolerable level.

At close quarters, Nelson's *Victory* engaged the French flagship *Bucentaure*, raking her with double-loaded guns that cleared her gundecks. As the *Victory* continued on its pass through the French line, the 74-gun *Redoutable* blocked her way. *Victory* ran into *Redoutable*, and the momentum opened the allied line for the ships under Nelson's command to follow. *Victory* suffered badly in the process.

The *Redoutable*'s marksmen, placed in the tops to fire on the enemy deck, were devastatingly effective at such close range. Admiral Nelson was among those who fell; a bullet pierced his lung before embedding itself in his spine. *Redoutable*'s crew might have been able to board the *Victory* in the confusion had not the HMS *Temeraire* (a ship previously captured from the French) come alongside her and killed many of *Redoutable*'s crew with a broadside.

As Nelson lay dying, his fleet carried on a five-hour mêlée. The British seamen proved more able to bring their ships within range of the enemy than the enemy's ships were to get away. British guns fired at around twice the rate of their French and Spanish counterparts. By the time Nelson died, he knew that he had won a great victory. By the end of the battle, 19 French and Spanish ships had been taken and one had blown up; no British vessels were lost. Even more effective proof of British artillery supremacy was that at least 5000 men of the Allied fleet were killed, compared to a mere 250 killed and 1200 wounded among the British ships.

Although most of the British prizes were lost in a storm that came up the same evening, the Battle of Trafalgar had effectively destroyed France as a major naval power. Napoleon continued to build ships in large numbers, especially between 1807 and 1812. But the program was ill-conceived. The French could not find enough sailors and the French ships, built too quickly, sometimes rotted before they were launched. The French were

The battle lines for Trafalgar are set out below. Ships are listed in the order in which they sailed on the day of the battle:

Nelson's Weather (left-hand) Column:

Victory (100 guns)	*Temeraire* (98)
Neptune (98)	*Leviathan* (74)
Britannia (100)	*Conqueror* (74)
Africa (64)	*Agamemnon* (64)
Ajax (74)	*Orion* (74)
Minotaur (74)	*Spartiate* (74)

Vice-Admiral Collingwood's Leeward Column:

Royal Sovereign (100)	*Belleisle* (74)
Mars (74)	*Tonnant* (80)
Bellerophon (74)	*Colossus* (74)
Achilles (74)	*Dreadnought* (98)
Polyphemus (64)	*Revenge* (74)
Swiftsure (74)	*Defiance* (74)
Thunderer (74)	*Defence* (74)
Prince (98)	

plus four frigates and two smaller boats.

Villeneuve's fleet:

Neptuno (80 guns)	*Scipion* (74)
Rayo (100)	*Formidable* (80)
Duguay Trouin (74)	*San Francisco de Asis* (74)
Mont Blanc (74)	*San Agustin* (74)
Héros (74)	*Santisima Trinidad* (136)
Bucentaure (80)	*Neptune* (84)
San Leandro (64)	*Redoutable* (74)
Intrépide (74)	*San Justo* (74)
Indomptable (80)	*Santa Ana* (112)
Fougueux (74)	*Monarca* (74)
Pluton (74)	*Algesiras* (74)
Bahama (74)	*Aigle* (74)
Swiftsure (74)	*Argonaute* (74)
Montanez (74)	*Argonauta* (80)
Berwick (74)	*Achille* (74)
San Ildefonso (74)	
Principe de Asturias (112)	
San Juan Nepomuceno (74)	

plus five frigates and two smaller boats.

Battle of Trafalgar
1805

The combined Franco-Spanish fleet of 33 ships of the line formed in line ahead, so that they could offer full broadsides to the British as they advanced. The British commander, Lord Horatio Nelson, responded with a bold plan: he divided his force into two columns, led by himself and by Vice-Admiral Cuthbert Collingwood, and led them to break the enemy line at two points. The result was a general mêlée as individual British and enemy ships engaged. In time, though, enough British ships managed to pass through the enemy line and reform leeward that the British could attack several French and Spanish vessels from both sides simultaneously, which helps to explain how the British could take or sink 22 enemy vessels while losing no ships themselves. Eleven French and Spanish ships made it back to Cadiz, but the French fleet was destroyed as an effective fighting force.

The Battle of Trafalgar was fought in the open Atlantic, off Cape Trafalgar in southwestern Spain, not far from the port of Cadiz.

2 Nelson sends several of his ships against the Franco-Spanish van in a feint to disguise his true battle plan.

4 The British leeward column, under the command of Cuthbert Collingwood in *Royal Sovereign*, move to cut off the rear of the Franco-Spanish fleet.

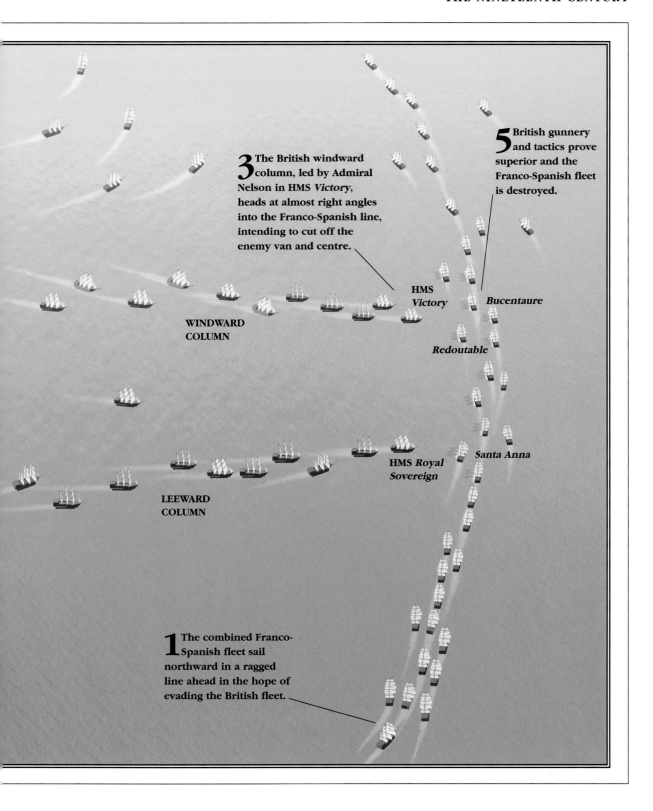

3 The British windward column, led by Admiral Nelson in HMS *Victory*, heads at almost right angles into the Franco-Spanish line, intending to cut off the enemy van and centre.

5 British gunnery and tactics prove superior and the Franco-Spanish fleet is destroyed.

HMS *Victory*

Bucentaure

WINDWARD COLUMN

Redoutable

Santa Anna

HMS *Royal Sovereign*

LEEWARD COLUMN

1 The combined Franco-Spanish fleet sail northward in a ragged line ahead in the hope of evading the British fleet.

unable to mount another large-scale naval action during the war.

Frigates and the War of 1812

The latter stages of the Napoleonic Wars saw Britain also engaged in an unfortunate struggle with the United States. The conflict was in large part provoked by British naval policy. The British government interdicted American trade with France, and compounded economic injury with national affront by stopping US shipping to search for Royal Navy deserters and to conscript supposedly English-born seamen. By 1812, Britain had seized about 400 American merchant vessels. The greatest resentment resulted from the infamous Chesapeake Affair of 1807, when the

British frigate *Leopard* stopped the USS *Chesapeake*, demanding that deserters be handed over. When her captain refused, *Leopard* opened fire on the unprepared vessel. The War of 1812 (which actually lasted 1812–15) would have been completely mismatched had Britain had not been so entangled in the war with France. In 1812, Britain possessed 100 ships of the line, 700 other ships, and 145,000 men in her navy. The United States confronted this force with six frigates, authorized by Congress in 1794 after Algeria seized some US shipping.

The frigate, a ship design developed in the mid-1750s, was a single-decked, three-masted warship comparable to later cruisers. It carried anything between 24 and 44 guns of various sizes. It was

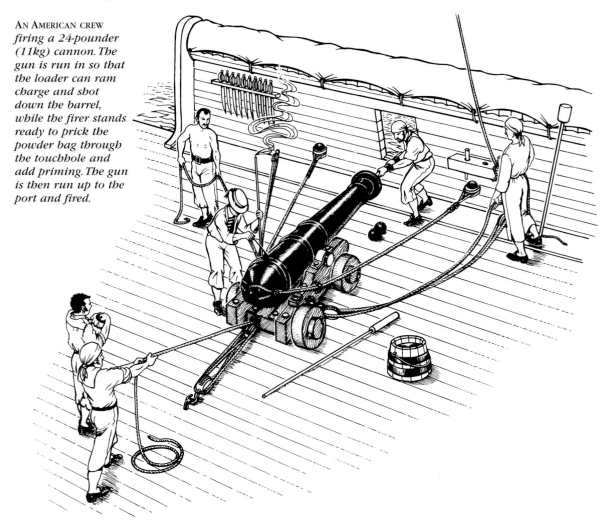

AN AMERICAN CREW *firing a 24-pounder (11kg) cannon. The gun is run in so that the loader can ram charge and shot down the barrel, while the firer stands ready to prick the powder bag through the touchhole and add priming. The gun is then run up to the port and fired.*

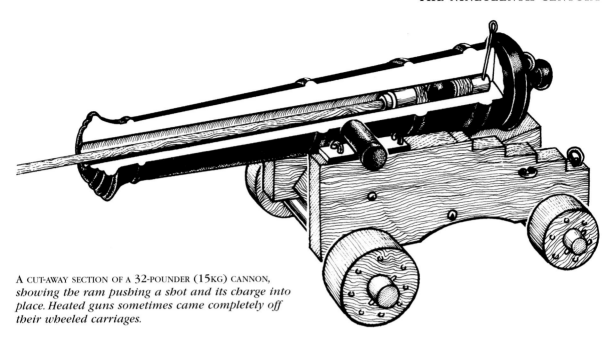

A CUT-AWAY SECTION OF A 32-POUNDER (15KG) CANNON, *showing the ram pushing a shot and its charge into place. Heated guns sometimes came completely off their wheeled carriages.*

fast and strong, intended for scouting and war against enemy trade. This is exactly what the Americans intended – seizure of British shipping. Britain responded by sending a few frigates to patrol and protect their interests in North American waters. The subsequent conflict resulted in some of the most interesting naval engagements of the early nineteenth century.

British Gunnery

British frigates had already been in a number of brushes with their European enemies, where they had shown the same strengths as British ships of the line: good discipline and a high standard of gunnery. For example, on 20 October 1793, Captain James Saumarez, commanding HMS *Crescent,* engaged in a duel with the French frigate *Réunion.* By the end of the engagement, 81 Frenchmen lay dead and wounded, while the only English injury was a crewman hit by the recoil of his own gun. Similarly, the First Battle of Lissa, a frigate action of 13 March 1811 during which four British frigates defeated a Franco-Italian frigate squadron nearly twice as large, showed the superiority of British gunnery.

By American standards, however, British naval artillery was less impressive. The training of gun crews was left to individual captains, who spent their own money on extra powder and shot; many captains preferred very close engagements where every shot would count, no matter how badly aimed or slowly fired. And the Royal Navy was used to dealing with enemies who had little experience shooting their guns on the open sea. In the US frigates, however, they faced volunteer seamen who were well trained and well paid, with plenty of sea experience. The US frigates were also the strongest and most heavily-built in their class. The most impressive of them all, USS *Constitution,* was 62m (204ft) long and displaced 2200 gross tons. She carried 44 guns, including the 24-pounder (11kg) cannons that were too heavy for most British frigates.

USS *Constitution* won her first encounter, against HMS *Guerrière.* The British frigate carried 18-pounder (8kg) guns, compared to *Constitution*'s 24-pounders (11kg) guns, and the American crew was considerably larger. Most of the British shot could not even penetrate *Constitution*'s hull, winning her the nickname 'Old Ironsides'. Even more impressive was *Constitution*'s victory over the HMS *Java* in December 1812, a ferocious duel in which the *Constitution*'s greater broadside weight and accurate gunnery proved too much for the smaller ship. Nonetheless, *Java* put up a tremendous fight,

surrendering only when 122 of her crewman lay dead or wounded. In the meantime, USS *United States* had captured HMS *Macedonian* after a long gunfight. These losses caused consternation in Britain. Although many of her strongest frigates were in the Mediterranean and the Channel, the most important lesson was that the Royal Navy should not feel complacent in her role as the natural master of the sea.

The balance was redressed when the frigate HMS *Shannon* met the USS *Chesapeake* in June 1813. The British captain Philip Broke had brought the *Shannon* to a very high level of efficiency during a long commission, paying special attention to gunnery training. By contrast, the *Chesapeake* was sailing with an untrained crew. In a fight that lasted only 11 minutes, *Shannon* swept the *Chesapeake*'s deck with two well-aimed broadsides and boarded. It was a bloody action, with 95 sailors killed on both sides and 128 wounded. The action was such a singular example of the damage a well-trained gun crew could do that the British Admiralty began to imitate Captain Broke in a regular system of training and introduced sights to help crews fix the enemy's position in the thick clouds of battle.

The United States and British navies also engaged in amphibious operations that demonstrated another side to the naval warfare of the period. Both navies built ships to fight on the Great Lakes along the border between British Canada and the United States. The US squadron on Lake Erie won a slogging match there in September 1813. Similarly, at the Battle of Lake Champlain on 11 September 1814, a British squadron failed to drive off the American ships, forcing British land troops to withdraw.

The British also bombarded several ports; the bombardment of Baltimore in 1814 was subsequently immortalized in the US National Anthem. Most notoriously, British Admiral Sir George Cockburn landed troops and sailors to destroy the military stores stockpiled at

THE SECOND BATTLE OF NAVARINO, *as painted by the Russian artist Ivan Aivozovsky in 1846. Such dramatic battle scenes were very popular throughout most of the nineteenth century.*

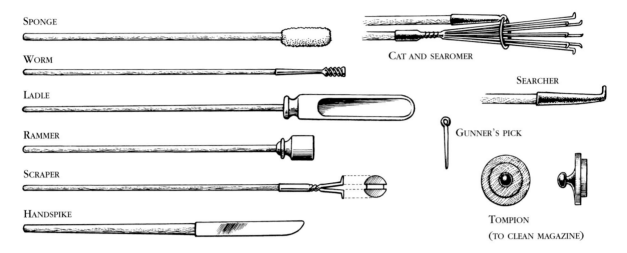

SPONGE

WORM

LADLE

RAMMER

SCRAPER

HANDSPIKE

CAT AND SEAROMER

SEARCHER

GUNNER'S PICK

TOMPION
(TO CLEAN MAGAZINE)

THE NECESSARY EQUIPMENT *for a ship gun. The worm was used to remove a charge from the gun; the crew aimed the gun by heaving it with the handspike.*

Washington. During the operation, they partially burned the building that came to be known as the 'White House' – after it was whitewashed to cover the scorch marks.

Rule Britannia

By the end of the Napoleonic Wars and the War of 1812, British supremacy at sea was assured. Over 22 years of war, Britain had lost only 5 ships of the line and 16 frigates, while her enemies had lost 92 line of battle ships and 172 frigates. Other fleets existed; for example, a Russian fleet under Admiral Senyavin destroyed the Turkish fleet off Lemnos in 1807. But no fleet could compare to the Royal Navy. Indeed, for a century following 1817, Britain held to the 'Two Power Standard' – that the Royal Navy should equal the combined strength of the next two world naval powers. Britain constructed a new battle fleet between 1815 and 1830, maintaining its size at a total of 250,000 gross tons displacement. France ran a distant second, with 84,000 gross tons in 1840. The Russian fleet had vessels amounting to 160,000 gross tons in 1840, but her ships were badly built and old-fashioned.

Britain applied some new lessons while rebuilding her fleet. The period after the conclusion of the Napoleonic Wars saw a shift to fewer, heavier guns, made possible because of a

major advance in the diagonal bracing of ships. The idea of Robert Seppings, it enabled ships to carry the greater weight. The early nineteenth century also saw an increasing standardization of armament, for example making all lower-deck guns 32-pounders (15kg), with all 12-pounders (5kg) on the upper deck; the change made for less confusion between different calibres of shot in battle. The War of 1812 also turned informed opinion against carronades, those heavy but short-ranged guns.

In a frigate action in 1814, HMS *Phoebe* and *Cherub* worked together to defeat USS *Essex* by slamming her with their long guns at a range at which *Essex*'s carronades could not respond. Carronades had also worked to British disadvantage in the Battle of Lake Erie. What won battles was firepower, as was demonstrated vividly at the Battle of Navarino in October 1827, when a combined British, French and Russian fleet under Admiral Sir Edward Codrington practically annihilated a Turkish-Egyptian fleet in a battle that effectively won Greek independence from Turkey.

The Steam Revolution

With the advent of the Industrial Revolution, it was inevitable that attempts would be made to operate ships using the new marvel of the age, steam power. James Watt patented a steam engine in 1769, and by 1807 Robert Fulton had created the first commercially successful steamboat, the *Clermont*. By 1815, he had constructed a steam vessel of 38 gross tons, with a central paddle wheel for the US Navy, which was named the *Fulton* after his death.

Yet most navies resisted the introduction of steam warships, and for good reason. A vessel like the *Fulton* could be useful for harbour defence, since it was able to manoeuvre against wind and tide with its 120 horsepower engine and top speed of 5.5 knots. But a steamship was dependent on a regular supply of coal, and early steam engines burned fuel extravagantly. The paddle wheel would be the weakest point of the warship should it come under attack; although the *Fulton*'s paddle wheel was protected within a double hull, it is probably fortunate that she was never employed in war. In fact, no paddle warship ever fought in a major battle, although a few were eventually constructed. Steam engines were heavy, requiring a particularly strong ship to carry one safely. Early steam engines also broke down frequently. Most terrifying of all was the danger of fire, especially onboard a warship with a large powder magazine. Early steam boilers were rather prone to explosions, even without the excuse of enemy fire.

Still, naval policy makers recognized that steam had its uses. Sailing ships cannot sail closer than six compass points (67.5°) into the wind, and for a thousand years naval enterprises had been frustrated when the wind blew in the wrong direction. Steam power could also take ships close in to the shore, making it much easier to carry war up rivers and into harbours. As European navies carried their nations' colonial aspirations around the world, this potential was highly desirable. Nonetheless, up until 1840, most navy steamers were used as dispatch boats or tugs. The Royal Navy ordered its first steamship, the *Comet*, in 1821 for use as a tender and to tow warships out of becalmed harbours. She was followed by paddle warships used to explore African rivers. Steam tugs

even made some appearances in battle. A French squadron bombarded Vera Cruz, Mexico, in November 1838, a feat possible only because steamers towed the warships into position in the harbour, where they could fire explosive shells. Similarly, in the first Opium War (1839–43), British Admiral Sir William Parker used Indian Navy steamships to tow British battleships into Chinese rivers, where they were able to destroy several major forts and land British troops to cut the Grand Canal.

> 'Heart of oak are our ships,
> Heart of oak are our men:
> We always are ready;
> Steady, boys, steady;
> We'll fight, and we'll conquer
> again and again.'
> — *ENGLISH PLAYWRIGHT DAVID GARRICK*

Steam engines became more powerful and reliable over time. In 1836, two inventors, Francis Smith and John Ericsson, independently patented the first screw propellers. Ericsson also constructed the steam sloop USS *Princeton*, launched in 1843, the world's first screw-propeller warship. Use of a screw propeller was both safer and more efficient, as the British Admiralty proved in 1845: fitting out two frigates with steam engines – one powering twin paddle wheels and the other a screw propeller – it then tried the two against each other. In a typical pattern for naval innovation in the period after 1815, it was an aspiring naval power that innovated, hoping the new invention would help offset Britain's naval superiority. But as soon as the British Admiralty had word of the novelty, they adopted it too.

The Royal Navy ordered its first screw-propeller warship in 1843. Britain then surged ahead, creating the first steam-driven battleship (as ships of the line were increasingly called) in 1846, converting the sailing ship HMS *Ajax* to steam power. France then joined the competition, launching a 90-gun steam battleship, the *Napoléon*, in 1851 – the first purpose-built steam battleship. Britain pulled even with *Agamemnon*, launched in 1852. Improvements continued into the 1880s when the turbine, the last major development of the steam engine, was put to use.

'AWFUL EXPLOSION OF THE "PEACE-MAKER" *on board the U.S. Steam Frigate* Princeton,' *an 1844 coloured lithography published by N. Currier, showing the gun explosion that killed seven dignitaries.*

Steam power created a very different strategic situation for the world's navies. Sailing ships had always needed access to some specialized materials to repair damage, but for the most part their only requirement from the land was food and water, which was available from any port. A steam vessel was dependent on coal, and needed secure bases with enormous stockpiles of fuel. Early steamships were extravagant in their needs; the early ironclad HMS *Warrior* burned 3.5 gross tons of coal per hour when cruising at 11 knots. She could carry barely enough coal to get her across the Atlantic. For reasons both of expense and of availability, hybrid ships became the norm in the early steam age. With masts and sails as well as a steam engine, they could adapt to a variety of

circumstances. Smaller warships that relied wholly on steam first appeared in the early 1860s, but the first mastless battleship, HMS *Devastation*, was not launched until 1871. Cruisers and gunboats continued to rely on sails long after battleships had been won over to the new technology, some of them depending mainly on sail as late as the 1890s.

The Explosive Shell

The gunnery developments of the Franco-British wars and the War of 1812 had mostly taken the form of improved training for gun crews, rather than changes to the guns themselves. For some time after 1815, the only significant innovation was the introduction of percussion caps to fire guns, introduced in the 1820s, followed by the creation of a British gunnery school in 1829. Improved designs, including experiments in rifling the bores of ship artillery and attempts to create a breech-loading gun, usually had discouraging results. A fundamental difficulty was that most cannon were made of wrought iron, which tended to have weak spots that could cause the gun to explode under high pressure. A particularly notorious example of an experiment that went wrong was the testing of the 'Peacemaker' gun aboard the US steam sloop *Princeton* in February 1844. The gun was fired successfully several times before it burst, killing eight people, including the Secretary of State and the Secretary of the Navy. After the Peacemaker explosion, the US Navy not only turned against further experimentation, but also ordered that naval guns should be fired with only half charges.

While still using essentially the same gun design, however, the adoption of explosive shells for shipboard use had a massive impact on naval warfare. In the early years of the nineteenth century, it was rare for a ship to be sunk in battle. A ship's great guns most often fired solid shot, which was essentially an anti-personnel rather than anti-ship munition. Even when a shot passed

BOMBARDMENT OF SEVASTAPOL. *The allied bombardment of Sevastopol in the Crimean War, a misguided effort that showed clearly the fragility of wooden ships against shore batteries.*

through the hull of a vessel, it made a clean hole that could usually be plugged. So long as enough of her sails and rigging remained in place to allow for manoeuvre and enough crewmen remained to handle the ship, man the guns and repel borders, a warship's ability to withstand to heavy fire was extraordinary. An extreme example is the British ship *Impregnable*, which more than lived up to her name in an August 1816 attack on Algiers. By the end of the day, she had suffered 233 large shots in her hull, but was still seaworthy enough to reach Gibraltar for repairs.

This all changed with the explosive shell. Shells had long been employed on land but had seen only limited use at sea, generally aboard bomb ketches for shore bombardment. In the 1820s, however, use of shells became more widespread, despite a general feeling among naval personnel that they were barbarous and cowardly. The explosive shell of the 1820s was fired at low velocity, intended to lodge in the side of a ship rather than going through. Once it was in place, the shell would explode, tearing a large, irregular hole that was hard to patch.

Once again, it was a weaker naval power, France, that took the lead developing the new technology, hoping to offset Britain's naval

superiority. Henri Paixhans developed an effective shell-shooting gun, which had the additional advantage of being lightweight since the shells were fired with only a small charge. These shell guns became part of the regular French armament in 1824. Britain responded with experiments, adopting a gun that could provide an 8in (20cm) shell in 1838. These new weapons were inaccurate and unreliable – but they could destroy a wooden ship in minutes.

The Lessons of the Crimea

The Crimean War, fought from 1854 to 1856 between Russia on one side and a British-French-Turkish alliance on the other, drove home the lessons of this new technology. In the Crimean War, ships and their crews were pushed to the limit of what wooden sailing ships could perform, and often beyond. Military technology was

beginning to make them obsolete. The utility of steam and the horror of explosive shells found an international showplace that led to a series of innovations, including the first ironclad ships.

Even before the Crimean War broke out, the Russian Navy demonstrated the military potential of explosive shells in no uncertain terms at the Battle of Sinope in November 1853. European navies had for some time enjoyed a crippling advantage over Ottoman Turkish fleets in terms of ship handling and fire discipline. Sinope moved this naval superiority to a new level. The engagement took place following a storm that forced the Turkish Vice Admiral Osman Pasha, with a squadron of seven frigates, two corvettes and several transports, to take refuge in the Black Sea port of Sinope. Russian Admiral Paul Nakhimov arrived with three line-of-battle ships and several smaller vessels.

Although the Turks were protected by shore batteries, the Russians entered the harbour in heavy mist, a manoeuvre that was possible only because some of the Russian vessels were steam powered. Once there, they opened fire on Osman

THE CONFEDERATE SHIP Stonewall, *an early ironclad that also saw service in the Japanese navy, renamed the* Kotetsu. *Note the combination of smoke stack and rigging.*

Pasha's flotilla. A furious six-hour fight ensued, the Russian ships relying heavily on shells rather than shot. At the end of the day, a single Turkish paddle steamer escaped the carnage. The rest of the Turkish squadron had been sunk, rather than disabled or burned

Although there were no fleet engagements in the Crimean War, the Allied navy played a key role not just in transporting troops, but also in attacking a number of ports. In 1854, the siege of Sevastopol made a mockery of naval aspirations. The British admiral who commanded a large squadron there was not willing to expose his ships to the fire from the major shore batteries; only the French admiral's threat to go in alone led the British to take grudging part. In fact, the technology was not up to the challenge. The French were able to move their heavily armed warships into a position from which they could bombard the shore only by lashing steam tugs to their sides – military planners were beginning to expect ships to be able to move against the wind.

THE USS *CASCO, a civil war ironclad of the Monitor class. The radical new design proved to be unseaworthy, and such vessels were used only for coastal duties.*

Yet, even when the Allied fleet began its bombardment, it did little damage; the naval commanders feared the plunging fire of shells from the batteries and stayed at the extreme range of their own guns. On the first day, Allied ships fired 700 gross tons of shot with little effect. The next day, they tried again, and again failed.

At first, matters were the same in the Baltic. An Anglo-French fleet bombarded the Russian naval base at Kronstadt, but it was able to withstand the onslaught. As had been the case for centuries, wooden ships had little protection against the heavy, often heated shot of shore batteries, not to mention shell. The Russian forts at Kinburn on the mouth of the Dnieper were, however, forced to surrender to Allied assault in October 1855. What turned the tide were the three

French 'floating batteries' – the *Dévastation*, *Lave* and *Tonnante*. These rectangular batteries, with 10cm (4in) of iron plate protecting 43cm (17in) of wood, were dragged into range of the shore batteries. There they set to work destroying the fortresses, suffering hardly any damage themselves in the process. These three vessels were the world's first ironclads.

Ironclads and Iron Ships

The use of plate iron in ship construction was not new in 1855. As early as 1822 a commercial steamship, the *Aaron Manby*, was launched with an iron-plate hull. Design improved rapidly. By 1832, a British merchant ship with an iron hull, the *Alburkah*, was able to complete an ocean voyage; in 1838, Britain also launched the transatlantic liner *Great Britain*. The *Nemesis*, the first iron warship, was put into service for the British East India Company in 1839. *Nemesis* was used with great success in the First China War (1841–43) on the Canton River, where it joined in the bombardment of Whampoa. The Royal Navy went

A CUT-AWAY SECTION *of CSS* Alabama, *a highly successful commerce raider, showing the placement of the steam engine amidships as well as the rigging for sail.*

on to order three shallow-draught iron ships in 1840 for work on the Niger River.

Iron construction had a serious disadvantage when it came to warships, however: iron is brittle and tends to break when hit by shot, unlike wood. As a result, navies were slow to adopt iron or even ironclad vessels (the latter with iron plate protecting a thick wooden hull, in an effort to combine the advantages of both wood and iron). It was the destruction of the Turkish fleet by Russian shells at Sinope in 1853 that renewed interest in providing warships with some sort of armour. When the results of the bombardment of the Kinburn forts by the iron vessels *Dévastation*, *Lave* and *Tonnante* became known, the French Navy again attempted to gain the technological edge over the numerically dominant British Navy. They immediately began converting the French fleet into ironclads by providing a girdle of wrought iron as protection against shells.

The first newly built ironclad was the French *Gloire*, launched in 1859. She was a steam screw frigate, with secondary sails, and was armed with 30 rifled breech-loading guns. What made *Gloire* dangerous, though, was her 11cm (4.5in) thick belt of iron, which ran horizontally the entire length of the ship and vertically from her upper

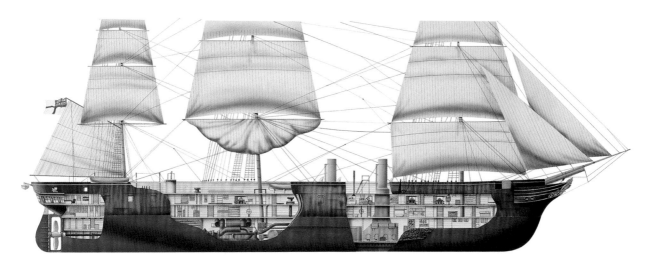

deck to well below the waterline. Britain immediately responded with HMS *Warrior*, which was launched in 1860. The *Warrior* was a distinct improvement over *Gloire*, which tended to roll so heavily that accurate gunnery was nearly impossible.

Warrior, at first classed as a frigate despite displacing 9210 gross tons (it classification was based on the number of guns), was iron-hulled and iron-armoured, with additional armour for guns and machinery. Unlike *Gloire*, *Warrior* was an ocean-going vessel, able to attain more than 14 knots under steam with her 1250 horsepower engine. She could have destroyed any ship afloat at the time of her launch. In the event, she never fired a shot in anger. Technological change came so rapidly that *Warrior* was obsolete by 1883. Clearly the age of the wooden warship had come to an end. By 1861, Britain and France between them had 28 ironclads either in service or under construction. The quest was also underway to find a way to defeat the enemy's ironclads; the French *Magenta* and *Solferino*, both launched in 1861, were the first ironclads built with a bow ram, an astonishing reversion to the tactics of the ancient Greek triremes.

Battle of the Ironclads: The US Civil War

Other navies soon acquired ironclads too. Spain, for example, launched the frigate *Numancia* in 1863. The best evidence for this new technology in action, however, came during the US Civil War of

HMS WARRIOR, *launched in 1860, was the first ocean-going ironclad warship. She was propelled by two powerful steam engines, but had sails that could be employed to save on the extravagant use of coal of early steamships.*

1861–65. At the outbreak of war, the Union enjoyed great naval superiority over the South, having the entire United States fleet of 90 ships and a majority of the commissioned officers. The Confederates did not have a navy at all, although many southern officers opted to stay loyal to their home states. The North also enjoyed overwhelming industrial superiority; the Confederacy had only one factory capable of producing the largest calibre of naval gun and found it very difficult to build steam engines, often taking the engines from civilian vessels instead. Like France after the Napoleonic Wars, the Confederacy attempted to counteract naval superiority with technical innovation, turning especially to the new ironclads.

The Confederate Navy's first attempt was the CSS *Manassas*, a tugboat converted into an ironclad ram. *Manassas* mounted only one gun, a 64-pounder (29kg) smoothbore that fired forwards through a bow peephole. Her primary weapon was her 6m (20ft) ram, attached to a bow of solid timber. *Manassas* was sent, with two armed steamers, in a surprise attack on a Union blockading squadron on the Mississippi in the night of 12 October 1861. She certainly had shock value. As *Manassas* closed, the Union ships fired

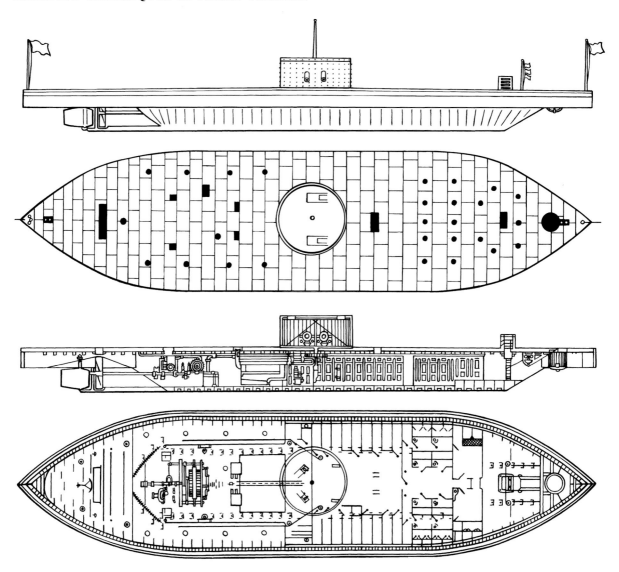

on her, only to find that both shot and shell bounced off her armoured sides. *Manassas* was able to ram the screw sloop *Richmond*, holing her below the waterline. In the process, however, the ram was damaged – clearly this was still an experimental technology. The Confederate squadron then sent fireships against the Union vessels, forcing them to slip anchor and head for the sea to avoid the danger. Two of the Union ships grounded; they were bombarded in the morning and escaped with heavy losses.

Throughout the war, the Confederacy's main naval concerns were to prevent attacks on ports

SEVERAL PLAN VIEWS *of USS* Monitor, *the brainchild of Swedish-American inventor John Ericsson. Her innovative plan rendered her largely impervious to enemy gunfire, although the* Monitor *proved to be sadly unseaworthy.*

and to break up Union blockades. To this end, the Confederate Navy built the ironclad frigate *Virginia*. The ship was constructed over the hulk of the wooden Union steam frigate *Merrimack*, burned to the waterline when Union forces evacuated the naval yard in Gosport, Virginia. The *Virginia* was an innovative ship, the first warship completely without rigging, and with a central

A TRANSVERSE CUT-AWAY *of USS* Monitor, *showing the most radical innovation in her construction—a gun turret that could rotate 360°, doing away with the limited field of fire of the traditional broadside.*

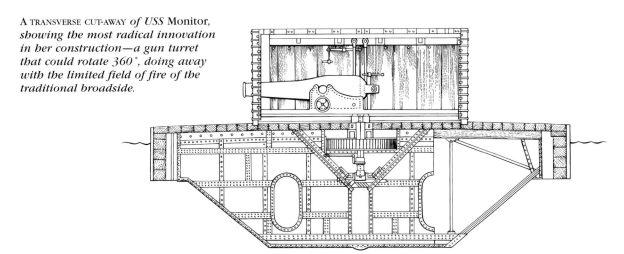

casemated structure built onto her hull. She was equipped with 10 shell guns, six 23cm (9in) Dahlgren smoothbore guns and four Brooke rifled guns. The Confederacy was perennially short of gunpowder, however, and placed their hopes on the *Virginia*'s heavy iron bow ram. Her steering was sluggish and her engines unreliable and inadequate, but her 5cm (2in) thick iron plates rendered her impervious to shot and shell.

In August 1861, when the North got word of the *Virginia*'s construction, an Ironclad Board was appointed to oversee the design and construction of light-draft ironclad vessels for coastal operations. The board ordered three experimental ships. The first to be completed was the *Monitor*, designed by the naturalized Swedish engineer John Ericsson. Ericsson's design, mocked as a 'cheesebox on a raft,' was so extraordinary that he had to promise to refund the government's money if his vessel failed to win the commission. The *Monitor* was a small vessel by contemporary standards, displacing only 987 gross tons and with a crew of just 49. She had no rigging or sails, allowing the use of her most innovative feature, a gun turret housing two 28cm (11in) smoothbore Dahlgren guns that could swivel in any direction. She was constructed entirely of iron.

First Clash of the Ironclads

In March 1862, the *Virginia* set out to break the Union blockade of the James River and the *Monitor* was sent to oppose her. The *Virginia* arrived first at Hampton Roads, accompanied by two small steam tenders and three gunboats, and launched a surprise attack on the Union squadron there. The *Virginia* quickly demonstrated the value of the ironclad concept. The guns of the USS *Cumberland* and *Congress* bounced off the *Virginia*'s side, allowing her to approach and ram the *Cumberland*, tearing a hole below the waterline. *Cumberland* nearly took the *Virginia* with her as she sank, but *Virginia*'s ram pulled off. The ironclad then succeeded in destroying the *Congress*, silenced several shore batteries, and sank several smaller ships. Although the *Virginia* had been hit over a hundred times she suffered only minor damage, including 2 dead and 8 wounded crewmembers.

The USS *Monitor* arrived later that evening, despite nearly sinking twice on the way. What followed the next morning was reminiscent of a duel between two medieval knights, each too well armoured for the blows to have any serious effect. For nearly four hours, *Monitor* and *Virginia* circled at very close range, trying and failing to ram each other and firing at point blank range. The battle was inconclusive. *Virginia* retired up the Elizabeth River after a strike from a 180lb (82kg) shell cracked the wood under her iron plate. Cracked plates and minor leaks were, however, the extent of the damage; there were no fatalities on either side. The new ironclad technology had already reached stalemate – but it had proven how deadly it would be against wooden ships. As

The Times of London reported on the battle, with only modest exaggeration, the Royal Navy had suddenly gone from 149 first-class ships to two – the ironclads.

Both the United States and the Confederacy rushed to construct more ironclads. The South put 21 ironclads vessels to sea during the war and began construction on 29 more. The Union built or started a total of 84 ironclads, 64 of them modelled on the *Monitor* (although another of the experimental vessels, the *New Ironsides*, was a superior design). They saw extensive coastal use as the Union Navy attempted to blockade 6000km (3500 miles) of coastline.

Dirty Tricks: Torpedoes and Submarines

Today we think of a torpedo as a self-propelling device, but the earliest torpedoes were simply underwater mines, taking their name from the electric ray fish that shocks its prey. Experiments with anti-ship mines began early in the nineteenth century. The ever-ingenious Robert Fulton tried to sell a plan for sea mines to Napoleon in 1801, turning to the British Navy when the French were not interested. In 1805, Fulton demonstrated his new mine by spectacularly exploding the captured Danish brig *Dorothea*, but the new weapon proved more difficult to use in battle. The United States made several unsuccessful attempts to use Fulton mines in the War of 1812, but their first appearance in combat was not until the Crimean War.

Russia used naval mines to protect her forts at Kronstadt – simple explosive devices sunk a few feet under the surface of the water and intended to explode on contact. Although the Russian mines succeeded in damaging a packet, the Allied forces attacking Kronstadt received word of the obstacles. They swept the area and recovered several mines – many of which were already waterlogged or corroded and would not have caused any damage anyway.

THE BATTLE OF HAMPTON ROADS, *between CSS* Virginia *(left) and USS* Monitor. *The two vessels battered each other for hours in an ultimately indecisive engagement in which neither vessel seriously damaged the other.*

Trying to protect their harbours without sufficient ships or guns, the Confederacy also adopted these stationary torpedoes during the US Civil War. The typical device was simple enough – a barrel, held in place by a weighted cable. They developed two detonation types: contact (a chemical reaction set off when a vessel hit the mine) and electric (ignited by an electrical connection with the shore). The devices were fairly small; for example, the mines used at Fort Henry on the Tennessee in 1862 were about 170cm (5.5ft) long and contained 35kg (75lb) of gunpowder; the largest had up to a ton of powder. Although most often stationary torpedoes failed to explode or washed away, they succeeded in sinking 32 Union vessels during the Civil War.

The Confederate Navy, ever inventive, also experimented with ways to deliver the torpedo to the hull of the enemy vessel, most notably with the spar torpedo - quite simply, a mine attached to the bow of a ship by a long pole. The ships chosen as 'delivery boys' were low and hard to see, pinning their hopes on approaching the enemy silently in the dark.

The desire for vessels that could deliver a spar torpedo unnoticed (preferably without being destroyed themselves in the process) led to experiments with submarines.

As early as the US Revolutionary War, the inventor David Bushnell had conceived an early submarine, hoping to use it to connect a detachable charge to the bottom of an enemy ship with a screw. Neither Bushnell's Turtle nor the mine-delivering submarine *Nautilus,* which Robert Fulton designed and tested for the French Navy in 1800–01, were very successful. Several submarine attempts in the War of 1812 and a German effort to create a viable submarine in 1850 also failed. The 1862 French submarine *Plongeur*, a vessel operated with a compressed air

'Familiarity with danger makes a brave man braver, but less daring.
Thus with seamen: he who goes the oftenest round Cape Horn goes the most circumspectly.'

— HERMAN MELVILLE

propeller and carrying a torpedo at the end of a 4.5m (15ft) spar, was also unsuccessful.

The Confederate Navy constructed several small submersible vessels, dubbed 'Davids.' These craft were not true submarines; instead of diving fully, they could move awash, the better to sneak up to an enemy vessel and make contact with the spar torpedo they carried over their bows. The officers of an Alabama volunteer regiment did, however, succeed in creating a submarine, the *HL Hunley*, in the spring of 1863.

The central section of this extraordinary vessel was made from a cylindrical iron steam boiler. Her propulsion was by muscle power, with eight crewmen to crank the propeller and a ninth to steer. She was intended for the defence of Charleston harbour, with a bold plan to travel under enemy ships and attach mines to their hulls. On 17 February 1864, the *Hunley* succeeded in attacking a Union sloop: by the time the crew of the *Housatonic* realized that the *Hunley* was not a floating log, she was too close for them to point their guns. The torpedo at the end of a spar attached to *Hunley* made contact and destroyed the ship. The *Hunley* herself did not return; it is thought that the force of the blast pressed her down into the water and her crew could not return to the surface.

On the whole, these experiments had little practical application until the great arms race that began in the 1880s. After a short flirtation with towed torpedoes, the Englishman Robert Whitehead designed a locomotive torpedo that could propel itself through the water, selling the plan to both Britain and France in 1872. The new device was impressive by contemporary standards, with a range of over 500m (1500ft) and an ability to travel at 17.5 knots. Britain launched its first warship with locomotive torpedoes, HMS *Lightning* (later renamed Torpedoboat No. 1) in 1876. It worked so well that the British Admiralty ordered a dozen more almost immediately. The first viable submarines appeared in the British, French and US navies only in the late 1880s.

War for the Ports

An important part of the Union war plan in the US Civil War was to deprive the Confederacy of ports. The techniques and risks of such a strategy can be seen particularly well in the siege of Charleston, the taking of New Orleans, and the Battle of Mobile Bay. The Union siege of Charleston, South Carolina, was in fact the longest campaign of the war, consisting of a series of indecisive naval battles that revealed both the Union Navy's inventiveness and its inexperience.

The Union forces first attempted to block the harbour by filling hulks with rocks and scuttling

THE ORIGINAL *MONITOR after her fight with the* Virginia. *Near the port-hole can be seen the dents made by the heavy shot from the guns of the* Virginia. *Hampton Roads, VA, July 1862.*

Battle of Mobile Bay
1864

US Admiral David Farragut was ordered to close Mobile Bay, one of three remaining Confederate ports, to blockade runners. He sent his squadron into the narrow channel that had been left open for blockade runners but was protected by mines, two forts and four Confederate ships. After one of his advance ships, USS *Tecumseh,* struck a mine and rapidly sank, taking 94 sailors down with her, Farragut led the way with his flagship and defeated the small Confederate flotilla under the command of Admiral Franklin Buchanan. A combined army-navy operation captured the two confederate forts a few weeks later. Although the city of Mobile remained in Confederate hands, the last blockade-running port on the Gulf Coast east of the Mississippi was shut down by the Federals.

Mobile Bay in the state of Alabama is one of the greatest seaports of North America. It was a major Confederate base.

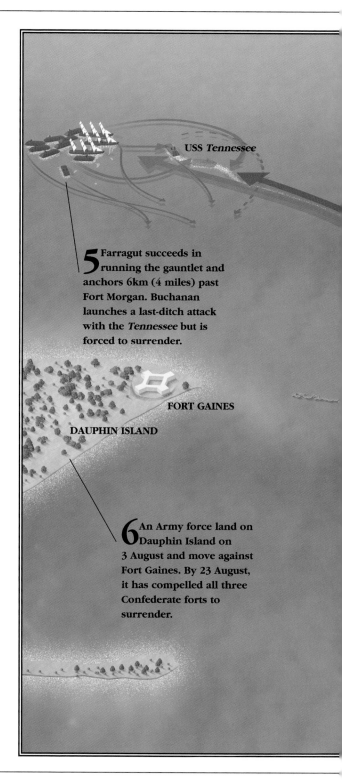

USS *Tennessee*

5 Farragut succeeds in running the gauntlet and anchors 6km (4 miles) past Fort Morgan. Buchanan launches a last-ditch attack with the *Tennessee* but is forced to surrender.

FORT GAINES

DAUPHIN ISLAND

6 An Army force land on Dauphin Island on 3 August and move against Fort Gaines. By 23 August, it has compelled all three Confederate forts to surrender.

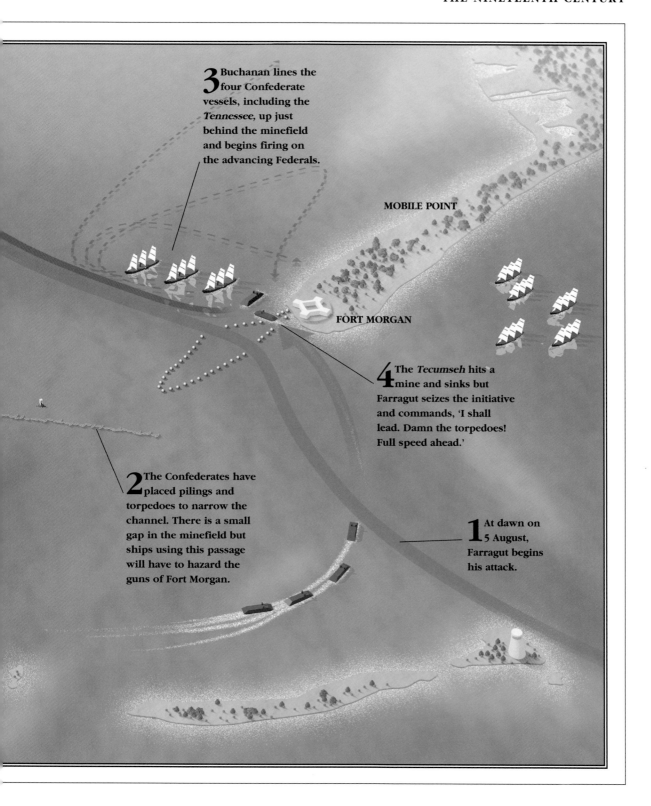

3 Buchanan lines the four Confederate vessels, including the *Tennessee*, up just behind the minefield and begins firing on the advancing Federals.

MOBILE POINT

FORT MORGAN

4 The *Tecumseh* hits a mine and sinks but Farragut seizes the initiative and commands, 'I shall lead. Damn the torpedoes! Full speed ahead.'

2 The Confederates have placed pilings and torpedoes to narrow the channel. There is a small gap in the minefield but ships using this passage will have to hazard the guns of Fort Morgan.

1 At dawn on 5 August, Farragut begins his attack.

them in the main channel, only to discover that their carefully placed obstructions soon washed away. Naval assaults failed, with several Union vessels running into sunken mines and sinking in minutes. The only counter-torpedo device available at the time was the 'boot-jack' – a raft fitted around the bow of a Monitor-class ironclad, with grapnels to snare the torpedoes.

While the siege of Charleston ground on inconclusively, Union commander David Farragut launched a bold attack on New Orleans. To reach the city, Farragut's squadron had to pass the forts at the mouth of the Mississippi River. He prepared his ships for the danger by landing all extra spars, rigging and boats – anything that could catch fire – and provided temporary armour in the form of cable chains draped over the sides of the vessels and bags packed around the boilers. This 17-vessel squadron set out shortly after midnight on 24 April 1862, surprising the forts' defenders (who had

expected an attack from upstream on the Mississippi, not from the Gulf of Mexico) and passing by the two forts and the unfinished ironclad *Louisiana*, which was moored as a battery. Farragut's squadron then fought the Confederate armed steamers above the forts. New Orleans itself was not well defended, and surrendered to the Union force two days later.

The Battle of Mobile Bay: 'Damn the Torpedoes'
Admiral David Farragut's most outstanding victory, however, is generally agreed to be the Battle of Mobile Bay, fought on 5 August 1864. The city of Mobile, Alabama, was vital for the Confederate war effort, a centre for iron manufacture and one of the Confederacy's few deep-water ports. In 1864, a joint navy-army expedition against the city was ordered. The army was to assault Forts Gaines and Morgan at the harbour entrance, after which the

AN 86MM (3.5IN) BOAT carriage gun. Note the advances in gun design, including screw mechanisms to aim the gun more easily, and a gun slide that was fixed to the deck. Before the Civil War, future Federal Rear-Admiral John A Dahlgren (1809-70) invented the Dahlgren gun, a rifled cannon, and boat howitzers with iron carriages. Dahlgren's boat howitzers were the finest guns of their time in the world and were used by both Federals and Confederates throughout the Civil War.

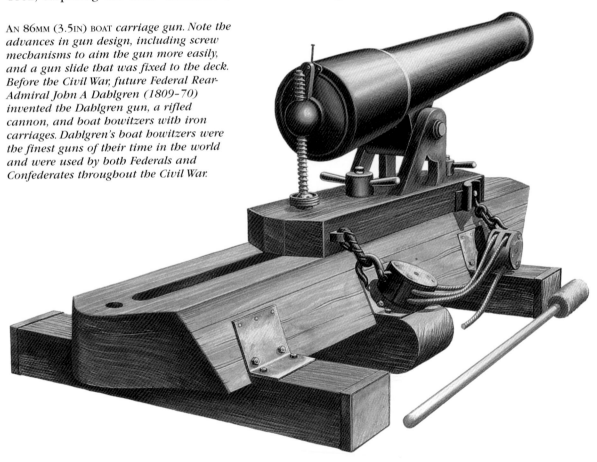

Petty Officer, US Navy (1865)

For the duration of the war enlisted Navy personnel wore the same uniform, consisting of dark-blue woollen overshirt, often worn over a red flannel undershirt, tucked into dark-blue woollen trousers. Sometimes, white tape or embroidery was used to decorate the shirt's collar and cuffs. The shirt was worn with a large black handkerchief. This sailor also wears the standard issue visorless cap. Usually, the name of the ship on which the seaman served was painted on the cap band in gold or yellow lettering. A white cap cover was worn in the summer months, while a double-breasted jacket was often worn in cold weather.

This Federal Petty Officer is armed with M1851 Colt Navy revolver, which was standard issue for officers and non-commissioned officers throughout the U.S. Navy. Officers and men would also be issued with an M1841 cutlass, and some ratings would also be armed with the M1861 Whitney Navy Rifle, for boarding actions and shore operations.

naval squadron under Farragut was to take Fort
Powell. They faced strong defences, including a
channel that had been obstructed with pilings and
180 submerged torpedoes, and a small
Confederate squadron in the bay. To force his way
into the bay, Farragut had five ironclads and
13 other warships.

In the ensuing action, Farragut displayed an
excellent understanding of the new naval and anti-
naval technologies. At the entrance into the bay, he
carefully positioned the ironclads under his
command to protect the wooden Union vessels
from the guns of Fort Morgan. As at New Orleans,
he draped heavy chain over the sides of the

wooden ships to provide temporary armour (the need for such extra protection was now generally recognized and the Confederate Navy even attempted 'cottonclads' – ships protected with bales of cotton). The seven smallest Union ships were lashed to the port sides of larger ships to protect them from the fort's shells.

Farragut's plan was to enter the harbour in line ahead, with two gunboat flotillas positioned to fire against the forts. The attack began when the first Union ship crossed the harbour bar at 6.00 a.m., taking advantage of both a southwest breeze and a flood tide.

The attack did not run smoothly. USS *Tecumseh*, a monitor, was brought forward to deal with the Confederate ironclad *Tennessee*. Before she could engage, *Tecumseh* struck a mine and sank in four minutes; 93 men died. The Union ships became bunched up in the channel, justifiably nervous about further mines, and suffered heavily in the fire from Fort Morgan. Farragut ordered the *Brooklyn* to dare the channel, but she did not respond even when the orders were conveyed three times. At this point Farragut ordered forward his flagship, the *Hartford*, with the cry, 'Damn the torpedoes, full speed ahead!' In the event, none of the mines struck by the *Hartford* exploded. Farragut then avoided the onslaught of the *Tennessee*. Despite heavy attack, the *Hartford* opened the way for the other Union vessels, driving off the Confederate gunboats.

By 8.30 a.m., all the Union ships were in the bay. The Confederate ironclad *Tennessee*, a six-gun vessel, attacked the entire Union fleet (mounting 157 guns in total). Two Union ships rammed the *Tennessee* on opposite sides, but failed to stop her; the *Hartford*'s ramming had little more effect. The *Tennessee* was then surrounded by Union vessels and subjected to fire from all directions. Even then, at close range, only one Union shot penetrated, but the barrage did succeed in knocking out the *Tennessee*'s steering and also knocked down her smokestack. She surrendered only when she ran out of ammunition.

Lessons of the US Civil War

European navies were quick to learn from the often confused and chaotic naval engagements of the US Civil War. All navies speeded their transition to iron-hulled and ironclad vessels. They were also

THE BATTLE OF MOBILE BAY *by William H Overend (1851–98). At the pivotal point of the battle, Admiral Farragut rose to the occasion and declared, 'I shall lead. Damn the torpedoes! Full speed ahead.'*

quick to adopt armoured turrets to protect the ships' guns and crews, an idea that had first been developed for the British Navy in the Crimean War. As early as 1864, the Danish fleet that attempted to halt the Prussian invasion of Denmark included a turret ship, the British-built *Rolf Krake*. The turret, designed by the Englishman Cowper Coles, turned on a roller path set into the lower deck. Coles went on to build the experimental HMS *Captain*, a seagoing turreted ship. *Captain* proved to be too top-heavy; she sank only four months after her launch with 473 fatalities, including her inventor. The first major warship with a central battery was HMS *Bellerophon*, launched in 1865. *Bellerophon* was constructed with a box casemate that held 10 23cm (9in) and five 18cm (7in) muzzle-loading rifled guns. She also had some defence against torpedoes in the form of a double hull, and a system of watertight compartments to help protect her if she was rammed.

In fact, the ships of the ironclad age had few opportunities to exercise their craft. The first and almost the only important fleet engagement between ironclad fleets at sea was the Second Battle of Lissa, waged between Austrian and Italian fleets on 20 July 1866. This rather farcical encounter certainly demonstrated that an effective anti-ironclad technique had yet to be developed. The prelude to the battle came when an Italian fleet under Count Carlo di Persano was sent with 12 ironclads, 14 wooden warships, and several smaller vessels to assault the Austrian-held island of Lissa in the Adriatic. An Austrian fleet under Admiral Wilhelm von Tegetthof arrived with seven ironclads, seven wooden warships and four scout ships to challenge the Italians.

Neither fleet had well-trained crews, but the Italians put their trust in superior numbers and possession of the only turret ship, the *Affondatore*, which also boasted a heavy bow ram. Unfortunately, the Italians also had an incompetent admiral, Persano, who decided at the last minute to transfer from his flagship to the *Affondatore*. Since he failed to inform his captains of the change, they ignored his signals during the battle. While transferring ships, Persano also opened a gap in the Italian line. Tegetthof exploited the gap, leading into it with his own flagship, the *Ferdinand Max*. A close-range mêlée ensued. The Austrian gunners had far more modern breech-loaders, but they still barely dented the Italian armour. So Tegetthof ordered his ships to ram the Italian ironclads. The wooden *Kaiser* rammed *Re di Portogallo*, but did more damage to herself than to the Italian vessel. Only when the ironclad *Ferdinand Max* rammed *Re d'Italia* did the Italian vessel sink, killing two-thirds of her 600-man crew. The Italians withdrew after a second armoured ship was lost.

Gunboat Diplomacy

Instead of great fleet engagements, the most immediate benefits of the technological revolutions of the nineteenth century were seen in a large number of colonial adventures, many of which involved coastal bombardment or amphibious operations. As early as 1816, an Anglo-Dutch fleet attacked the harbour defences of Algiers and burned the Algerian pirate fleet; the French went on to conquer the city in 1830. Such encounters did not really require traditional warships; instead, a premium was placed on manoeuvrability within harbours, the ability to move up rivers, and the possession of heavier firepower than their less technologically advanced opponents. Thus in the Second Seminole War in Florida in the 1830s, the US Navy positioned steamboats on the larger rivers, the better to reach the enemy. Similarly, in the First Opium War (1839–42) Chinese junks could not prevent British ships from attacking their coastal forts or from cutting the Grand Canal with a combination of ships of the line and steamers.

The year 1840 was decisive in demonstrating naval superiority as a key element of colonial policy. In that year, the British Navy drove an Egyptian army from Palestine, took Acre after a bombardment, and destroyed 74 Chinese junks in the Pearl River. In the 1850s, the French used river flotillas to move up the Senegal River in West Africa, benefiting greatly from steam-powered river craft.

Nineteenth-century navies gave Western powers a 'strategic reach': the imperialist powers held on to their empires thanks to defensible coastal enclaves that could easily be supplied, and

A WHITEHEAD TORPEDO, *invented by the English engineer Robert Whitehead in 1866. It could travel 914m (1000yd) at a speed of about 6 knots.*

the ability to shift troops rapidly from one place to another.

By the late 1850s, it had become common for European navies to disembark much of a ship's company along with some of the ship's guns to destroy enemy land forces. British ships played an important role during the Indian Mutiny of 1857-58, for example, even though their draughts were too deep to sail upriver. Instead, the ships' companies were put on shore or towed upriver on rafts, along with many large guns from the ships. Marines, who had long been present on naval ships, finally came into their own.

The other key development of the colonial age was the use of ironclad vessels, much better protected than their flammable predecessors, to bombard land positions. Thus in 1864 a Western Allied fleet forced the Strait of Shimonoseki in Japan, softening up the coastal forts with bombardment before landing detachments to spike or carry off their guns. The British Mediterranean fleet also successfully bombarded the forts that defended Alexandria in Egypt, on 11 July 1882.

Building a Better Gun

One of the key factors that allowed Western navies to dominate around the world was the revolution in gunnery, a process that began in about 1850 and reached its pinnacle in the 1870s and early 1880s. Naval gun designers had long recognized that their weapons could be much improved if they could be loaded without the need to run the gun inboard, and if the barrels of guns could be rifled, adding the spin that would give their projectile greater force and accuracy. A solution to the

OPPOSITE: A BOY SEAMAN *aboard USS* New Hampshire. *Navies employed large numbers of boys, who thus received a long apprenticeship as sailors.*

problem was much harder to identify, however, and required major improvements in metal-working technology.

The 1850s saw a new interest in rifled guns, but it was difficult to transfer the idea to the big guns of a warship. High pressures (caused by the snugger fit of the charge in the barrel of the gun) had a disconcerting habit of making the gun blow up. Sweden and Sardinia introduced rifled guns in the 1840s - another example of smaller navies trying to gain a strategic advantage over Britain. Other navies only gradually adopted rifled guns, often using rifled and smooth-bore weapons together. In the United States, for example, John Dahlgren developed a rifled ship gun, but also invented a more reliable smooth-bore shell gun, with improved venting. The US Navy also introduced a second rifled gun, the Parrott gun, which could fire 132-175lb (60-80kg) of shot.

An even greater challenge was the creation of a reliable breech-loading big gun - it was extremely difficult to form a perfect seal when the chamber was closed after loading. The French Navy adopted breech-loaders in 1858. As always, the British Navy responded by developing their own version. A number of accidents with breech-loading guns during the bombardment of Kagoshima in 1863, however, gave Admiralty planners second thoughts; Britain returned to muzzle-loaders. Improved breech-loaders were developed only in the late 1870s; by 1884, the largest breech-loading guns could fire 41.25cm (16.25in) shells weighing 1800 pounds.

The New Arms Race

Competition was often fierce between European navies as they scrambled to match each other technologically and to compete with British naval dominance on their own terms. Outright naval war, however, was for the most part restricted to the periphery. By the 1880s, however, the colonial scramble led to increasing tensions among the European powers, especially as a newly united Germany tried to claim her share of colonies in Africa and Asia.

By that time, many basic technological difficulties had been resolved. Britain launched the first mastless man-of-war, the *Devastation*, in 1873, while France created the first steel-hulled warship, *Redoubtable*, in 1878. Changes in doctrine accompanied technological advance. The French *Jeune École*, in particular, developed a naval strategy based on using the most advanced technology possible. The result, by the late nineteenth century, was a reinvigorated arms race that would take the navies of Europe up to World War I and beyond.

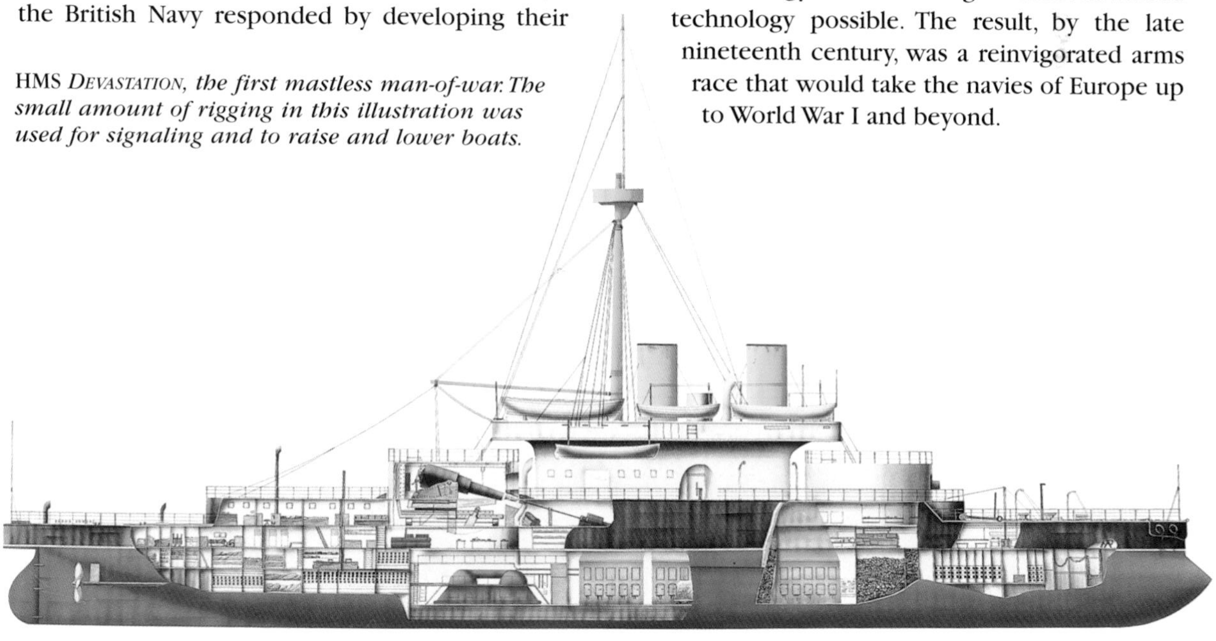

HMS DEVASTATION, *the first mastless man-of-war. The small amount of rigging in this illustration was used for signaling and to raise and lower boats.*

CHAPTER 5

THE MODERN ERA

The first armoured warships rapidly demonstrated that they could sweep the seas clear of wooden ships in combat, but staying afloat was a more significant problem. Many designs had inadequate seakeeping qualities and were limited to coastal protection duty. Some were designated 'floating batteries' rather than being considered true warships. In time, ocean-going armoured warships became the norm, and the modern era of naval warfare had begun.

M ost early armoured vessels were grossly underpowered and possessed a sailing rig in addition to their steam plant. This added to the topweight of an already overloaded vessel and made ocean deployments hazardous. Gradually however, fully steam powered warships emerged that were capable of long ocean cruises, providing a suitable source of coal was available.

A DEPTH CHARGE EXPLODES *astern of a US destroyer in the North Atlantic, 1943. Experiments using an obsolete submarine as a target showed that the standard 300lb (136kg) depth charge was insufficient. By the time the Pacific war broke out, a 600lb (272kg) charge was available.*

This in turn led to the need for coaling stations around the world, at least for those nations with overseas possessions.

From Ironclads to Armoured Ships

By the beginning of the twentieth century, the gun-armed warship was beginning to take on its classic form. Some weapons were carried in limited-traverse mounts along the ship's sides, other in fully rotating turrets. Many vessels carried their armament in unprotected deck mounts that served much like an artillery piece on land.

The largest of these armoured warships were termed, predictably, battleships, but many navies could not afford such expensive vessels. Even those navies that could afford battleships also needed lighter vessels capable of undertaking long patrol cruises. The colonial powers of the time invested in armoured cruisers for this purpose

THE INFLUENCE OF THE TORPEDO *on early twentieth century naval thinking was profound. Admiral 'Jacky' Fisher for a time advocated a navy made up entirely of submarines and torpedo boats like these small British craft.*

while lesser navies used cruisers as a substitute for capital ships.

In this era, vessels still communicated with one another by visual means – flags and lamps – although radio gradually became common. This meant that vessels on a distant station were effectively unable to communicate with their home nation. The problem was partially overcome by setting up telegraph stations on remote islands, connected to one another by cables laid on the ocean bed. New orders could be received and reports sent by sailing to one of the stations, but in between times the distant vessels had to operate on the initiative of their commanding officer. The telegraph stations were also vulnerable to attack from hostile raiding vessels.

Changes in Naval Weapon Systems

The Automobile (self-propelled) Torpedo was first demonstrated in 1866 by Robert Whitehead. The self-propelled torpedo offered even minor craft the chance to sink large vessels such as battleships, and its importance was such that the term 'torpedo' quickly came to refer solely to such

weapons. Static explosive charges, previously known as torpedoes, became known as mines instead.

The first successful torpedo attack was made in 1891 during the Chilean Civil War, albeit from a rather short range of less than 100m (300ft), and soon specialist vessels were developed to carry torpedoes into action. Most were short-ranged craft intended mainly for coastal defence, but more seaworthy torpedo boats soon followed. Before the nineteenth century was over, the new torpedo boats had attacked and sunk many vessels much larger than themselves.

The counter to the torpedo boat was a specialist vessel, termed a torpedo boat destroyer, intended to intercept torpedo craft and sink them with gunfire. Gradually the torpedo boat destroyer evolved into a general-purpose light warship capable of escort duties as well as making torpedo attacks of its own. The light torpedo boat remained in existence and served as a coastal patrol and defence craft.

As late as the end of the nineteenth century, many vessels were still built with ramming in mind, but the gun was now the weapon of choice. Armament for a cruiser or battleship normally consisted of one or two heavy guns at each end of the ship, sometimes in armoured turrets and sometimes in open-topped mounts. These were backed up by multiple lighter weapons. The thinking at the time was that an enemy vessel could be most expeditiously dealt with by smothering it in a rain of lighter shells. Given that many ships had open gun mounts, this was not an unreasonable assumption.

Although the theories behind the development of battleships, cruisers and destroyers were sound and the vessels had been tested in small actions from time to time, naval strategists waited for a

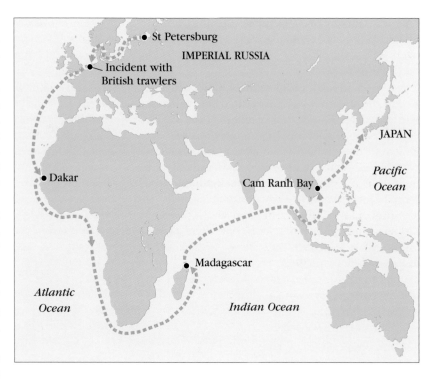

THE LONG VOYAGE *of the Russian Baltic fleet to Tsushima adversely affected the fighting capabilities of its ships and men. Early in the voyage, the Russian ships fired on the Dogger Bank fishing fleet in the North Sea, mistaking British trawlers for Japanese torpedo boats.*

major naval clash to determine quite how effective these new iron ships would be. In the early years of the twentieth century, the Russo-Japanese War would provide just such a testing ground.

The Battle of Tsushima

After centuries of isolationism, Japan leaped into the modern era with a programme of industrialization that included the acquisition of advanced warships from the best yards in Germany and Britain. The crews of these new ships were sent to train with the Royal Navy.

The Japanese fleet was still small when war with China broke out in 1894. This conflict was characterized by aggressive handling of good ships by the Japanese, and at times a lack of competence and fighting spirit on the part of their enemies. The largest clash, at the Yalu River, involved 10 heavy ships on each side plus supporting vessels.

Japanese training and discipline enabled them to achieve a decisive victory in a hard fight.

Naval Build-up

Concerned about Russian influence spreading in Korea, the region whose allegiance the Japanese had recently fought the Chinese over, Japan continued to build up her navy. This build-up included the purchase of six excellent battleships of British design. These represented the ultimate development of the pre-dreadnought battleship, with twin turrets fore and aft housing two 12in (30cm) guns each behind 14in (35cm) of armour. The ships were capable of 18 knots and carried 14 6in (15cm) guns in single mounts, seven on each side, as a secondary armament. The Japanese battle fleet also included a number of cruisers and some destroyers, which at the time tended to be very small vessels, though armed with torpedoes.

With this big stick in hand, Japan entered into negotiations with Russia from 1902 onwards. The main bone of contention was the ownership of the Liaotung Peninsula and the naval base at Port Arthur. Negotiations cane to nothing, and the decision was made to resolve the issue by other means.

Elimination of the Russian Pacific Fleet

Attacking on 8 February 1904, the Japanese fleet was able to inflict considerable damage on the Russian force at Port Arthur. The weakened Russian fleet was blockaded in Port Arthur and although mine warfare and some minor actions inflicted casualties on both sides, it was not until August that the Russians came out to fight. The resulting action became known as the Battle of the Yellow Sea.

The Russians had reserves elsewhere, so Vice-Admiral Heihachiro Togo, commanding the Japanese fleet, knew that he could not afford to lose too many ships. Nevertheless, he took an aggressive stance as soon as the opportunity presented itself. Despite suffering a pounding from the Russian guns, the superb Japanese battleships were able to remain in action. Meanwhile, repeated hits on the Russian flagship sent her out of control and threw the Russian battle line into chaos. Togo pressed home the advantage and hammered the Russian fleet until darkness allowed the survivors to escape.

Although significant elements of the Russian fleet remained intact, morale had collapsed and the fleet hid in Port Arthur until it fell to land forces in January 1905. The Russian fleet in the Pacific had been eliminated, but while the Japanese had only one battle force, the Russians had another, and it was already en route.

Enter the Baltic Fleet

In order to restore the situation in the Pacific, the Russian Baltic Fleet set sail in October 1904, making a long and arduous passage around Africa to meet the Japanese fleet at the Straits of Tsushima between Japan and Korea. The core of the Russian fleet, under Admiral Rozhestvenski, was built around four excellent modern battleships and three older capital ships. However, much of the fleet was obsolete or in poor repair. Some vessels were decades old, making them relics in an era when technology was advancing rapidly year by year.

The Baltic Fleet had sailed a very long way, with vessels that were not all in very good condition. The crews were not at a peak of efficiency either. Thus, the Russian fleet hoped to

> *'It is absurd to think of steaming victoriously into Vladivostok. Or of getting command of the sea! The only possible chance is a dash through, and having dashed through, after two, three or at the most four sallies we [...] shall have to prepare for a siege, take our guns on shore...'*
>
> — NAVIGATING FLAG LIEUTENANT FILIPPOVSKY, KNYAZ SUVOROV

slip through the Tsushima Narrows and enter port at Vladivostok undetected, giving them the opportunity to undergo maintenance and training before engaging the Japanese. Unfortunately for the Russians, the fleet was spotted by an auxiliary cruiser, which notified the Japanese Admiralty of the sighting. Soon the whole Japanese battle fleet was at sea and a fight was inevitable.

Contact between the fleets came early in the afternoon of 27 May 1905. The Russian

THE RUSSIAN *KNIAZ SUVOROV (top) and Japanese* Fuji *(lower) were both new ships built to a modern design, with almost identical main and secondary armament. Suvorov's main armour belt was considerably thinner than that of Fuji, but her turrets were better armoured. This did not prevent all her main guns from being disabled by enemy fire.* Suvorov *was sunk at Tsushima;* Fuji *was hit 11 times but survived.*

commander tried to use a patch of fog to conceal his approach, but disorder ensued among his ships due to poor training. Togo was quick to press this advantage, and closed rapidly with the enemy.

It was clear that this would be the decisive clash of the war. There was no other Russian fleet, so Togo could risk losing some of his ships if it led to a complete victory. He had four battleships and eight armoured cruisers in his main battle force, all of which had benefited from good maintenance and training while awaiting the arrival of the Russian fleet. Togo's force could make a battle speed of 15 knots. The Russian fleet, however, was limited to just 9 knots by its obsolete vessels, though its main striking power rested in four battleships, which were a match for those Togo commanded.

Aggressively seeking total victory, Admiral Togo made the historic signal, 'The future of the Empire

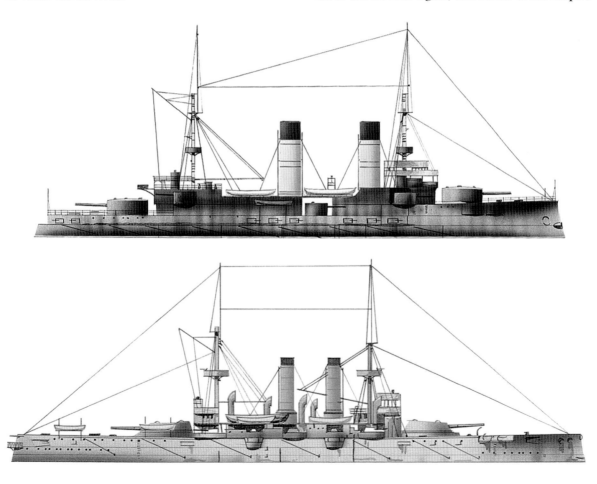

Battle of Tsushima

1905

The Russian Admiral Rozhestvenski did not want to engage the Japanese fleet until his ships had been refitted and their crews rested at Vladivostok. He hoped to slip through the Tsushima Narrows and pass by undetected. The Japanese fleet, conversely, was well rested and ready for battle aboard ships that had been well-maintained in their home ports. Moreover, since there were no more Russian fleets if this one was defeated, Admiral Togo could afford to take fairly heavy losses if, by doing so, he achieved his strategic aim of driving the Russians from the seas around Japan. The Russian fleet was in poor shape for a naval battle, with only four new Borodino class battleships, and many other outdated models. The long voyage and the lack of maintenance meant their bottoms were heavily fouled, much reducing their speed. The Japanese ships were almost twice as fast, and Togo used the superior manoeuvrability of his fleet to advantage, 'crossing the T' twice.

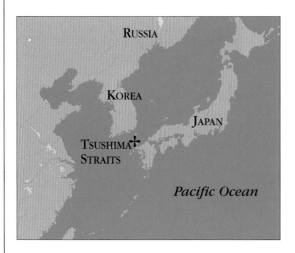

Although not of the same strategic significance as the Gibraltar Strait, the Tsushima Straits remain important to navigation in the region. They funnel naval and mercantile traffic into a narrow sea area.

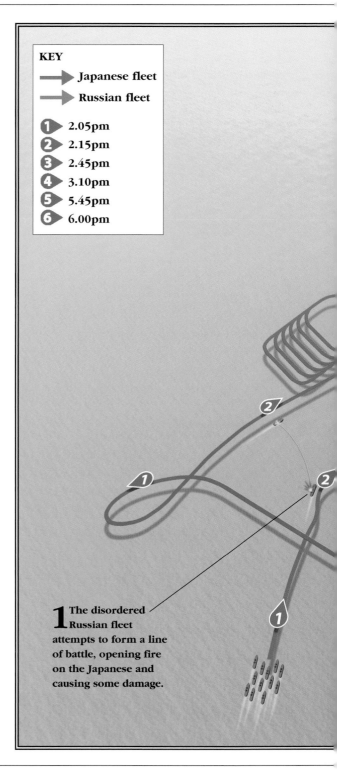

KEY

→ Japanese fleet
→ Russian fleet

1 2.05pm
2 2.15pm
3 2.45pm
4 3.10pm
5 5.45pm
6 6.00pm

1 The disordered Russian fleet attempts to form a line of battle, opening fire on the Japanese and causing some damage.

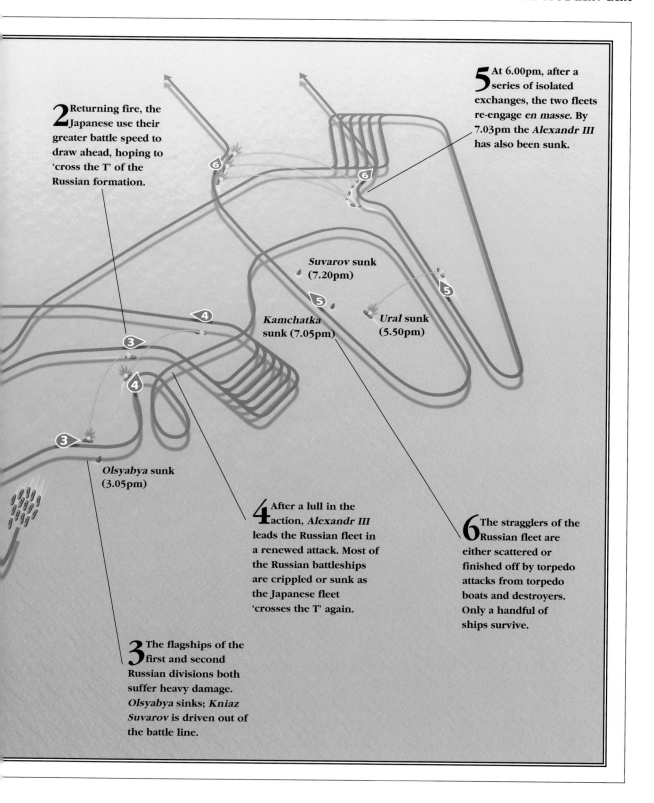

2 Returning fire, the Japanese use their greater battle speed to draw ahead, hoping to 'cross the T' of the Russian formation.

5 At 6.00pm, after a series of isolated exchanges, the two fleets re-engage *en masse*. By 7.03pm the *Alexandr III* has also been sunk.

Suvarov sunk (7.20pm)

Kamchatka sunk (7.05pm)

Ural sunk (5.50pm)

Olsyabya sunk (3.05pm)

4 After a lull in the action, *Alexandr III* leads the Russian fleet in a renewed attack. Most of the Russian battleships are crippled or sunk as the Japanese fleet 'crosses the T' again.

6 The stragglers of the Russian fleet are either scattered or finished off by torpedo attacks from torpedo boats and destroyers. Only a handful of ships survive.

3 The flagships of the first and second Russian divisions both suffer heavy damage. *Olsyabya* sinks; *Kniaz Suvarov* is driven out of the battle line.

THE JAPANESE NAVY made extensive use of torpedo boats, some of which mounted up to six tubes. The large torpedo boat Kotaka *was capable of ocean operations and is sometimes considered to the world's first destroyer.*

rests on this battle', and led his fleet onto a parallel course at a range of about 6000m (20,000ft). His plan was to use his superior speed to draw ahead and 'cross the T' of the Russian fleet, allowing his ships to use all their guns while the Russians could reply only with their fore turrets.

The Fleets Clash

The two fleets opened fire a little after 2 p.m. At such a close distance, hits were frequent and Togo's flagship *Mikasa* was hit several times, taking serious casualties. One of the twin guns in her fore turret was disabled, but none of the Japanese ships was forced out of line despite accurate gunnery on the Russian part.

Meanwhile, the Russians were taking a pounding. The battleship *Kniaz Suvarov*, flagship of the Russian fleet, was badly damaged and caught fire, as did the older battleship *Oslyabya*. The latter was forced out of the battle line at 2.50 p.m. and sank soon afterwards. This deprived the Russian second division of its flagship. Shortly afterwards, the *Suvarov* was also forced out of action. Fleet command was already disrupted at this point, as the admiral and his staff were all dead or wounded.

Japanese destroyers closed in on the burning *Suvarov*, but the flagship was tough and well-constructed. Although crippled and dead in the water, she was able to beat off numerous destroyer attacks with her remaining armament. It was not until several hours later that she sank, by which time the rest of the fleet had also ceased to exist. Other Russian ships also gave good account of themselves. As the *Suvarov* drifted out of the line, the battleship *Alexandr III* turned towards the Japanese fleet, leading the remaining force. She became the target for heavy fire as she closed to less than 3000m (10,000ft) before being forced to turn away. Seriously ablaze, *Alexandr III* was forced out of the fight for a time.

The Endgame

The two fleets lost contact and hope began to emerge that some of the Russian ships might get through to Vladivostok after all. It was not to be. As the fleets sighted one another again, *Alexandr III* led her sisters *Borodino* and *Orel* back into action. However, by this time the outcome was already settled. There was no longer any chance of victory for the Russians, if there had ever been one. The question was simply which of their vessels, if any, would survive.

The action re-opened at about 6.00 p.m. Again the superior speed of the Japanese ships proved its worth, and Togo was able to dictate the course of the engagement. *Borodino* and *Alexandr III* were pounded to pieces and sank by 7.20 p.m. The older battleship *Sissoi Veliki*, damaged by several heavy shells, was torpedoed by a destroyer and crippled. She was scuttled and abandoned.

As night fell, the major Japanese units withdrew, but the fight – if it could still be termed as such – went on. Destroyers had already finished off *Suvarov* and *Veliki*. During the night, they also claimed the battleship *Navarin* and the cruisers *Vladimir Monomakh* and *Makhimoff*, and maintained contact with some of the survivors among the Russian force. As a result, by the following morning the *Orel* and two older battleships found themselves facing Togo's entire force and wisely surrendered.

Few Russian ships survived the battle. Of these, one light cruiser and two destroyers managed to reach Vladivostok. Three old cruisers slipped away and reached Manila, only to be interned.

Aftermath

Russian prestige was severely dented by the defeat at Tsushima and it was a major contributing factor to the revolution that swept through Russia in 1905. The consequences for Japan were rather more positive. Having shattered two battlefleets belonging to a major world power, Japan was now firmly established on the political stage. Morevoer, she received the Liaotung Peninsula and sovereignty over Korea as part of the peace settlement with Russia as well as ownership of Russian assets in Manchuria.

The Imperial Japanese Navy had established itself as a world-class force and faced the coming years with a confidence that would not be dented until the Battle of Midway. Indeed, some historians contend that the defeat of the Russian fleets in 1904–5 bred a dangerous overconfidence among the Japanese commanders, which ultimately led to Japan's defeat in 1945.

Dreadnoughts and Battlecruisers

Experience of battles such as Tsushima demonstrated that most of the time capital ships were able to shrug off hits from medium-calibre weapons without coming to harm. In addition, a mix of gun types complicated fire control. Reducing secondary armament in favour of more big guns would both simplify the fire-control equation and increase the chances of inflicting damage on an enemy vessel. Consequently, various nations began working on 'all-big-gun' warships. First to be completed was the HMS *Dreadnought*, and she gave her name to a new kind of battleship.

HMS *Dreadnought* carried 10 12in (30cm) guns in twin turrets, rather than the usual two big-gun turrets and large numbers of medium-calibre guns. She also used newly developed steam turbines to drive her at 21 knots, a high speed for a capital ship of the time. This enabled a dreadnought force to dictate the range of an action and to chase down or escape from enemies as the need arose. The creation of HMS *Dreadnought* made all other capital ship designs obsolete, and to a great extent levelled the playing field. Navies with dozens of pre-dreadnoughts no longer had an unassailable lead in the naval arms race, and large numbers of all-big-gun capital ships were laid down in many nations.

Meanwhile, other changes were occurring. The British First Sea Lord, Admiral 'Jackie' Fisher, had long held that 'speed is armour' and he pushed for a class of fast vessels equipped with guns that could take on capital ships. The theory was that these battlecruisers, as they became known, would outrun any vessel they could not outfight, and the combination of heavy firepower and high speed would allow them to smash their foes before significant damage was taken.

The British Invincible class was equipped with twelve 12in (30cm) guns (as compared to 10 guns aboard *Dreadnought*) but had no more armour than the preceding class of armoured cruisers. With less weight and larger engines on a comparable displacement, this made the Invincible class faster than the *Dreadnought*, at a speed of 25 knots. They were, however, very susceptible to damage.

With their battleship-grade armament, battlecruisers were capable of sinking most existing capital ships and all cruisers. This made them excellent commerce raiders and, equally, ideal vessels to chase down and sink enemy raiders. They were also useful for fleet reconnaissance, as they could punch through an enemy cruiser screen, obtain sightings, and withdraw without being caught and brought to action. Designs varied considerably. While the British felt that speed alone was sufficient protection, German designers preferred to compromise somewhat and built better-protected vessels. Thus HMS *Lion* (laid down in 1908) carried eight 13.5in (34cm) guns while her German equivalent *Derfflinger* (laid down 1912) was armed with eight 12in (30cm) weapons.

On several occasions, the concept of a 'fast battleship' was put forward, essentially combining battlecruiser and battleship into a single fast, well-protected – and expensive – package. However, this idea did not come to fruition for many years.

Major Operations in World War I

The naval component of the Great War started in a small way on 5 August 1914. HMS *Lance*, a destroyer on patrol off the Thames Estuary, spotted a German vessel laying mines and opened fire. The vessel was a liner hurriedly converted to the minelaying role and had no guns. She was chased down and sunk, but one of her mines claimed the cruiser *Amphion* the following day.

The Royal Navy had been hoping for a dramatic clash to open the war; Britain had 20 dreadnoughts compared to only 13 in the German Navy, and a large superiority in other classes of ship. Wisely, the High Seas Fleet remained entrenched behind its minefields and coastal batteries. This suited the British purposes to an extent since it allowed the Royal Navy to blockade German ports unchallenged, gradually strangling German industry. However many in the British Admiralty preferred to seek out a decisive victory, so a plan was hatched to draw out and smash the German fleet.

The British plan was to penetrate the Heligoland Bight with a force of cruisers, destroyers and submarines and attack the patrols that operated there, hopefully drawing a few 'big fish' out of port to join the fight and leading them into a submarine ambush. The plan went awry for several reasons, not least because the Admiralty added elements to it without informing the commanders already at sea. Although they assigned a potent force of four battlecruisers to support the operation, orders were somewhat unclear as to what role the battlecruisers would play, while the lighter British forces had no idea that they had been assigned at all.

Meanwhile, the raid had been detected and German light forces, including several cruisers, were waiting to pounce on the raiders. Nevertheless, the initial clash went heavily in the British favour, with a force of German destroyers and torpedo boats driven off and chased towards land. As the German cruisers raced to join the battle, things became very confused. The arrival of the British battlecruisers caused particular consternation among the British light forces, who were still unaware of their presence and initially identified them as German cruisers.

On the face of it, the battle of the Heligoland Bight looked like a success

HMS DREADNOUGHT *revolutionized naval warfare with her speed and armament, though she was not the first all-big-gun ship to be designed. The American South Carolina class, with the main armament on the centreline, was designed earlier but entered service two years after* Dreadnought.

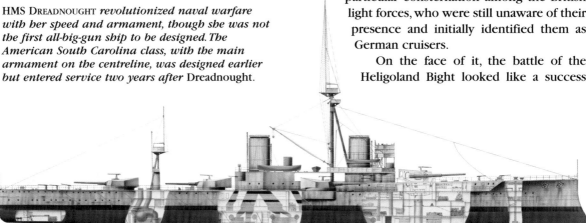

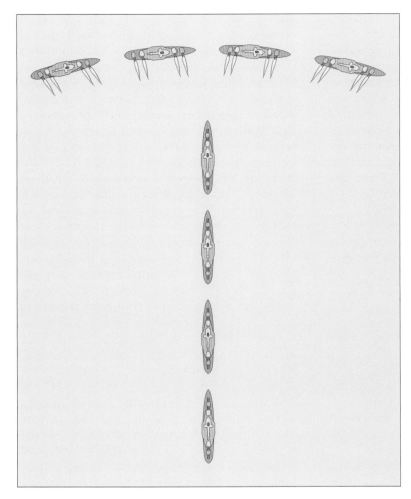

'CROSSING THE T' *allowed a fleet to engage with all its guns while the opposing force could reply only with forward-mounted guns. The faster fleet had a good chance of getting into this advantageous position, meaning that in some ways superior speed translated into more firepower.*

for the Royal Navy, but in fact it was a chaotic business in which British ships had pursued one another by mistake and British cruisers were attacked by their supporting submarines. Firepower, dash and aggression made up for the lack of coordination, but there were clearly important lessons to be learned from the action.

Meanwhile, there were problems in other theatres. The German East Asia Squadron, under the command of Vice-Admiral Maximilian von Spee, was on the loose in the Pacific. One of its

vessels, the light cruiser *Emden*, made a spectacularly successful raiding cruise in the Indian Ocean. The rest of the squadron, comprising the armoured cruisers *Scharnhorst* and *Gneisenau* plus supporting light cruisers, was also capable of causing mayhem among the Pacific trade routes.

The British sent the West Indies Squadron to find and destroy Spee's force. It was to be reinforced by the pre-dreadnought battleship *Canopus*, but she was slow and had not caught up with the British force – of two armoured cruisers, a light cruiser and an armed liner – when they encountered Spee's squadron off the island of Coronel. Another reinforcing vessel, the armoured cruiser *Defence*, was also still en route.

Although badly outgunned, the British commander, Rear-Admiral Cradock, decided to give battle. The German force was easily able to run ahead of the British squadron, keeping the range open. This was to their advantage as Cradock could engage with only two 9in (23cm) guns whereas Spee's force had 16 guns to shoot back with, albeit of slightly smaller calibre. The result was a foregone conclusion. One British armoured cruiser had sunk and the other was crippled when the lighter British vessels gave up and slipped away in the darkness. The only consolation was that the battle had used up around half of Spee's ammunition and resupply was not possible.

The Falkland Islands

The disaster at Coronel shook British morale, and the response was swift. The Royal Navy despatched Rear-Admiral Sturdee with a powerful squadron to the Falkland Islands, where it was to resupply before launching a search for the German squadron. As matters transpired, the search was unnecessary. Spee had decided to raid the Falkland Islands, intending to deprive the British of the wireless station there as well as the coaling facility.

At the time the raid was planned, the Falklands were entirely unprotected, but by the time Spee approached with his squadron the situation was very different. Spee ordered a ranging shot be fired at the wireless station; to his horror, heavy shells came back at him. One shell skipped off the water and punched through *Gneisenau*'s funnel without detonating. Now aware that he faced a major warship, Spee aborted the operation and made a run for it. It was too late.

The ageing *Canopus* had been sent to the Falklands and was now acting as a shore battery. More seriously, Sturdee's squadron, built around the battlecruisers *Inflexible* and *Invincible* and also containing three armoured cruisers and two light cruisers, was at the Falklands, undertaking resupply. The British were caught without steam up, complacently coaling, but hurriedly raised steam and began pursuing Spee's ships.

Detaching some of his lighter units to chase down the enemy supply ships, Sturdee went after the main German force. Three hours after leaving harbour, the range had fallen to the point where fire could be opened, and the battle proper began. Spee ordered his light cruisers to scatter and make a run for it, and their British equivalents went after them. The British light units played no further part in the main battle, though they did destroy most of the German light cruisers; only one escaped.

This left Sturdee with two battlecruisers armed with 12in (30cm) guns chasing two armoured cruisers armed with 8.2in (20.8cm) guns. The cruisers had thinner armour and a top speed some three knots slower than the battlecruisers, and half their ammunition was gone. Realizing he was being overtaken, Spee decided to fight it out. His ships turned to form a rather small line of battle

> *'No greater single step towards efficiency was ever made than the introduction of the turbine. Previous to its adoption, every day's steaming at high speed meant several days' overhaul of machinery in harbour.'*
> — ADMIRAL SIR REGINALD BACON

and opened fire with all their guns. The British battlecruisers turned up parallel and replied in kind; a fleet action in miniature.

Although the German guns were lighter, their fire control was much better, and salvoes straddled the British warships while the battlecruisers' fire was wayward at best. However, even the relatively light armour of a battlecruiser was sufficient to protect her from the 8.2in (21cm) guns of the German vessels.

Unable to escape and being battered to pieces at long range, *Scharnhorst* and *Gneisenau* came about and ran headlong at their opponents instead, bringing on a point-blank gunfight. After an hour, *Scharnhorst* was heavily afire and had lost many of her guns. Yet her battle ensign still flew as she turned in a final charge at HMS *Invincible*. Like many large ships of that era, *Scharnhorst* carried torpedoes and she made a last, gallant attempt to get close enough to launch them. During her lunge, the armoured cruiser rolled over and sank with all hands.

Sturdee then opened the range once more and began the methodical destruction of *Gneisenau*. She lasted over an hour, ceasing fire only when her ammunition was gone. Finally, *Gneisenau* capsized and sank, fortunately slowly enough that some of her crew were able to abandon ship. The defeat at Coronel was now avenged, and it seemed that the battlecruiser concept was proven. The big ships had indeed run down and sunk raiders using a combination of big guns and high speed.

Minor Naval Operations in the Great War

Traditionally, weaker fleets tend to engage in raiding operations rather than seeking a head-on clash that is likely to result in defeat. Although the German High Seas Fleet was a potent force in 1914, it was not sufficiently powerful to be able to take on the British Grand Fleet and break its power. The German Navy thus mainly undertook *guerre de course,* or 'cruiser warfare' (as raiding operations against commercial traffic are sometimes known). This took the form of raids by surface forces and submarines against shipping belonging to or destined for the British Empire.

The British fleet also operated mainly against German commerce, though in an entirely different way. As a result of geography as much as anything else, the British fleet was in an excellent position to blockade the German coastline and greatly impede the movement of food and essential war material by sea. So long as the blockade was maintained, Germany could be slowly strangled. For most of the war, therefore, naval operations were fairly small-scale, taking the form of raiding cruises by surface vessels and submarine campaigns, plus operations against these threats.

The classic surface-raiding cruise was carried out by the light cruiser *Emden*, detached from the East Asia Squadron. Taking with her a collier, *Emden* made her way into the Indian Ocean and caused havoc in the shipping lanes there. Over the course of several months, *Emden* sank more than 100,000 gross tons of merchant shipping and 23 British vessels, as well as a Russian cruiser and a French destroyer. She also harassed shore facilities, attacking oil storage tanks at Madras.

It was while attacking a shore installation that she met her end. *Emden*'s captain decided to attack the wireless and cable station at the Cocos Islands, which would severely disrupt enemy communications in the region. There she was intercepted by HMAS *Sydney*, an Australian light cruiser. *Sydney* was newer, bigger and better armed than *Emden*, with 6in (15cm) guns to the German vessels's 4.1in (10cm) weapons. Despite the disparity in fighting power, *Emden* put up a determined fight, trying to close for a torpedo

ADMIRAL ALFRED VON TIRPITZ *intended to create a fleet sufficiently strong that the Royal Navy would not be able to challenge it without risking unacceptable losses. The result was a naval arms race that contributed to the outbreak of World War I.*

attack before finally being disabled. However, *Emden*'s real contribution to the war went beyond the merchant ships she sank. During her cruise, *Emden* brought shipping in the Indian Ocean almost to a halt and tied down no less than 78 naval vessels hunting for her. It is also worth noting that her captain and crew behaved honourably and with compassion towards the merchant crews they attacked.

Leutnant-Capitan, German Navy (1916)

The uniform shown here was established within the German Navy in the early part of the twentieth century, though a full-length dress coat became popularly replaced by the double-breast tunic seen here.

The typical dress of a German naval officer in World War I was the blue tunic with matching trousers, a white shirt with wing collar and black tie, black shoes, and the naval peaked cap. The cap was blue in colour and had a black mohair surround and leather brim. It also featured Imperial cockade surrounded by oak leaves and surmounted by a crown.

The rank of this officer is indicated by the rings on the sleeve capped by the Imperial crown, though naval officers during this period often had rank displayed through shoulder-boards and shoulder-straps.

Another light cruiser, *Konigsburg*, was less successful as a raider, although she surprised a British cruiser in harbour and sank her before being bottled up in the River Rufiji in East Africa. Even then, she tied down several ships that could otherwise have been used elsewhere, and considerable resources were expended to eliminate her. *Konigsburg*'s crew then joined German land forces fighting in the region. Other surface raiders were not originally warships at all. Various vessels were converted into raiders by fitting a few obsolete guns. This was entirely sufficient to take on unarmed merchant ships of course, and there were never enough warships to escort every vessel.

One answer to the threat posed by surface raiders was to arm liners and other merchant ships as 'auxiliary cruisers' or 'armed merchant cruisers'. In truth, liners were not necessarily the best choice for this role because they had a very high silhouette, which made an easy target. On the other hand, they did tend to be fast. These converted civilian ships escorted unarmed merchant ships, patrolled distant stations and

TORPEDO BOATS *were capable of operations in the North Sea but generally remained close to the coast most of the time. This was still a hazardous duty. Some 67 German boats were lost during the war, most of them to mines.*

freed warships for more dangerous roles. However, they did sometimes have to fight.

In September 1914, the liner *Carmania*, serving with the Royal Navy as an auxiliary cruiser with 4.7mm (0.18in) guns aboard, came across her peacetime rival *Cap Trafalgar*. She, too, was a liner, fighting for Germany as a commerce raider and armed with eight 4.1mm (0.16in) guns. *Carmania* gave chase and a fight between the former liners ensued. Although their guns were old and not very powerful, the two liners had no trouble punching holes in one another's hulls. By the end of the action, both ships were on fire and so close to one another that machine-gun fire from *Cap Trafalgar* interfered with firefighting operations aboard *Carmania*. Finally, as *Cap Trafalgar* began to sink, her captain was forced to beach her.

Prelude to Jutland:
The Battle of the Dogger Bank

Unable to defeat the British Grand Fleet in a straight fight, the German Navy set out to weaken it until a decisive action might become possible. The strategy was to launch fast raids, drawing out parts of the Grand Fleet to be destroyed piecemeal. Although initially unsuccessful, the plan was repeated with slight variations. In January 1915, a portion of the High Seas Fleet set out to 'trail its coat' by attacking fishing vessels and naval

patrols on the Dogger Bank. The Germans planned to draw out elements of the Grand Fleet and whittle down its strength.

However, the German Navy's codes had been broken and the British fleet was already at sea, hoping to spring a trap. The main element in this endeavour was a battlecruiser force of five ships and supporting vessels consisting of seven light cruisers and 35 destroyers.

The main German strength resided in three powerful battlecruisers, *Seydlitz*, *Moltke* and *Derfflinger*. A fourth ship, *Blücher*, was also designated a battlecruiser but was really an

THE GRAND FLEET of the Royal Navy in the North Sea. The fleet steamed in columns to facilitate communication by visual signal, which could take a long time to be repeated all down a lengthy line.

armoured cruiser, armed with 8.2in (20.8cm) guns rather than the 11in (28cm) and 12in (30cm) guns of her squadron mates. She was also much slower, capable of 23 knots rather than the 28 knots of the other ships. The force also included four light cruisers and 22 destroyers.

As the two forces encountered one another, the German commander, Admiral Hipper, realized that he was in trouble and ran for home. *Blücher* was left further and further behind by her faster squadron mates. The British battlecruiser force, under Rear Admiral Beatty, gradually closed the gap and opened fire. The British flagship, HMS *Lion*, scored a direct hit on *Blücher* at about 20,000m (65,600ft) – at that time, the longest range hit that had been recorded. As the range dropped, a gunnery duel ensued in which both sides suffered badly. Fears of a U-boat attack

caused Beatty to order his ships to turn away, and Hipper took this opportunity to flee. The unfortunate *Blücher* had to be abandoned to her fate. She did not go quietly, however. The first destroyer to attempt a torpedo run against her was hit with an 8.2in (20.8cm) shell in the boiler room. A more calculated attack got the desired results, with three destroyers making coordinated torpedo attacks, a light cruiser closing to short gun range, the distant battlecruisers hurling salvoes and finally every other vessel in range firing at the doomed cruiser. Finally *Blücher*'s last gun was silenced and she slowly capsized and sank.

The other battlecruisers, although badly battered, were too close to home to be caught now, and the British force returned to port. HMS *Lion* had to be towed home, so great was the damage she had suffered.

The Battle of the Dogger Bank offered an opportunity to achieve a decisive victory over the High Seas Fleet, but due to a combination of confusion on the British side and superior German gunnery, the opportunity was lost. However, in strategic terms the British were still winning. With the blockade of the German coastline causing increasingly serious shortages, Germany needed a victory at sea to clear the ports. All the Royal Navy had to do was to avoid defeat, and thus far it was in no danger in that regard.

The Battle of Jutland

On 30 May 1916, Admiral Reinhard Scheer, commanding the German High Seas Fleet, sent a decoy force under Admiral Hipper northwards, close to the Norwegian coast. He hoped to draw a British response to what looked like a raiding sortie and then pounce on it with his main battle fleet. The British fast battlecruisers, with light cruisers and destroyers as escorts, would be the most likely warships to come out after the raiders. If they could be lured into a trap, this would deprive the Grand Fleet of their heavy reconnaissance assets as well as a significant number of big guns.

Had the British not known something was afoot, then things might have gone as Scheer predicted. However, the British Admiralty was aware from intercepted wireless signals that a major operation was in the offing. The commander of the British Grand Fleet, Admiral John Jellicoe, came up with a plan remarkably similar to Scheer's. As Hipper trailed his coat, hoping to draw out part of the British fleet, his opposite number was doing much the same thing. This was Vice-Admiral David Beatty, commanding a force of four battleships and five battlecruisers. Both commanders now believed that the opposing main force was still in port, when in fact both forces were quite close to one another off the Jutland Peninsula.

The Initial Skirmish

First contact occurred just after 2.20 p.m. on 31 May, when British light cruisers and German destroyers, which had both been sent to investigate a neutral steamer, caught sight of one

Battle of Jutland

1916

The Battle of Jutland was the only full-scale clash of battleships in World War I, and the last major fleet action between battleships in any war. Both sides sought the same outcome at Jutland – to draw out a portion of the enemy fleet and destroy it before the main force could intervene. Both sides used light decoy forces to achieve this end. Battlecruisers played a key role in the battle, which demonstrated the strengths and weaknesses of the ships on both sides. British battlecruisers had bigger guns but tended to explode and sink more easily when hit. German vessels were more modestly armed but very robust; one struggled home under her own power despite shipping 5000 tons of water due to battle damage. Overall, 14 British and 11 German ships were sunk with great loss of life on both sides.

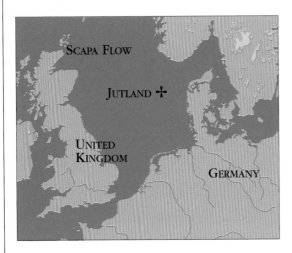

Few naval battles occur far from land, and for their outcome to be considered decisive it must have an influence on events on land. The Battle of Jutland was part of the Royal Navy's strategic aim of prevent supplies from reaching the German ports, and in this, they succeeded.

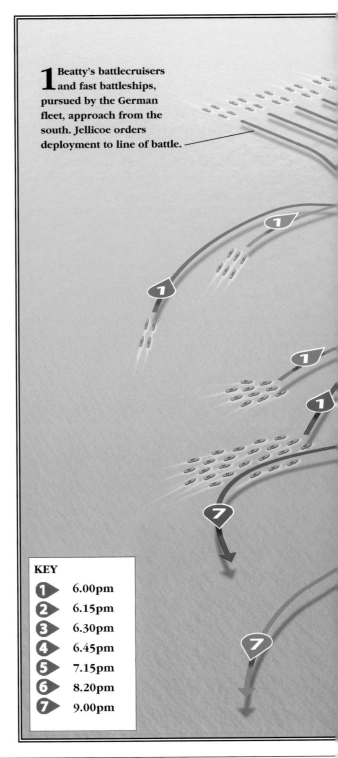

1 **Beatty's battlecruisers and fast battleships, pursued by the German fleet, approach from the south. Jellicoe orders deployment to line of battle.**

KEY

1	6.00pm
2	6.15pm
3	6.30pm
4	6.45pm
5	7.15pm
6	8.20pm
7	9.00pm

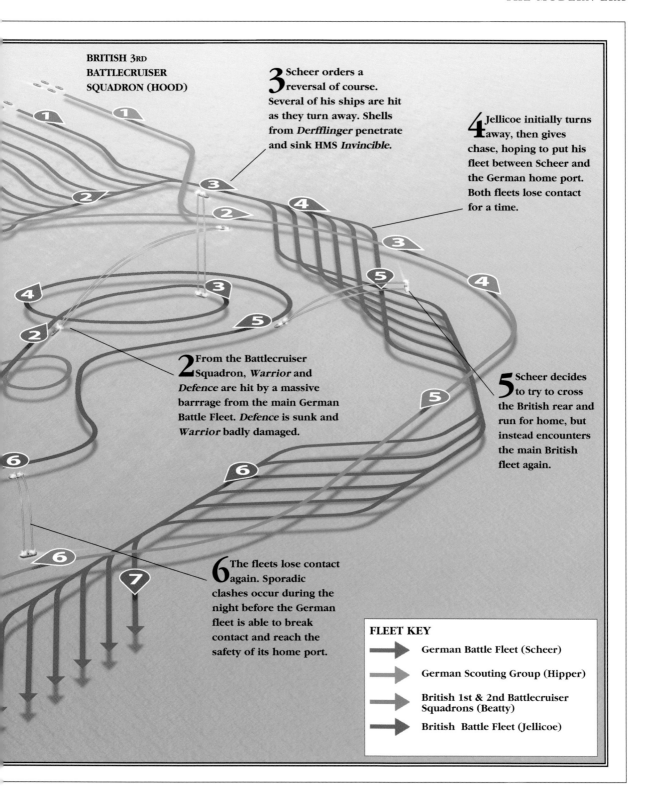

BRITISH 3RD
BATTLECRUISER
SQUADRON (HOOD)

3 Scheer orders a reversal of course. Several of his ships are hit as they turn away. Shells from *Derfflinger* penetrate and sink HMS *Invincible*.

4 Jellicoe initially turns away, then gives chase, hoping to put his fleet between Scheer and the German home port. Both fleets lose contact for a time.

2 From the Battlecruiser Squadron, *Warrior* and *Defence* are hit by a massive barrrage from the main German Battle Fleet. *Defence* is sunk and *Warrior* badly damaged.

5 Scheer decides to try to cross the British rear and run for home, but instead encounters the main British fleet again.

6 The fleets lose contact again. Sporadic clashes occur during the night before the German fleet is able to break contact and reach the safety of its home port.

FLEET KEY

→ German Battle Fleet (Scheer)

→ German Scouting Group (Hipper)

→ British 1st & 2nd Battlecruiser Squadrons (Beatty)

→ British Battle Fleet (Jellicoe)

another. Reports were flashed back to the fleets, and an escalating skirmish began as more light cruisers from both sides joined the fray. The British force began to retire and their opponents gave chase. Admiral Hipper, leading the German battlecruiser force, also went after them. This was exactly what the British had wanted; Hipper was unknowingly making the mistake he had been sent out to entice Beatty into making.

Beatty decided to use his battlecruisers and fast battleships to cut off the German retreat. Unfortunately, a signalling error caused the British battleships to become detached from the battlecruisers and they were somewhat left behind. As a result of course changes on both sides, the two battlecruiser formations came into sight of one another at about 3.20 p.m. It was immediately obvious that these were heavy ships, not light cruisers out on a raid. Beatty now realized that he was too far north to cut off the German retreat and instead turned towards Hipper's force. Destroyers on both sides accelerated to maximum speed to try to get into their proper position ahead of the battlecruisers.

As the British force began deploying into line of battle, Hipper turned away to try to draw Beatty onto the guns of the main German fleet. The British had still not sighted the main German force; indeed, Beatty believed that it was still in harbour.

The Run to the South
The battle proper opened with Beatty steaming south in pursuit of Hipper's force, which was on a parallel course 14km (9 miles) to the east. Hipper closed the range to reduce the advantage of his opponent's bigger guns and opened fire. Beatty's force replied at once.

Fire control proved a problem for the British due to the smoke produced by their own guns and funnels, while the wind conditions favoured the German force by blowing the smoke away from their rangefinders. Possibly as a result, German gunnery was superior to that of the British force. One of the German battlecruisers was left unengaged due to an error in the reading of the flag signals hoisted aboard Beatty's flagship, HMS *Lion*. Worse, the rangefinders overestimated the

range. As British shells howled far over their targets, Hipper's gunners had found the range and were firing as fast as they were able.

Beatty's ships were hit repeatedly. Most of the hits did relatively little damage, but several guns were put out of action. HMS *Lion* was badly hit and lost one of her turrets. She was saved from total annihilation by the prompt flooding of her magazine, which prevented an explosion. Aboard *Indefatigable*, shells penetrated the aft magazines and caused a crippling explosion. Soon after, a salvo struck the fore magazines and detonated them, destroying the vessel. *Queen Mary* also exploded as a result of shells reaching her magazines. Perhaps too much protection had been sacrificed in favour of speed and huge guns.

The German battlecruisers proved more resilient than their British counterparts. When Beatty's fast battleships finally arrived to join the fight, finding their range faster than the battlecruisers, *Seydlitz* was hit by a 15in (38cm) shell but was not forced out of action, despite already having taken penetrating hits from the battlecruisers.

The range between the two forces had shortened sufficiently that some of the battlecruisers were able to launch torpedoes. *Lion* narrowly escaped a salvo fired from *Moltke*. The torpedo tracks fed British paranoia about submarines. Various vessels reported spotting periscopes, even though there were no U-boats in the area. Meanwhile a vicious destroyer action was unfolding between the two battlecruiser forces as the light vessels on both sides savaged one another with guns and torpedoes, hoping to break through and make a torpedo run on the heavy ships. One destroyer put a torpedo into *Seydlitz*, but despite damage the battlecruiser remained in action.

This phase of the battle was now drawing to a close. Although his ships were taking a beating, Hipper had sunk two enemy vessels and damaged several others. More importantly, he had fulfilled his main task: Beatty's force was now coming into range of the entire High Seas Fleet.

The Run to the North
Realizing he was running into a trap, Beatty ordered a 16-point (180°) turn, which kept his

THE BRITISH COMMANDERS *Jellicoe and Beatty (above left) have been criticized for over-caution during the Battle of Jutland, but in truth they did not need to take risks. All the Royal Navy needed to do was to avoid a catastrophic defeat.*

battlecruisers just out of effective range of the main German fleet. Now aware that the High Seas Fleet was out in force, Beatty ran northwards, hoping to stay out of range and to draw the enemy onto the guns of the Grand Fleet. However, Beatty's battleships continued to head south, having not received the order to reverse course. By the time the signal was passed by flag and the battleships began to turn, it was inevitable that they would pass into gun range of the massed High Seas Fleet.

Despite the hammering they had already taken, the German battlecruisers also came about and began heading northwards. This took them into range of the British destroyers, which had not yet

withdrawn. *Seydlitz* was hit by another torpedo but remained in the battle line, now listing somewhat. Two British destroyers made an attack on the German battle line, though without success, and soon afterwards another pair tried their luck, also to no effect. Their opposite numbers, just as daringly, launched torpedo attacks on Beatty's force, though they too obtained no hits.

The action became a running fight as Beatty's force raced for the protection of the Grand Fleet. Smoke from the funnels and fires aboard *Lion* and *Tiger* obscured the battlecruisers to a great extent, and gradually they moved out of effective range. Now the fast battleships of Beatty's force became the main target for their enemies. At the rear of the line, the battleship *Malaya* took the worst of it and was very seriously damaged. The British battleships hit back, of course, causing further damage among the German battlecruisers. *Von*

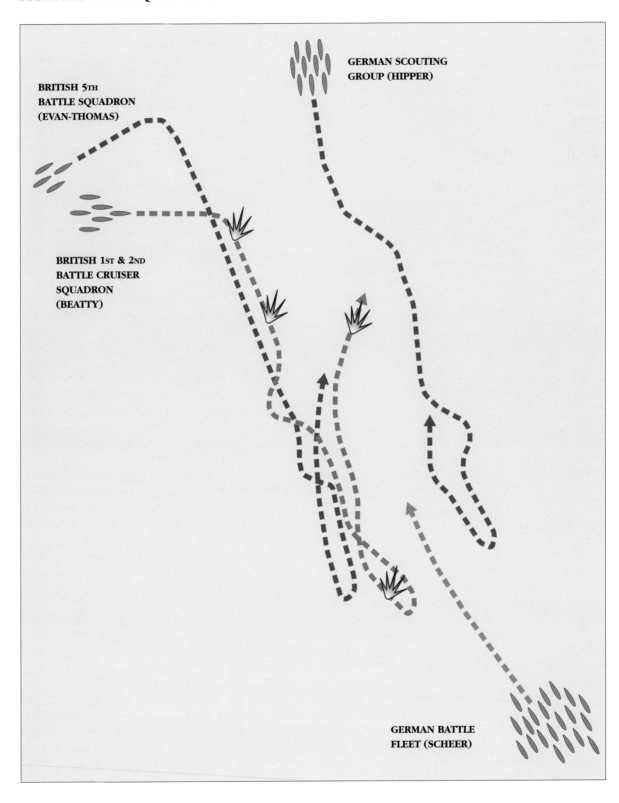

BRITISH 5TH
BATTLE SQUADRON
(EVAN-THOMAS)

GERMAN SCOUTING
GROUP (HIPPER)

BRITISH 1ST & 2ND
BATTLE CRUISER
SQUADRON
(BEATTY)

GERMAN BATTLE
FLEET (SCHEER)

OPPOSITE: DURING THE 'RUN TO THE SOUTH', *Hipper tried to draw Beatty's squadrons onto the guns of the High Seas Fleet's battleships. He almost succeeded; Beatty's reversal of course was made only just in time.*

Der Tann's big guns were all disabled, but her captain chose to stay with the squadron, drawing fire away from the other vessels.

As the range opened, Beatty altered course to meet the Grand Fleet, which caused the range to drop again, and the battlecruisers resumed shooting at one another. Meanwhile Scheer had ordered his force to slow somewhat, closing up the gaps that had developed between his ships. By this time, it was hard to see the British vessels on the darkening horizon. This mainly affected Hipper's battlecruisers, which were in range of the enemy but often could not see their targets.

Hipper's battlecruisers were again knocked about as they pursued Beatty northwards,

DERFFLINGER (TOP) AND *HMS LION* (BOTTOM). *Although the German battlecruiser* Derfflinger *and her British equivalent* Lion *were constructed on similar displacements, their design philosophy was different.* Lion *mounted eight 13.5in (34cm) guns and had a 9in (230mm) armour belt.* Derfflinger *carried eight 12in (30cm) guns and was more thickly armoured all round, with a 12in (300mm) belt.* Derfflinger *and her sister* Seydlitz *took tremendous punishment at Jutland, surviving hits by shells of up to 15in (38cm) calibre, some of which penetrated. By comparison,* Lion *was crippled by a 12in (30cm) hit at the Dogger Bank and almost sunk at Jutland when a shell penetrated 'Q' turret.*

although choked boilers and exhausted stokers made it increasingly difficult to maintain high speed. Meanwhile, reports were reaching Jellicoe from his scouting cruisers that the enemy was approaching from the south. There was still much uncertainty, however. Jellicoe could hear the sounds of combat but at one point wondered who it was and what they were shooting at.

The Fleet Action

Jellicoe's ships were still in their cruising dispositions of parallel columns. This could be dangerous if an enemy deployed for battle were encountered. Thus when Beatty's ships came into sight, Jellicoe demanded to know where the enemy was. Beatty had lost contact, however; all he knew was that Scheer was somewhere southeast of him and closing fast.

Finally, Beatty was able to establish the enemy's position and at 6.10 p.m. Jellicoe ordered a deployment from parallel columns to line of battle. This put his line across the 'T' of the approaching High Seas Fleet, allowing Jellicoe's ships to engage with all their guns against only the forward armament of their opponents. In addition, the British were partially hidden by the dark sky behind them and clouds of smoke from the German vessels.

Scheer ordered an immediate 16-point battle turn. His ships turned individually through 180° and began running southwards, reversing their order in the battle line. Several took

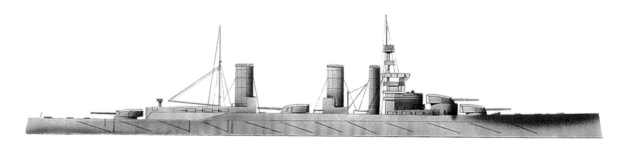

punishing hits, but a salvo from *Derfflinger* penetrated deep into HMS *Invincible* and detonated her magazines, breaking the battlecruiser in half. Jellicoe, worried about mines and destroyer attack, also ordered a reversal of course, causing the fleets to separate. The British then reformed into columns and began to pursue, attempting to get between the High Seas Fleet and its home port.

As the light faded and the mist rose, Scheer tried to cross behind the British rear and run for home, but instead crossed his own 'T' with his ships silhouetted against the lighter western sky. Action resumed at around 7.15 p.m. with the High Seas Fleet taking a battering from the massed British guns. To cover his disengagement from this desperate situation, Scheer ordered his battlecruisers to charge at the enemy line. Meanwhile, destroyers laid smoke and then attacked with torpedoes, allowing the German battlecruisers to break off and flee.

The High Seas Fleet Escapes

As darkness fell, the fleets lost contact, though for a time they were sailing parallel just 10km (6 miles) apart. Finally, Scheer decided to make a run for home. A little before midnight on 31 May,

the lead elements of the High Seas Fleet met a rearguard of destroyers following Jellicoe's main force. The resulting action was chaotic, as vessels fired on shapes dimly seen in the dark or illuminated by starshell. A British destroyer rammed the battleship *Nassau*; another torpedoed and sank the pre-dreadnought *Pommern*.

Cruisers were also lost. The German *Elbing* was run down by the battleship *Posen*; the British *Black Prince* was sunk when she encountered what she thought was a friendly force, only to be shattered by fire from four enemy battleships. The confused fighting went on for about four hours before Scheer disentangled his fleet and headed for home.

Aftermath

Both sides claimed victory at Jutland. In terms of ships and men, the High Seas Fleet had come off best. The British had lost three battlecruisers, three light cruisers and eight destroyers, with six other vessels severely damaged. By contrast, the High

THE LIGHT CRUISER HMS CHESTER was only three weeks into her commission when she fought at Jutland, suffering severe damage while in action in support of the 3rd Battlecruiser Squadron.

Seas Fleet had lost one obsolete battleship, one battlecruiser, four light cruisers and five destroyers, while four other vessels were severely damaged.

German gunnery was generally better than the British. Their armour-piercing shells were highly effective while the British equivalents included far too many duds. In terms of protection, the German ships were also superior; British battlecruisers had tended to explode when hit with 12in (30cm) shells while German vessels survived hits from much bigger guns.

The High Seas Fleet had fought an action on unfavourable terms and inflicted significant losses on the enemy. However, the Germans had not achieved their ultimate strategic aim. Germany needed to weaken the Grand Fleet to the point where the British blockade could be broken. Although he had not won a spectacular tactical victory, Jellicoe had done enough to prevent Scheer from achieving this strategic aim, which was ultimately victory enough.

The High Seas Fleet was not beaten. Its ships sallied out on three more occasions to attack British shipping and its presence near the mouth of the Baltic prevented the British sending help to the troubled government in Russia in 1917. However, there was no further major fleet action.

The Submarine War

While the powerful British fleet could deal with surface raiders, submarines were more of a problem. Britain was dependent upon sea trade, and thus vulnerable to blockade. When German U-boats were deployed as commerce raiders, the losses of Allied merchant shipping began to rise to unsustainable levels. The submarines of the day were primitive, capable only of low speeds and short duration underwater. A submerged submarine would quickly be left behind by its target. To set up an attack, it was necessary either to lie in wait or to get ahead on the surface. The most common practice was to attack on the surface, either with torpedoes or deck guns, rather than from underwater. Although this made the submarine somewhat vulnerable to gunfire or ramming, their low silhouette made for a difficult target. There were at that time no specialist weapons or sensors for use against submarines and no way to track or to attack a U-boat while underwater. However, anti-submarine weapons were quickly developed and introduced. Depth charges could be dropped behind a warship and set to detonate at various depths, hopefully hitting a submarine as they sank and breaching its pressure hull. Tracking was by hydrophone, a microphone lowered into the water to listen for the sounds of a submarine. Neither the sensors in operation nor the weapons that followed up a contact were very effective, but if a submarine could be forced down, merchant vessels in the area could escape. A submarine might be attacked for hours without result, though some were sunk as a result of depth-charge attacks. Others were forced to the surface with damage.

As there were never enough escort warships available, armed merchant ships were used as escorts for other commercial vessels. Not all armed merchants carried their guns overtly. Some vessels, known as Q-ships, carried concealed weapons. To lure enemy submarines into range,

> *'Invincible was overwhelmed by the same awful catastrophe that had already overtaken the Indefatigable, Queen Mary and Defence. At 7.33, Lutzow's third full salvo struck the battlecruiser between the midships turrets, pierced the armour and detonated inside the ship, hurling the roof of a turret into the air and igniting the charges beneath it.'*
> — GERMAN OFFICIAL HISTORY OF THE BATTLE OF JUTLAND

many Q-ships used a 'panic party', who would abandon ship amid great confusion, hoping to convince the enemy commander to come in close to finish off the merchant vessel with gunfire. At this point, the guns on the Q-ship were uncovered and the submarine hopefully crippled by rapid, accurate fire.

The German Navy at times attempted to use submarines according to international law, giving merchant ships a chance to surrender, but this resulted in unacceptable losses. A policy of unrestricted submarine warfare was therefore implemented, but then rescinded after American protests. However, it soon became apparent that the only way to effectively blockade Britain was to permit submarines to operate without regards to international law and the policy was reintroduced in 1917. The submarine blockade was highly effective, and came close to forcing Britain out of the war. However, the attacks on Allied and neutral shipping also played an important part in bringing the United States into

ALTHOUGH U-BOATS *were better suited to attacking merchant vessels than warships, the threat they posed was taken very seriously. When a U-boat successfully penetrated the Grand Fleet anchorage at Scapa Flow, the entire fleet was re-based to the west coast of Scotland.*

the conflict. Submarine operations against naval assets were less effective. There were isolated successes, such as when U-9 sank three elderly British cruisers in the North Sea, but for the most part the submarines of World War I were not up to the task of taking on major naval units.

Interwar Developments

Naval expansion continued after World War I, resulting in an arms race that threatened to bankrupt the participants. Battleships became ever larger and more powerful, and each round of building provoked other nations to build their own bigger and better battleships. Even lesser naval powers saw fit to provide themselves with modern heavy ships.

The naval race was eventually brought to a halt by the Treaty of Washington in 1922. This agreement bound the participants (Britain, the United States, Japan, France and Italy) to a set tonnage of ships of various types, and imposed limits on the size and armament of capital ships. Germany was still bound by the terms of the Treaty of Versailles. Although Italy and Japan violated the terms of the Washington Treaty, it did serve its purpose in slowing down the pace of naval building.

There were other, unintended outcomes too. Some older ships were paid off early to free up tonnage for more modern vessels; some projects were cancelled; and some vessels were converted into other types. Several vessels intended as cruisers and battlecruisers were converted into aircraft carriers. Although the importance of naval airpower was not yet recognized, the end result was that these navies received vessels of strategic importance rather than thinly armoured and vulnerable battlecruisers. It would turn out to be a good trade.

In 1936, the London Naval Treaty, which would have relaxed tonnage limits but continued to restrict battleship sizes, was not ratified by the Japanese and it collapsed. Gradually, bigger ships with larger guns began to emerge. More significantly, improvements in construction techniques saved weight while better engines increased speeds. The battleship and battlecruiser roles merged into the classic capital ship of the period, the fast battleship.

In the meantime, Germany had been quietly violating the terms of the Versailles Treaty, building cruisers that were larger than the official figures claimed. Eventually the treaty was disregarded entirely and full-scale battleships of advanced design were constructed.

German Surface Operations in World War II

At the outset of World War II, the German Navy was still relatively small. This did not prevent it from supporting the invasion of Norway, however, and inflicting losses on the Royal Navy. In June 1940, the British aircraft carrier *Glorious* was sunk by gunfire from the battlecruisers *Scharnhorst* and *Gneisenau* as she returned to Scapa Flow from Norway.

For the most part, however, the German surface fleet attempted to inflict strategic damage by attacking commercial traffic. Many of its vessels were well suited to this role. The three Deutschland-class cruisers or 'pocket battleships', for example, carried six 11in (28cm) guns in two triple turrets rather than the 8in (20cm) guns of most comparable vessels. The most famous of

SMALL, FAST BOATS *were used by the Royal Navy's coastal forces in both world wars. This is CMB121, a 12m (40ft) Coastal Motor Boat launched in 1916. The boats used in World War II tended to be larger and better armed.*

these cruisers, *Graf Spee*, conducted a raiding cruise in the South Atlantic at the start of the war before being brought to action by two British light cruisers and one heavy cruiser at the Battle of the River Plate in December 1939. *Graf Spee* was damaged and sought refuge in Montevideo. Duped into thinking that a huge British force was waiting outside, her captain scuttled his ship rather than fight a losing battle.

Another pocket battleship, *Admiral Scheer*, made a number of wide-ranging raiding cruises, inflicting considerable damage on Allied shipping. In late 1940, she attacked a convoy of 37 merchant ships escorted only by the converted liner *Jervis Bay*. Although equipped with obsolete 6in (15cm) guns and totally unprotected by armour, *Jervis Bay* bought sufficient time for the convoy to scatter, allowing 32 of her charges to escape.

Other convoys were rather better protected. The Allies eventually began sending older capital ships along with some convoys, making attacks a dangerous prospect for even the heaviest raiders. Most surface raiders were converted merchant craft and unable to take on any warship with a decent prospect of wining. However, the big ships were still a threat to convoys. Locating a ship in

ESCORTS HAD TO DEVELOP *ever more effective means to counter the U-boat threat in World War II. Here, two Canadian destroyers combine to force U-744 to the surface in the North Atlantic, 6 March 1944.*

the vast ocean was difficult, and once found it was necessary to have sufficient powerful vessels nearby to deal with her. Thus the big raiders tied down large numbers of Allied forces that might have been useful elsewhere.

The May 1941 sortie by the battleship *Bismarck* and the heavy cruiser *Prinz Eugen* resulted in a desperate scramble to locate them before they got in among the Atlantic convoys. The raiders were spotted by British cruisers but fought off the initial attempt to stop them, sinking the battlecruiser HMS *Hood*. Finally, *Bismarck* was damaged by air attack and brought to action by a greatly superior force. *Prinz Eugen*, which had slipped away earlier, had to return to port with engine trouble.

The greatest damage done by a surface raider was inflicted without leaving port. *Tirpitz*, *Bismarck*'s sister ship, spent much of the war in Norway. She was well positioned there to sortie against the Arctic convoys to Russia, and tied down considerable forces to ensure she was contained. This is the basis of the 'fleet in being' strategy – however much damage *Tirpitz* might have done if she had come out, she had an impact just by remaining a threat, keeping busy many ships that were needed elsewhere.

In July 1942, convoy PQ17 was en route from Britain to northern Russia when word came that *Tirpitz* had sortied with other heavy ships. The light escort accompanying the convoy could not

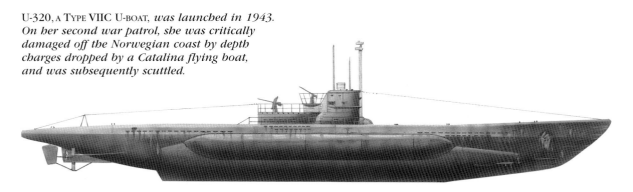

U-320, A TYPE VIIC U-BOAT, *was launched in 1943. On her second war patrol, she was critically damaged off the Norwegian coast by depth charges dropped by a Catalina flying boat, and was subsequently scuttled.*

defend it against such powerful forces, so the order was given to scatter. The sortie turned out to be a false alarm, but by then the merchant ships and escorts were separated, making the task of U-boats and enemy aircraft much easier. PQ17 suffered massive losses as a result.

The German battlefleet was gradually worn down during the war, though some ships survived to the end. Shortages of fuel and likelihood of destruction kept most vessels in port, where they nonetheless exerted some influence as a fleet in being. Some ships, such as *Prinz Eugen*, served as floating artillery batteries, shelling Russian forces advancing along the Baltic coast.

Commerce Protection

If sufficient damage could be inflicted on her commercial sea traffic, Britain could be starved into surrender. A policy of unrestricted submarine warfare was therefore implemented almost from the very beginning of World War II.

Anti-submarine technology was more advanced than in the previous war, and even though submarines were also more capable, the balance had swung somewhat. New developments included projector weapons that fired contact-fused bombs ahead of a ship, rather than behind like the depth charge, and ASDIC echolocation, nowadays more commonly known by the American designation SONAR. However, the Allies chose not to implement a policy of escorted convoys immediately. Instead, they used their anti-submarine assets to hunt down U-boats and set up patrols in areas the submarines had to pass through. This policy failed, and eventually a convoy system was implemented. However, escorts were

in short supply, and in the early years of the war losses to U-boats were very high.

The 'Battle of the Atlantic' was critical to the Allies, but other convoy routes were also important. Supplies, troops and materials moving to and from the Pacific had to come around the Cape of Good Hope, and this provided a 'choke point' where shipping was easy to find. The Arctic runs to northern Russia and through the Mediterranean were also of great importance. The latter routes were exposed not just to submarine attack but also to land-based air units along the route. In the Mediterranean, the Italian Navy's destroyers and torpedo boats were a constant threat.

Yet the convoys had to keep moving. Just as Britain needed supplies, so war material had to be shipped to Russia to keep the Soviet Union in the war. The critical island of Malta, which helped block Axis supply lines to North Africa, was under a constant state of siege and Allied convoys had to fight their way through to bring in supplies.

The humble escort ship took the brunt of the convoy battles. These small vessels defended their charges from air and submarine attack as best they could. Even if a submarine was not destroyed, the escorts might be able to keep it out of firing position while the convoy passed. All kinds of vessels served as escorts, from custom-built escort destroyers and frigates down to lightly armed trawlers. Despite this, there were never enough escorts available, and so various expedients were tried. Arming merchant ships with guns was nothing new, but some were fitted with a catapult that could launch a fighter plane. The aircraft could not land again, so the pilot had to bail out

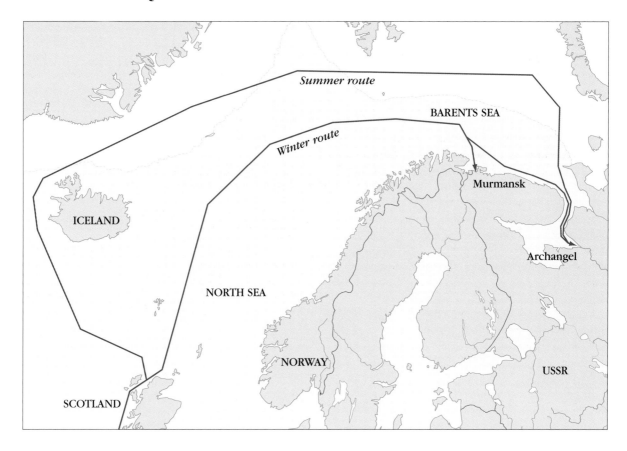

near to the ship and the plane would be lost. Nonetheless, these Catapult Armed Merchantmen (CAM-ships) were useful in bringing down enemy reconnaissance aircraft that could otherwise call in U-boats. It was the aircraft carrier, more than anything else, that finally tipped the balance of these convoy battles. Starting with Merchant Aircraft Carriers (MAC-ships) that were equipped to fly off a few aircraft, the Allies eventually fielded large numbers of escort carriers. These were small and were able to carry only a few aircraft, but the presence of an escort carrier with a convoy allowed for reconnaissance, air defence and attacks on U-boats.

The Battle of Cape Matapan

The Mediterranean Sea was important to both the Allies and the Axis powers. It provided a quick route to the Far East via the Suez Canal and a means to move troops and supplies to the North African theatre. The Allies held both ends of the

CONSTRAINED BY PACK ICE *to the north, the Murmansk convoys were forced to run a gauntlet of U-boats and air attacks out of occupied Norway. In the summer, with constant daylight, the convoys were easy for aircraft to find.*

Mediterranean, with fleet bases at Gibraltar and Alexandria, but the central region lay close to Italy and was, in theory at least, dominated by the powerful Italian fleet.

The beleaguered island of Malta lay on the Axis supply routes to the armies fighting in North Africa. Its fortunes in turn affected the war there; when Malta was fighting for survival, the Axis supply routes past the island were little hindered. However, when the Allied forces on Malta felt able to project power outwards, the logistics situation of the Afrika Corps and supporting Italian forces became more perilous and this contributed to their eventual defeat.

The Italian fleet possessed good, modern battleships and cruisers. These vessels were largely able to operate under friendly air cover and benefited from air reconnaissance. Lighter craft such as torpedo boats were also able to harass the Allied convoy routes.

Despite this, the Italian fleet was somewhat timidly handled. Naval operations in the Mediterranean generally took the form of attacks on convoys or indecisive skirmishes. The latter occurred either because one side felt outmatched and thus retired at speed, or as a deliberate tactic to try to draw the opposition over a submarine ambush. Major battles were very rare.

However, in March 1941, Italian and British naval forces clashed off Cape Matapan. After inflicting a serious defeat on Axis forces in North Africa, the Allies had begun transferring troops to Greece. Overestimating the losses suffered by British naval forces in the region, the Italian fleet came out to attack the troop convoys. In fact, the Allies fielded a far stronger force than the Italians had realized, including three modernized World

War I battleships, seven light cruisers and a large destroyer force.

Significantly, an aircraft carrier, HMS *Formidable*, was also available. The Italian fleet was commanded by Admiral Angelo Iachino in his flagship *Vittorio Veneto*. She was armed with nine 15in (38cm) guns and supported by six heavy cruisers and two light cruisers plus destroyers.

HMS *Hood* (TOP) *was a product of the general fascination with battlecruisers in the early years of the twentieth century. Although huge and armed with eight 15in (38cm) guns, she was scantily armoured despite extra protection added as a result of the experiences of World War I. Hood was fast - 31 knots on her trials in 1920 and 29 knots in 1941 as age took its toll. She was, however, the product of an earlier age. KMS Bismarck (middle) belonged to the new generation of 'fast battleships', which essentially combined the battleship and battlecruiser concepts. The cruiser Zara (bottom) was also of a new, faster type favoured by the Italian Navy. She was sunk at the battle of Cape Matapan in a night engagement.*

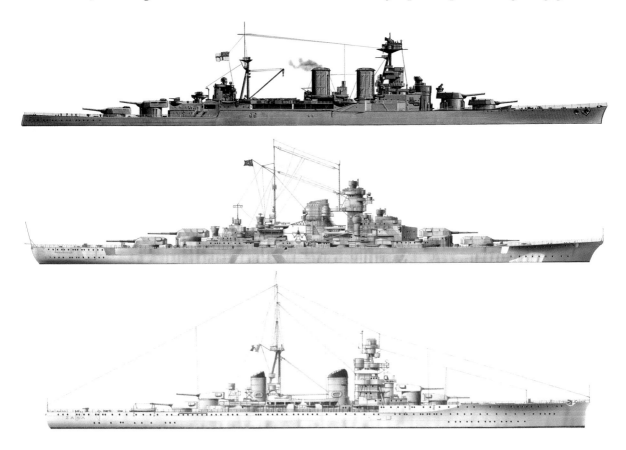

HMS ILLUSTRIOUS *launched the famous Taranto Raid, in which her Swordfish torpedo aircraft inflicted crippling damage on the Italian fleet in its own harbour.* Illustrious *later survived intense attempts to sink her whilst berthed at Malta.*

was still too far away to join the battle, but the British cruisers were leading the enemy towards Cunningham's three battleships. And Cunningham possessed one weapon that could strike at such a distance – Albacore torpedo-bombers from HMS *Formidable*.

The Air Strikes

The first strike concentrated on *Vittorio Veneto,* but did not achieve a hit. However, the manoeuvres taken to avoid the torpedo attack slowed the Italian fleet. Just after midday, losing contact with the fleeing cruisers and mindful that his own air cover could not reach him, Iachino turned back for friendlier waters. This was undoubtedly the right decision, for just after 3.00 p.m. a second strike resulted in a hit to the Italian flagship, temporarily disabling her. For 90 minutes, *Vittorio Veneto* lay dead in the water as the damage was repaired and water was pumped out of her hull.

The Italian ship was able to get underway once again before Cunningham's ships could reach her, but she came under air attack for a third time at 7.30 p.m. This attack included a couple of aircraft from Crete as well as *Formidable*'s torpedo bombers. The battleship escaped further damage, but a hit on the heavy cruiser *Pola* brought her to a dead stop. Iachino decided to get his damaged flagship home to Taranto and pressed on, but he detached a large force of cruisers and destroyers to assist *Pola*. He did not know at that time that Cunningham's force was still in pursuit.

The Surface Action

Unlike the Italian vessels, several of the British warships were equipped with radar. At 10 p.m., the leading British ships picked up a group of contacts that seemed to be stationary in the water.

The First Clash

Shortly before 8.00 a.m. on 28 March 1941, a force of four British and Australian cruisers and supporting destroyers under Vice Admiral Pridham-Wippell encountered Iachino's fleet. Greatly outgunned, the cruisers fled and were pursued by the Italian cruisers. After an hour-long pursuit in which long-range gunfire achieved no results, the Italians broke off pursuit.

Pridham-Wippell's cruisers immediately came about and began following the Italians. This led the cruisers into range of *Vittorio Veneto's* massive guns. No direct hits were made, but the cruisers took some damage as they turned and withdrew, the Italians again in pursuit. At this point, the main Allied force under Admiral Andrew Cunningham

Lieutenant, Italian Navy (1941)

At the outbreak of World War II, the Italian Navy fielded an impressive fleet of over 300 combat vessels (including 6 battleships) and, by August 1943, 259,000 personnel. However, its contribution to Axis combat efforts was fairly minimal. Its greatest achievements lay in dangerous resupply missions to Italian troops across the Royal Navy-dominated Mediterranean.

This officer of the Taranto command wears the blue reefer jacket and matching trousers and peaked cap, the standard dress of Italian Navy officers. The cap badge is the Italian naval insignia: an oval shield bracketed by laurel leaves and surmounted by a crown, all in gold embroidery.

Rank is shown on the navy-blue shoulder-straps (more senior officers would have their straps outlined in gold embroidery), and on the cuffs, the silver stars on the collar being common to all ranks.

Battle of Cape Matapan
28/29 March 1941

The Battle of Cape Matapan was significant partly because it was the first time aircraft carriers had taken part in a major sea battle, and partly because the main action took place at night. After an abortive attack on British troop convoys bound for Greece, the Italian fleet began to retire as a large British force tried to bring it to action. Attempts to slow down the Italians with a carrier-launched air strike were partially successful, allowing British capital ships to engage a group of cruisers and destroyers lying stopped. The Italians had no radar and were unaware that the British were present until they opened fire. The resulting action was less of a battle than an execution by firing squad. Within minutes, two Italian cruisers, *Fiume* and *Zara*, and two Italian destroyers, *Vittorio Alfieri* and *Giosué Carducci*, were sunk. Two other destroyers, *Gioberti* and *Oriani*, managed to escape with some damage.

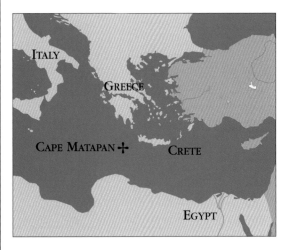

As Allied ships of the Mediterranean Fleet covered troop movements to Greece, intelligence reports showed an Italian battle fleet was moving to attack the convoys. British cruisers and an aircraft carrier from Greek waters and Alexandria, Egypt, confronted the Italian fleet west of Crete on the 28th March.

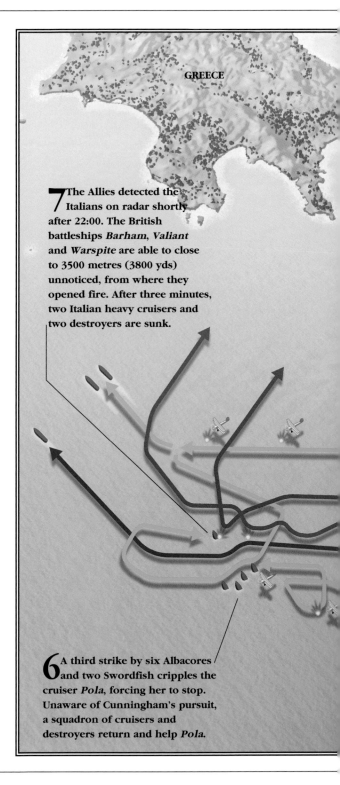

7 The Allies detected the Italians on radar shortly after 22:00. The British battleships *Barham*, *Valiant* and *Warspite* are able to close to 3500 metres (3800 yds) unnoticed, from where they opened fire. After three minutes, two Italian heavy cruisers and two destroyers are sunk.

6 A third strike by six Albacores and two Swordfish cripples the cruiser *Pola*, forcing her to stop. Unaware of Cunningham's pursuit, a squadron of cruisers and destroyers return and help *Pola*.

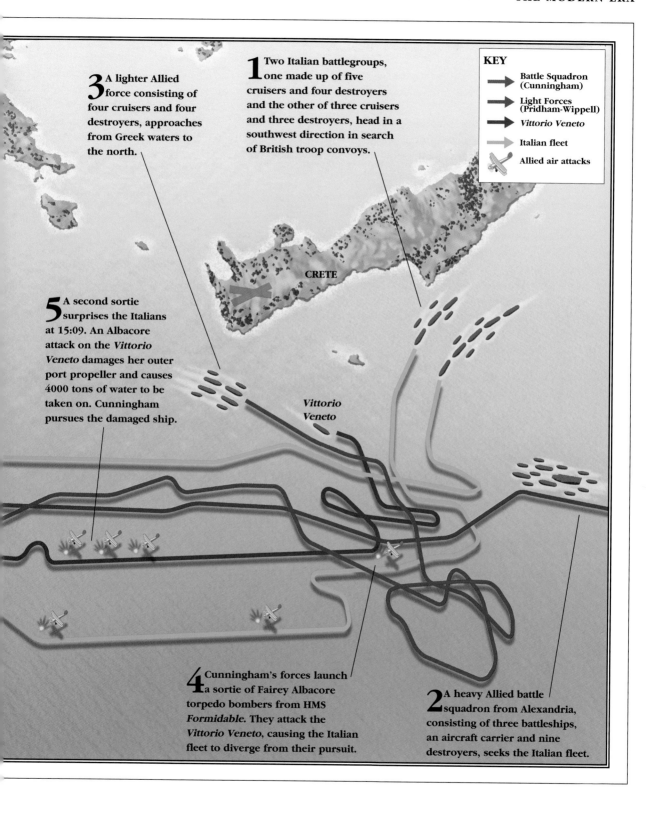

3 A lighter Allied force consisting of four cruisers and four destroyers, approaches from Greek waters to the north.

1 Two Italian battlegroups, one made up of five cruisers and four destroyers and the other of three cruisers and three destroyers, head in a southwest direction in search of British troop convoys.

KEY

→ Battle Squadron (Cunningham)

→ Light Forces (Pridham-Wippell)

→ *Vittorio Veneto*

→ Italian fleet

✈ Allied air attacks

CRETE

5 A second sortie surprises the Italians at 15:09. An Albacore attack on the *Vittorio Veneto* damages her outer port propeller and causes 4000 tons of water to be taken on. Cunningham pursues the damaged ship.

Vittorio Veneto

4 Cunningham's forces launch a sortie of Fairey Albacore torpedo bombers from HMS *Formidable*. They attack the *Vittorio Veneto*, causing the Italian fleet to diverge from their pursuit.

2 A heavy Allied battle squadron from Alexandria, consisting of three battleships, an aircraft carrier and nine destroyers, seeks the Italian fleet.

Unsure whether he had caught the damaged *Vittorio Veneto* or some other ship, Cunningham nevertheless seized his opportunity. His darkened battleships *Warspite*, *Valiant* and *Barham* closed to just 3500m (11,500ft) from the Italian cruisers before opening fire.

What followed could more accurately be described as an execution – not combat. Searchlights from the British ships illuminated the enemy vessels at point-blank range, with guns already laid on target. The shock among the Italian crews can only be imagined as the big guns blasted out, especially as they had never trained for night action. First to go were the heavy cruisers *Zara* and *Fiume*, sisters of the crippled *Pola*. Neither was able to fight back – their guns were trained fore and aft and were not loaded, and their crews were not at action stations. As the two cruisers were shattered by heavy gunfire, the crews of the remaining Italian vessels struggled to man their weapons and get underway.

Unable to move, *Pola* fired back with some of her minor armament as two of her escorting destroyers were quickly despatched. Other destroyers did their best, attempting a torpedo attack on the British warships. A combination of shock and a lack of training for night combat, coupled with the difficulty of attacking an escorted battle force, prevented success and the surviving destroyers made off. *Pola* was captured afloat, but Cunningham decided to sink her by torpedo and withdraw after picking up the survivors. His force was within range of aircraft based in Italy and he wanted to be away before daylight brought retribution.

Aftermath

The Italian Navy had always been hesitant about coming out to fight the British, to the point where heavy forces had in the past been seen off by aggressively handled destroyers and light cruisers. In the wake of the disaster at Cape Matapan, morale slumped even lower. Although some further operations were undertaken, the Italian battle fleet largely ceased to be a factor in the Mediterranean war.

The Battle of Cape Matapan demonstrated that aircraft could contribute effectively to a naval action, albeit in a supporting role. The usefulness of radar was also proven beyond doubt. Without it, Cunningham's fleet could not have found their opponents in the darkness, nor sneaked into position for a killing strike.

The fact that the Italian Navy did not expect to fight at night was also a factor, as was the fateful decision to leave several heavy cruisers dead in the water rather than taking *Pola* under tow as quickly as possible. Whatever the reason for this decision, it probably seemed safe enough at the time. An attack during the night had seemed unthinkable, and by morning air support would have been available.

Overall, Cape Matapan was a fairly minor action that took on greater strategic significance due to its effects on Italian morale and naval thinking. Italy still had powerful battleships, but to a great extent Cape Matapan rendered them impotent.

Air Operations

In the early years of World War II, aircraft were recognized as having a useful role to play in support of conventional operations at sea. Aircraft were carried for reconnaissance by many larger vessels, and it was not uncommon to include a carrier in a battle squadron. However, it quickly became apparent that carriers were destined to be far more than just support platforms. In November 1940, obsolete Swordfish torpedo aircraft from a British carrier attacked the Italian fleet in its base at Taranto. For the loss of just two aircraft, an Italian battleship and a heavy cruiser were sunk and two more battleships were damaged. The Italian fleet was not only weakened but was also forced to move north to Naples, reducing its strategic capabilities.

Aircraft were instrumental in other naval actions. The battle of Cape Matapan in March 1941 had hinged on the contribution of air power. In May 1941, the German battleship *Bismarck* was damaged by air attack, slowing her sufficiently that she could be caught by surface forces and sunk. In December of the same year, HMS *Repulse* – which had chased the *Bismarck* – and HMS *Prince of Wales*, were sunk by Japanese aircraft off Singapore. The loss of two powerful capital ships to Japanese torpedo aircraft and bombers, with no

THE SWORDFISH BIPLANE *was known as a 'stringbag' because, like its namesake, it could be used for just about anything. Although performance was modest, the Swordfish was a reliable and robust aircraft that gave good service in difficult times.*

hostile surface vessels present, demonstrated what was to come. The era of the big-gun capital ship was almost over, and for the later part of the war battleships served mainly as escorts to the carriers, often as giant floating anti-aircraft batteries. They also bombarded shore positions in support of amphibious operations.

In part, this move from guns to air power occurred out of necessity. The air attack at Taranto was studied with great interest by the Imperial Japanese Navy, which was then anticipating the forthcoming battle against the US Navy and searching for a means to even the odds. The answer was a surprise strike by carrier-launched bombers and torpedo-bombers against the US fleet base at Pearl Harbour. The attack left the US fleet temporarily crippled, since it took time to rebuild the fleet strength and repair damaged ships. In the meantime, the US Navy's main strategic assets were the aircraft carriers, which had fortuitously been away from port at the time of the attack.

As the Japanese forces overran southeast Asia and advanced southwards towards Australia, the

Allies gathered their strength to halt them. The decisive clash occurred in May 1942, in the Coral Sea, northeast of Australia. This was the first major action in which the opposing fleets did not see one another nor exchange direct fire. It was fought entirely by aircraft that flew off carriers on both sides.

The US Navy lost a fleet carrier at the Coral Sea in exchange for a lighter Japanese carrier. However, the Japanese advance was halted and Allied morale rose after months of defeats. The lessons learned at the Coral Sea helped other US carriers to resist battle damage. Perhaps most importantly, the Japanese fleet was still weakened when the fleets clashed again at the Battle of Midway a month later.

The Battle of Midway

At the Battle of the Coral Sea, the US fleet carrier *Lexington* was sunk and *Yorktown* damaged. In exchange, the Japanese Navy lost the smaller and less capable *Shoho,* and the carriers *Shokaku* and *Zuikaku* were damaged. The Japanese commander, Admiral Isoroku Yamamoto, felt that with *Lexington* sunk, *Yorktown* out of action and *Saratoga* in harbour for repairs after being torpedoed, the Japanese Navy now had an opportunity in which it was the superior power. He accordingly planned a two-pronged attack against the Aleutian Islands and the US base at Midway Island.

However, the US fleet was not as weak as it seemed. Although *Yorktown* had taken serious damage that would need weeks of work to repair, she was patched up and made battleworthy in just three days and was available for action in time for Midway. The damaged Japanese carriers *Shokaku* and *Zuikaku,* on the other hand, were still unavailable at the time of the battle.

Deployments

Flying his flag in the giant battleship *Yamato*, Admiral Yamamoto sailed at the head of a battleship force that also contained the carrier *Hosho*. The remainder of the fleet sailed in several

USS YORKTOWN (TOP) *was arguably the first modern US carrier. She carried about 90 aircraft; a mix of fighters, torpedo bombers and dive-bombers. At the Battle of the Coral Sea, she evaded no less than eight torpedoes but was hit by a bomb that penetrated due to her lack of an armoured flight deck. Repaired in record time, she fought at Midway, where she was sunk by air attack. USS* Intrepid *(bottom) was part of the Essex class developed from* Yorktown *and her sisters. She was somewhat larger, with better air defences but much the same air group.* Intrepid *was commissioned in 1943 and survived the war.*

groups: the main striking force with four carriers, two battleships and three cruisers; the Midway invasion force with two battleships, a carrier and five cruisers; and the close-support force with four heavy cruisers. There was also an occupation force with two seaplane carriers and a minesweeper group, and a cordon of 10 submarines deployed forward at Midway.

At the same time, a related operation was unfolding against the Aleutian Islands. This involved two carriers, four battleships and several cruisers. As a result, although the Japanese force was powerful, it was not well coordinated. Indeed, the elements assigned to the Aleutian operation were unavailable for action off Midway. Separating the battleships from the carriers was another questionable tactic, as their large anti-aircraft batteries could have provided valuable defensive firepower for the carriers.

Meanwhile, the US Navy could deploy no battleships at all, and only three carriers. The 13 cruisers present were important chiefly as anti-aircraft escorts; had they faced the enemy fleet in a conventional gun action, they would have been quickly overwhelmed. However, the US forces could also deploy land-based aircraft out of Midway Island, which went some way towards evening the odds.

As a result of radio intercepts and good reconnaissance, the US commander, Admiral

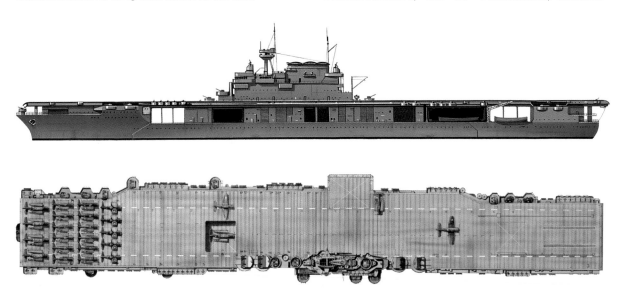

Petty Officer First Class, US Navy (1942)

The US Navy in World War II used a similar system of enlisted rates to other navies. The term 'rank' is applied to officers only; enlisted personnel are 'ratings'. The Petty Officer First Class (PO1) depicted here belongs to the most senior classification of Petty Officers. Below him are Second Class and Third Class Petty Officers, with less responsibility, and below them are the three Seaman rates – Seaman Recruit, Seaman Apprentice and Seaman. In time and with diligence, this PO1 can hope to be promoted to Chief Petty Officer, Senior Chief Petty Officer and, possibly, even Master Chief Petty Officer.

As a rating, he can be seen wearing the standard navy-blue square rig uniform which consisted of blue pullover with white-striped flap collar, black knotted scarf, matching blue trousers, black shoes and white cap. His rank is displayed through the red chevrons on his left sleeve, above which is worn a radio speciality badge. The cuffs do not refer to rank, but to seaman grades, and the three stripes 120mm (4.7in) long with each stripe 5mm (0.2in) wide), joined together by vertical edge stripes, correspond with Seaman 3rd Class. The rest of the uniform remains unadorned.

Chester Nimitz, had a good idea of his enemy's strength and dispositions. Yamamoto, on the other hand, was working with very little information.

Opening Moves

The battle began on 3 June 1942, when reconnaissance aircraft out of Midway located the Japanese invasion force. A flight of B-17 bombers departed to make an attack. However, high-level bombing against moving ships was rarely effective and the B-17s did no damage. A torpedo strike by PBY flying boats during the night damaged a Japanese transport. As dawn broke the next day, the main Japanese striking force began launching its planes against Midway Island. The strike force, which consisted of 36 'Kate' level bombers and 36 'Val' dive-bombers, was soon picked up on radar. However, the A6M 'Zero' fighter escort accompanying the bombers roughly handled the obsolete US fighter planes based at Midway. Ground-based anti-aircraft fire was more effective, downing many Japanese aircraft, and despite heavy damage the airbase remained operational.

Strike aircraft from Midway were already in the air as their base was coming under attack, having taken off just minutes before the Japanese strike arrived. This force mainly comprised Vindicator dive bombers, which were reaching the end of their operational lives, plus six Avenger torpedo bombers. The Avenger's combat debut was not spectacular, with five shot down. Indeed, the entire strike did no real damage to the Japanese carriers.

However, the commander of the Japanese striking force, Admiral Nagumo, now had a tough decision to make. In accordance with Japanese practice at the time, he had held half of his aircraft in reserve. These were armed with torpedoes and armour-piercing bombs for use against any surface ships that might try to interfere with the raid. Informed that Midway needed a second strike to put it out of action, Nagumo had to decide whether to rearm his reserve planes or wait for the first strike to return.

Nagumo opted to rearm his reserve and send it against Midway. Just 15 minutes after he gave the order, information reached him from the fleet's scouting aircraft. Enemy vessels, including at least one cruiser, had been sighted. An hour later,

Nagumo was warned that one aircraft carrier was present – even then, he had no idea that three US carriers were actually facing him. Nagumo ordered the rearming process halted, leaving him with part of his force equipped to attack Midway and part armed for an anti-shipping strike. Bombs and torpedoes were left on deck or in the hangars rather than being moved back to their magazines. This would have serious consequences later in the battle.

The Midway strike force was at this time on its way back, low on fuel and needing to land very soon. Nagumo thus had to decide whether to send off his reserve without much in the way of fighter cover and carrying a mix of weapons, or to send the reserve aircraft back to the hangars and bring the first strike home, sending out a properly organized and equipped force a little later. He chose the latter option.

The US Carriers Strike

Nagumo believed that he had time to recover his strike force and rearm properly for renewed offensive operations. As the first aircraft landed at around 8.30 a.m., things seemed to be going well. During the previous 90 minutes, some 130 US aircraft from Midway had attacked the carrier force without causing any hits. Unknown to the Japanese, however, the US carriers *Enterprise* and *Hornet* had already launched a strike force at around 6.30 a.m. from extreme range. *Yorktown* launched her own strike at 8.40 a.m., having been delayed by the need to recover her scouting flights.

The task of recovering one strike and preparing another was complicated by the need to keep a properly armed Combat Air Patrol in place. The repeated attacks from Midway were not getting though, but they were causing the Zeroes on Combat Air Patrol (CAP) to expend a lot of fuel and ammunition. Finally, however, Nagumo was ready to launch his strike against the US carrier force. At 9.17 a.m, he ordered his carriers to turn into the wind, ready to launch their anti-shipping strike against the US carriers. Just minutes later, the first US carrier strike arrived.

Most of the 98 attack aircraft committed by *Enterprise* and *Hornet* were Devastator torpedo bombers, an obsolete design by this time. The remainder were Dauntless dive-bombers. The escort force comprised 20 Wildcat fighters. The strike should have been a coordinated assault by torpedo bombers at low level and dive-bombers coming down from above with the fighters keeping the Zeroes on CAP busy. However, the groups of aircraft became disjointed. As a result, the Devastators courageously attacked without fighter cover and suffered accordingly. *Yorktown*'s strike arrived around 40 minutes later and was similarly massacred. In all, 31 out of 45 Devastators were shot down without achieving anything other than to drag the CAP down to a low level and force a high expenditure of ammunition.

The Dauntless dive-bombers had become detached from the torpedo strike planes, and at first failed to locate the target. Low on fuel, they searched what appeared to be an empty ocean until a fast-moving Japanese destroyer was spotted. Correctly guessing that the destroyer was headed back to the fleet, the Dauntless squadrons took a best guess and headed in what they hoped was the right direction.

They arrived, by chance, at the perfect moment. The Wildcat fighters accompanying *Yorktown*'s strike had by then became involved in a dogfight with the CAP, distracting its pilots at what turned out to be the critical moment. The CAP was down low and the Japanese fleet was disorganized due to the torpedo attacks. Starting at

USS *YORKTOWN* survived bomb hits at the Coral Sea, and again at Midway. Even after being torpedoed by a Japanese submarine, she sank slowly enough that most of her crew were saved.

Battle of Midway
1942

Japanese dispositions before the Battle of Midway worked in the favour of their enemies. Instead of concentrating the carriers as a striking group, the Japanese dispersed them in such a way that some could not contribute to the battle at all. This offset the numerical advantage enjoyed by the Japanese navy at that time. The Japanese also suffered from a lack of information, which resulted in a number of apparently sound decisions leaving the main Japanese carrier force open to attack. Similarly, correct decisions made by US airmen searching for their targets were critical to the outcome of the battle. At Midway, the Japanese failed in their primary aim of eliminating the remaining US carrier forces, while suffering a severe blow to their own naval power, with the loss of four out of their six fleet carriers, as well as many highly-trained aircrews, which were difficult to replace.

NAGUMO –
FIRST CARRIER
STRIKE FORCE

Hiryu

Kaga

Akagi

Soryu

1 Nagumo's first strike, consisting of 72 bombers and 36 fighters, is launched at 4.30 a.m. on 4 June. Its target is Midway, some 380km (240 miles) away. Half of the available aircraft are held back in reserve as per standard Japanese operating practice. They are armed for an anti-shipping strike.

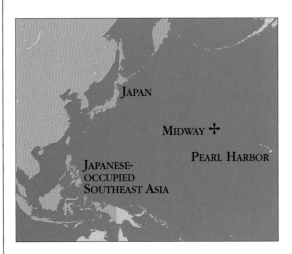

JAPAN

MIDWAY ✛

PEARL HARBOR

JAPANESE-
OCCUPIED
SOUTHEAST ASIA

The Japanese hoped to draw out and destroy the US fleet by attacking a target it had to defend. Midway would have been the base for an assault on Pearl Harbour which, if successful, would drive the US navy all the way back to San Diego.

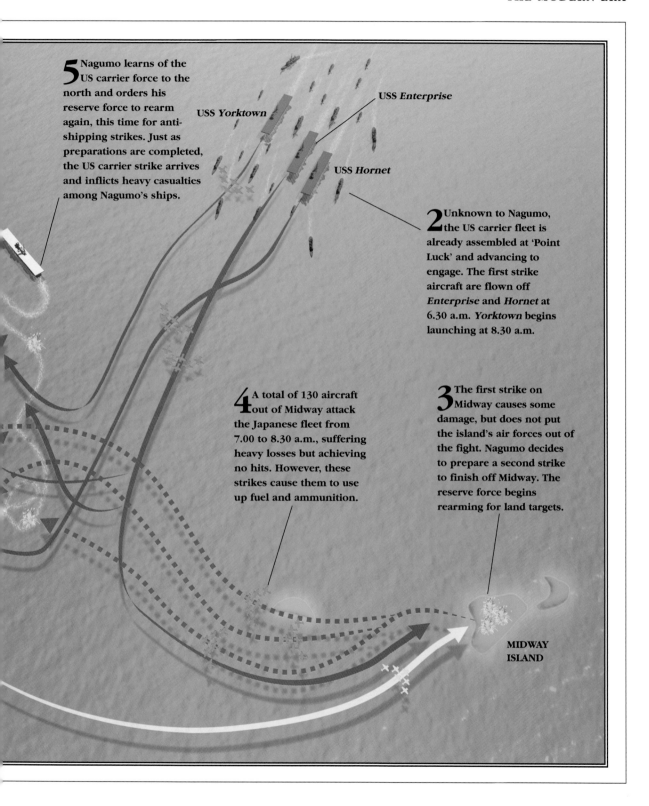

5 Nagumo learns of the US carrier force to the north and orders his reserve force to rearm again, this time for anti-shipping strikes. Just as preparations are completed, the US carrier strike arrives and inflicts heavy casualties among Nagumo's ships.

USS *Yorktown*

USS *Enterprise*

USS *Hornet*

2 Unknown to Nagumo, the US carrier fleet is already assembled at 'Point Luck' and advancing to engage. The first strike aircraft are flown off *Enterprise* and *Hornet* at 6.30 a.m. *Yorktown* begins launching at 8.30 a.m.

4 A total of 130 aircraft out of Midway attack the Japanese fleet from 7.00 to 8.30 a.m., suffering heavy losses but achieving no hits. However, these strikes cause them to use up fuel and ammunition.

3 The first strike on Midway causes some damage, but does not put the island's air forces out of the fight. Nagumo decides to prepare a second strike to finish off Midway. The reserve force begins rearming for land targets.

MIDWAY
ISLAND

As THE TIDE TURNED AGAINST JAPAN, *increasing numbers of Kamikaze attacks were launched. Any aircraft, however obsolete, could be packed with explosives and plunged into an enemy vessel.*

10.22 a.m., the dive-bombers delivered their attack on the Japanese carriers. *Akagi* took two hits, which set fire to aviation fuel, resulting in internal explosions. She was later torpedoed by the submarine *Nautilus*. *Soryu* also burned after being hit by three bombs. *Kaga* took four hits and was disabled. All three carriers were abandoned.

Trading Blows

Nagumo transferred his flag to the cruiser *Nagara* and informed the fleet commander of his losses. At the same time, he ordered his remaining carrier, *Hiryu*, to launch a strike against the US carrier force. The Japanese strike force found *Yorktown* about midday and delivered three hits with bombs, temporarily putting the carrier out of action. Damage-control crews set to work

immediately, and within two hours *Yorktown* was underway again with her fires out. The repairs were so good that when a second strike arrived at 2.45 p.m. and hit *Yorktown* with two torpedoes, the pilots thought that they had found an undamaged carrier. The second strike put *Yorktown* out of action once again.

The Japanese at this point thought they had sunk two carriers, but were rudely disabused of this notion when a strike from *Enterprise*, which included some of *Yorktown*'s former air group, successfully attacked *Hiryu* and sank her at 5 p.m. A strike from *Hornet*, arriving a little later, attacked the escorts without success.

Endgame

During the carrier-versus-carrier battle, the massive Japanese battleship force remained unengaged. Yamamoto, in overall command, issued orders first to concentrate his forces and then to suspend the operation. At 5.30 p.m. he changed his mind and ordered the Aleutians force to proceed, then at 7.15

p.m. he decided on a 'general advance' eastwards in the hope of making a battleship attack or at least bombarding Midway. Early in the morning on 5 June 1942, Yamamoto finally called off the Midway invasion and began a withdrawal. His fleet was found by air reconnaissance and attacked by carrier and land-based aircraft, sinking a heavy cruiser and damaging another. While attempts were underway to save her, *Yorktown* was torpedoed by a Japanese submarine and sunk. Most of her crew and air group were saved. The same was not true of the Japanese carriers. The loss of so many skilled pilots gravely reduced the fighting ability of the Imperial Japanese Navy, and it never recovered.

Aftermath

Midway marked the end of the period of Japanese dominance in the Pacific and paved the way for the Guadalcanal campaign and the gradual island-hopping advance towards the Japanese Home Islands. Although the Aleutians operation was a success, it was ultimately of no consequence: the course of the war passed the Aleutians by and the Japanese garrison was withdrawn before US forces arrived to retake the islands. Midway was not only the turning point of the Pacific war, it was the end of an era. No more would the battleship with its big guns dominate the oceans. Now the crown had passed to the aircraft carrier. Although Japan possessed many battleships, including the biggest and best in the world, it was the US Navy's carrier force that would determine the outcome of the war.

Support for Amphibious Operations

After Midway, the tide slowly turned in the Pacific War. There were further battles, but there was no point at which the US Navy and its allies risked defeat in a fleet action. The strength of the Japanese carrier arm had been broken and although significant numbers of battleships and cruisers remained, these were unable to significantly influence the course of the war. In addition, the US submarine campaign against Japanese merchant traffic greatly reduced the availability of supplies and fuel.

The Allies were therefore able to begin an advance against Japan, capturing islands as bases and gradually reducing the wide perimeter established in 1942. Naval power was essential to support and protect these operations. During the battles for Guadalcanal in the Solomon Islands, for example, Japanese attempts to land more troops on the island were thwarted by naval power, albeit at considerable cost.

Surface actions still occurred, of course. Off Guadalcanal in November 1942, USS *Washington* – her consort *South Dakota* crippled by electrical failure – fought a brilliant action against a Japanese squadron. The battle of Leyte Gulf in October 1944 involved hundreds of ships, torpedo boats and aircraft. But in truth the capital ship was moving into a secondary role as an escort for the carriers and a bombardment platform to support amphibious operations.

It became increasingly apparent that even the best-protected battleship could not survive long enough in the face of heavy air attack to reach gun range. As the Allies landed on Okinawa in April 1945, the super-battleship Yamato was sent to oppose the operation. She was sunk by air attack along with a light cruiser and half the escorting destroyers. This took considerable effort but cost the Allies only 10 aircraft. Cruisers and battleships protected the Allied invasion fleet from conventional attack by aircraft and from suicide attacks by Kamikaze planes – though carrier-based aircraft were important in making early interceptions. The aircraft carrier had established itself as the major instrument of power projection at sea, with other surface ships moving into a supporting role.

The Missile Era

After the end of World War II, the United States and the Soviet Union, former allies, now emerged as

> *'We can run wild for six months or a year, but after that I have utterly no confidence.'*
>
> — ADMIRAL ISOROKU YAMAMOTO

the chief rivals for naval supremacy. As the Cold War superpowers faced off over ideological differences, so too did their respective navies develop along very different lines.

The US and its allies chose the aircraft carrier as the main tool of power projection. Carriers proved their worth in Korea and Vietnam, acting as impregnable bases from which aircraft could be launched against land targets. Carrier aircraft were also the primary means of engaging surface ships. Western warships were armed for surface action, but did not really expect to fight against other ships. For the most part, surface vessels were there to protect and support the carriers.

To counter the carriers, the Soviet Union and its allies relied on land-based long-ranged bombers, submarines and powerful 'surface action groups' capable of launching long-range missiles. Even then, some naval air power was necessary; scouting helicopters were carried by many ships to find targets for the missiles. Soviet ships also expected to be attacked from the air and they carried heavy anti-aircraft armament.

The navies of the various Cold War powers became specialized to a great extent. The Royal Navy, for example, assumed a large share of the responsibility for preventing Soviet submarines getting into the Atlantic through the Greenland-Iceland-United Kingdom (GIUK) Gap, and developed excellent anti-submarine capabilities at the expense of some other areas.

The development of missile submarines capable of launching nuclear weapons against land targets also necessitated a shift in naval priorities. On both sides of the Iron Curtain, attack (or 'hunter-killer') submarines were developed to find and sink enemy missile submarines and surface craft, and specialized anti-submarine escorts became common. Larger anti-submarine cruisers, often carrying large numbers of helicopters, were also fielded by some powers. The advent of nuclear power allowed for a new generation of submarines, able to travel vast distances without surfacing. Although not as quiet as a conventional submarine running on its batteries, a nuclear boat was capable of going almost anywhere. This made them ideal raiders as well as reconnaissance platforms.

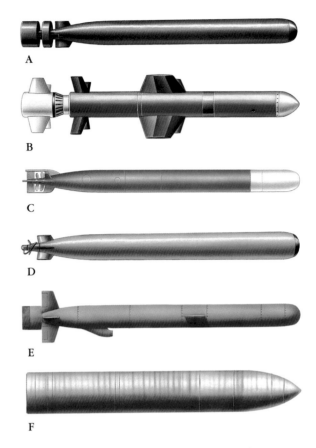

A – DCTN F17; B – HARPOON; C – FFV TYPE 61
D – DCTN L5; E – TOMAHAWK; F – SS-N-18

ABOVE: MODERN NAVAL MISSILES *and torpedoes provide surface ships and submarines with 'standoff' attack capability coupled with precise guidance. Wire-guided torpedoes typically have a range of around 20km (12 miles). Anti-shipping missiles such as the Harpoon extend a vessel's striking range out to 100km/60 miles (or more, in the case of extended-range weapons). Cruise missiles such as the Tomahawk can be used for anti-shipping strikes or to attack fixed land targets out to about 1100km (680 miles) while submarine-launched ballistic missiles are strategic weapons with a range of thousands of kilometres.*

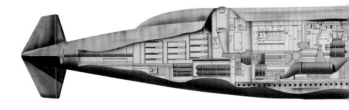

Many World War II era destroyers and a few cruisers were modernized and then gradually passed down to other nations whose navies could not afford first-line units. Other modernization projects were more ambitious. The US Navy updated four battleships of the Iowa class, adding missile-based air defences and long and medium range missiles for land attack and surface combat. The big guns remained, and saw action in the 1991 Gulf War, conducting shore bombardment.

This was the last hurrah for the battleship. Mothballed for a time, the last of these great ships were finally stricken from the US Navy list in 2006. One reason for their demise was the large number of highly skilled crewmembers they absorbed; each battleship required enough personnel to man four cruisers.

The dangers of over-specialization were highlighted during the 1982 Falklands War between Britain and Argentina. The Royal Navy task force sent to the South Atlantic was not ideally suited to fighting a conventional war. It was primarily an anti-submarine force and while many vessels were excellent in that role, they lacked all-round capability and, in particular, air defences. As a result, Argentinean air attacks sank several vessels and the ability of the force to support army units ashore was somewhat limited.

The controversial sinking of the cruiser *Belgrano* by the nuclear attack submarine HMS *Conqueror* illustrates how much naval warfare had changed by 1982. *Belgrano* was an ex-US heavy cruiser, armoured to resist hits from 8in (20cm) guns. Aboard the Royal Navy task force, there were no weapons that could sink her. However, torpedoes fired from a submarine could do the job. Indeed, the Mark 8 unguided torpedoes used to sink her had last been used in anger to sink the Japanese heavy cruiser *Haguro* in 1945.

Naval Warfare in the Modern World

As armoured ships faded from the scene, the need for weapons that could punch through heavy armour also receded. There are now very few armoured ships left in service anywhere in the world, and most of those that remain are museum pieces. Instead of steel plate, modern warships are protected by other means. Ideally, the 'kill chain' can be broken before an enemy can fire his weapons, or else the enemy can be deprived of information upon which to base a firing solution. 'Stealth' technologies make it difficult to pick up vessels on radar, while good EMCON (EMissions CONtrol) can limit the amount of radio and radar emissions from a ship.

If a naval force is attacked, the first line of defence is its aircraft, if any are available. Anti-air escorts can shoot at incoming aircraft or missiles using medium- and long-range missiles – a technique that is known as 'area defence'. Any threats that 'leak' through the area-defence perimeter can be engaged by short-range point-defence missiles. The Close-In Weapon Systems (CIWS) offers a last-ditch defence, essentially

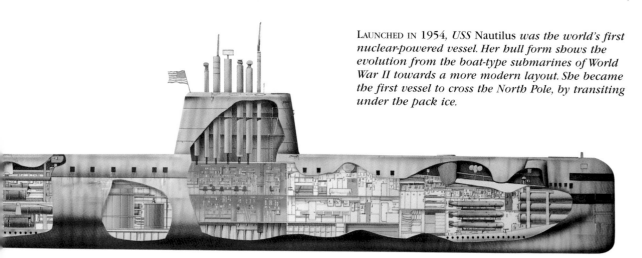

LAUNCHED IN 1954, *USS* Nautilus *was the world's first nuclear-powered vessel. Her hull form shows the evolution from the boat-type submarines of World War II towards a more modern layout. She became the first vessel to cross the North Pole, by transiting under the pack ice.*

A BOW-ON VIEW *of the battleship USS New Jersey leading the US Navy battle line. She is followed by the battleship USS* Missouri *and the nuclear-powered guided missile cruiser USS* Long Beach *with other screening vessels following astern of the cruiser. In the 1980s, the US Navy rebuilt four battleships as 'missile battleships' mounting a formidable armament of cruise missiles and shorter-range missiles while retaining their massive gun armament. These vessels played a part in the 1991 Gulf War but are no longer in service, not least because each one absorbed enough skilled crewmembers to operate four cruisers.*

acting as a goalkeeper to shoot down missiles just before they strike home. Electronic warfare, jamming and decoys also contribute to defence, by distracting homing weapons from their target, by obscuring the target, or by overloading the seeker head of the missile so that it cannot operate effectively.

There is nothing entirely new in these techniques, of course – smokescreens have long been used to obscure ships from enemy fire and escort vessels have always attempted to shoot down incoming aircraft. In that respect, nothing has really changed; major warships have a job to do and escorts are there to protect them. However, modern naval forces do face a broad range of threats, including torpedoes, mines and guns, as well as missiles and unguided weapons such as bombs and rockets. Many of these can be launched from air, surface or underwater platforms.

In addition, the naval warfare environment is constantly changing. During the Cold War, fleets expected to face large-scale threats involving sea-skimming cruise missiles launched from ships or long-range bombers, and high-capability attack submarines. The expectation was that engagements would take place in the open sea ('blue water') for the most part.

Today, ships are increasingly forced to operate close to the shore ('brown water') in support of military operations, disaster relief, humanitarian intervention, and anti-terrorism or anti-drug operations. This adds yet another dimension to the naval equation. For example, some British destroyers in the 1980s carried no medium-calibre guns, but only missiles for surface combat. However, an expensive missile is not the ideal choice of warning shot when apprehending drug runners or suspected pirates. The 'small boat threat' is also very real. Warships equipped to take on fast jets and large surface combatants sometimes lack the capability to engage small targets, low on the water and moving fast. US warships operating in the Persian Gulf in the late 1980s had little difficulty crippling an Iranian corvette with missiles and guns but struggled to hit the much smaller Boghammar-class armed speedboats. Thus many modern warships carry light, fast-slewing weapons for use against smaller targets and in 'enforcement' duties, such as when chasing down suspected drug runners. There is also a move back towards armour of a sort, albeit light materials such as Kevlar over critical areas of the ship rather than the thick steel plate of previous incarnations.

This change in design philosophy reflects the sort of threats faced by modern warships. At a time when the likely threat was a large missile, which could cripple a ship even with a near miss, the most effective defence was to destroy the threat before it arrived. Faced with the likelihood of hits by lighter weapons, however, it makes sense to fit lightweight protection suitable for defeating such a threat.

The design of warships continues to change as the threat evolves, and the threat continues to evolve as weapons designers try to circumvent warships' defences. What has not changed and is not likely to change is the role of the warship. It is still a symbol of political and military might and a means to project power across the globe.

Thus the warships of today and in the foreseeable future must be able to attack an enemy and to protect friendly ships and shorelines. Whether nuclear-powered or hauled along by oar and sail; whether filled with archers, carrying guns and torpedoes or festooned with missiles, warships must be able to defeat other vessels while resisting attack. It might be that any admiral or captain, from any era, would issue very similar orders. The means may have changed enormously over the centuries, but the mission – to locate the enemy and sink his ships – has not.

AN F/A -18 HORNET FIGHTER-BOMBER *lands aboard the aircraft carrier USS Coral Sea (CV-43) during heavy seas. Carrier-based air power remains a key means of power projection for modern navies.*

Select Bibliography

Adams, Simon. 'The Battle that Never Was: the Downs and the Armada Campaign' from M. J. Rodriguez-Salgado & Simon Adams, eds., *England, Spain and the Grand Armada*, 1558-1604. Rowman & Littlefield: 1991.

Andrews, K.R. 'Elizabethan Privateering', from *Raleigh in Exeter X: Privateering and Colonization in the Reign of Elizabeth I*. Joyce Youngs (ed). London: David Brown: 1985.

Anglim S., Jestice P.G., Rice R.S., Rusch S.M., Serrati J. *Fighting Techniques of the Ancient World, 3000BC - AD 500*. New York: Thomas Dunne Books, 2002.

Armstrong, Richard. *The Early Mariners*. New York: Frederick A. Praeger, Inc, 1968.

Banks, Arthur. *A World Atlas of Military History*. London: Seeley Service & Co, 1973.

Barker, Philip. *The Armies and Enemies of Imperial Rome*. Worthing: War Games Research Group, 1981.

Barraclough, Geoffrey (ed.). *The Times Atlas of World History*. London: Times Books Ltd., 1979.

Bradford, Ernle. *The Sultan's Admiral: The Life of Barbarossa*. New York: Harcourt, Brace & World, Inc, 1968.

Bruce, Robert B. et al. *Fighting Techniques of the Napoleonic Age, 1792-1815*. New York: Thomas Dunne Books, 2008.

Davis, James C. (ed). *Pursuit of Power: Venetian Ambassadors' Reports*. New York: Harper & Row, Publishers, 1970.

Delgado, James P. *Lost Warships: An Archaeological Tour of War at Sea*. New York: Checkmark Books, 2001.

Galuppini, Gino. *Warships of the World: An Illustrated Encyclopedia* (English translation by Arnaldo Mondadori). New York: Military Press, 1989.

Graff, David Andrew (ed). *A Military History of China*. Revised Paperback Edition. Boulder: Westview Press, 2002.

Guilmartin, John Francis. *Gunpowder and Galleys: Changing Technology and Mediterranean Warfare at Sea in the Sixteenth Century* (revised edition). Annapolis: Naval Institute Press, 2004.

Hakluyt, Richard. *Voyages and Discoveries: The Principal Navigations, Voyages, Traffiques and Discoveries of the English Nation* (Jack Beeching, editor). Harmondsworth: Penguin, 1987 edition of 1600 original.

Hale, J. R. (ed). *Renaissance Venice*. Totowa: Rowman and Littlefield, 1973.

Herodotus. *The Histories* (translation George Rawlinson). London: Everyman's Library, Random House, 1910.

Holmes, Richard. *World Atlas of Warfare*. London: Mitchell Beazley International Ltd., 1988.

Hough, Richard. *Fighting Ships*. New York: G. P. Putnam's Sons, 1969.

Jörgensen, Christer et al. *Fighting Techniques of the Early Modern World, 1500-1763*. New York: Thomas Dunne Books, 2005.

Kelsey, Harry. *Sir Francis Drake: The Queen's Pirate*. New Haven: Yale, 1999.

Lane, Frederic C. *Venice: A Maritime Republic*. Baltimore: The Johns Hopkins University Press, 1973.

Lloyd, Christopher. *Ships and Seamen*. London: Weidenfeld & Nicolson, 1961.

Marsden E.W. *Greek and Roman Artillery*. London: Historical development, OUP, 1969.

Martin, Colin and Parker, Geoffrey. *The Spanish Armada* (revised edition). Manchester University Press, 2002.

Martinez-Hidalgo, Jose Maria. *Columbus' Ships*. Barre: Barre Publishers, 1966.

Mattingly, Garrett. *The Armada*. Mariner Books, 1974.

McNeil, William H. *The Pursuit of Power: Technology, Armed Force and Society Since A.D. 1000*. Reprint edition. Chicago, University of Chicago Press, 1984.

Needham, Joseph. *Science and Civilization In China*. Volume 4: 'Physics and Physical Technology', 'Part III: Civil Engineering and Nautics'. Cambridge: Cambridge University Press, 1971.

Nelson R.B. *Warfleets of Antiquity*. Worthing: War Games Research Group, 1973.

_____. *Armies of the Greek and Persian Wars*. Worthing: War Games Research Group, 1975.

Nolan, John S. 'English Operations Around Brest' from *Mariner's Mirror*, 1994.

Oliphant, Margaret. *The Atlas of the Ancient World*. London: Ebury Press, Random House, 1992.

Parker, Geoffrey. 'Letters and Gunpowder' from *MHQ*, 1998.

Parker, Philip (ed.). *Atlas of Military History*. London: Collins, 2004.

Plutarch. *Roman Lives* (translation Robin Waterfield). Oxford: Oxford University Press, 1999.

Rodger, N.A.M. *The Safeguard of the Sea: A Naval History of Britain*, Vol I, 660-1649. New York: Harper Collins, 1997.

Rodgers, William Ledyard. *Naval Warfare Under Oars, 4th to 16th Centuries: A Study of Strategy, Tactics and Ship Design*. Annapolis: Naval Institute Press, 1967.

Sawyer, Ralph D. *Fire and Water: The Art of Incendiary and Aquatic Warfare in China*. With the Collaboration of Mei-Chun Lee Sawyer. Boulder: Westview Press, 2004.

Stillman, Nigel and Nigel Tallis. *Armies of the Ancient Near East, 3000 BC to 539 BC*. Worthing: War Games Research Group, 1984.

Throckmorton, Peter (ed). *The Sea Remembers: Shipwrecks and Archaeology from Homer's Greece to the Rediscovery of the Titanic*. New York: Smithmark Publishers, 1987.

Turnbull, Steven. *Fighting Ships of the Far East (2)*. With Illustrations by Wayne Reynolds. New Vanguard 63. Oxford: Osprey Press, 2003.

_____. *The Samurai: A Military History*. New York: Macmillan, 1977.

_____. *The Samurai Invasion of Korea, 1592-1598*. With illustrations by Peter Dennis. Campaign 198. Oxford: Osprey Press, 2008.

Unger, Richard W. *The Ship in the Medieval Economy: 600-1600*. London: Croom Helm, Limited, 1980.

Villiers, Alan. *Men, Ships, and the Sea* (2nd ed). Washington: National Geographic Society, 1973.

Wernham, R.B. 'Elizabethan War Aims and Strategy' pp. 340-368 in *Elizabethan Government and Society: Essays presented to Sir John Neale* (Bindhoff, Hurstfield and Williams, eds.). London, 1961.

Wingfield, Anthony. 'The Counter Armada of 1589' from *The Expedition of Sir John Norris and Sir Francis Drake to Spain and Portugal, 1589* (R.B. Wernham, ed.). Naval Records Society: 1988.

Index

Page numbers in *italics* refer to illustrations, those in **bold** type refer to maps and information displays with illustrations and text. Abbreviations are as follows: (B) - battle; (NB) - naval battle; (S) - siege.